The Psychology Major's Companion

Everything You Need to
Know to Get You Where
You Want to Go

Dana S. Dunn
Moravian College

Jane S. Halonen
University of West Florida

worth publishers
Macmillan Learning

Vice President, Social Science: Charles Linsmeier
Executive Acquisitions Editor: Christine Cardone
Editorial Assistant: Melissa Rostek
Media Editor: Laura Burden
Marketing Manager: Katherine Nurre
Director of Content Management Enhancement: Tracey Kuehn
Managing Editor: Lisa Kinne
Senior Project Editor: Jane O'Neill
Photo Editor: Sheena Goldstein
Permissions Editor: Chelsea Roden
Director of Design, Content Management: Diana Blume
Senior Design Manager: Vicki Tomaselli
Interior Designer: Lee Ann McKevitt
Art Manager: Matthew McAdams
Senior Production Supervisor: Paul Rohloff
Media Producer: Eve Conte
Composition: codeMantra U.S. LLC
Printing and Binding: RR Donnelley
Cover Art: Andrzej Wojcicki/Science Photo Library/Getty Images

Library of Congress Control Number: 2016940035

ISBN-13: 978-1-319-02143-6
ISBN-10: 1-319-02143-3

Printed in the United States of America

First printing

Worth Publishers
One New York Plaza
Suite 4500
New York, NY 10004-1562
www.macmillanhighered.com

For
David G. Myers
Doug Bernstein
Ludy T. Benjamin, Jr.
Bill McKeachie

Brief Contents

Contents

CHAPTER 9
What Career Options Are There for Students with a BA or BS in Psychology? 129

CHAPTER 10
How Do You Apply To and Get Into Graduate Programs in Psychology? 147

Preface

One of our favorite childhood books is *Oh, the Places You'll Go!* by Dr. Seuss. We have always been impressed by the open-ended prospects that the phrase invokes; we always smile when we hear it. We both experience that same sense of optimism when we hear students identify psychology as their chosen major.

Selecting a major is one of the most significant decisions one can make in young adulthood. Selecting the wrong major is an expensive and inefficient means of getting through the undergraduate years. In contrast, selecting the right major can make those years rich in present experiences and prepare you for your future.

Although psychology is a popular major, it is also hugely misunderstood. That misunderstanding is held not just by loved ones who worry about career opportunities but also by some who major in psychology. With good advising, hard work, and focused energy, a degree in psychology can open a wide range of amazing possibilities for any student. However, poor advising and lackluster performance in psychology can reinforce some people's perceptions that it is a weak major. Therefore, the objective of this book is to help students to declare the psychology major if it is in their best interest to do so, to successfully leverage what they learn in the major, and to prepare for a psychology-related future.

NOTE TO STUDENTS

We wrote this book for you, whether you are a traditional-aged college student or a more seasoned adult learner interested in exploring the options associated with being a psychology major. You might be a college-bound student fresh out of high school who is curious about psychology. Or perhaps you are already enrolled in college and about to decide on an academic major area of study and you want to know if majoring in psychology is right for you. Some readers may have already taken the plunge and want some guidance about what careers are available to psychology majors or advice on how to pursue graduate study in psychology.

Whatever your background, *The Psychology Major's Companion: Everything You Need to Know to Get You Where You Want to Go* is designed to satisfy your needs. We address a variety of key questions, including:

- What do psychologists do? Where do they work?
- Is majoring in psychology the right choice for you?

- ■ What skills and benefits does an undergraduate degree in psychology provide?
- ■ How can I get the most out of my psychology major while becoming a focused, high-performing student?
- ■ How can I leverage my major by pursuing the right organizational memberships, summer jobs, and internships?
- ■ What can I do with a major in psychology after graduation?
- ■ What jobs are available to BA- or BS-level psychology majors who decide not to pursue an MA or a PhD?
- ■ How do I begin a job search right out of college?
- ■ If I decide to go to graduate school in psychology, what's involved in the application process?
- ■ What area of psychology should I pursue there after college?
- ■ How can I make my application a compelling one?
- ■ Of what benefit will psychology be to my life beyond my education and my career?

We strongly believe that both prospective and current psychology majors should know what to expect from the undergraduate major, the larger discipline, and the marketplace beyond campus. This book will give you a good start in planning your future once psychology piques your interest.

NOTE TO INSTRUCTORS AND ADVISORS

We wrote this book to serve multiple purposes for the psychology instructor. First, we think the text can serve well in psychology courses that introduce students to the major. Such courses are often titled *Introduction to the Psychology Major* or *Careers in Psychology*. Our book could be the main text or a supplemental text in these courses. The book provides a solid foundation for students interested in the discipline. We also hope that students will find the *Companion* valuable enough that they will use it to help them make the decisions that will follow their entry into the major.

Some instructors may wish to use the *Companion* as a supplemental text in introductory psychology courses exclusively aimed at psychology majors, research methods in psychology courses, and in psychology seminars. We purposefully designed the book to allow teacher-instructors to discuss and delve into academic as well as practical issues with students.

Instructors may also find the *Companion* useful as a supplemental text in capstone courses. A very strong trend in psychology curricula over the past few years is to require a course that encourages students to integrate what they have learned across their psychology courses. Because the *Companion* focuses on preparation for the steps after graduation—whether those might involve entering the workforce or pursuing graduate or professional school—we think it can provide appropriate guidance about the important decisions that lie ahead.

We included some special features that should help students engage and personalize their learning. Each chapter has a feature called "A Major Success Story" that profiles former students who have successfully navigated life after graduation. We hope these will be inspirational and provide some good exemplars to cite when students discuss their choice of the psychology major.

The *Companion*'s "Reality Check" features will help students personalize the learning in each chapter. The Reality Checks provide an opportunity to apply the principles of the chapter to their own course and career planning.

We are proud that the *Companion* uses emerging best practices from the collaborative national work on the undergraduate psychology curriculum from the American Psychological Association (APA). Our discussions of curriculum design and assessment strategies reflect recent work from the APA's Puget Sound Conference and the *Guidelines for the Undergraduate Psychology Major, Version 2.0*. As participants in those efforts, we wanted to ensure that our work here reflects the most current and helpful content.

Supplements

To support instructors in student assessment and in teaching, we have written a test bank comprised of multiple choice and essay questions as well as lecture slides that summarize the content of each chapter. These materials are password protected and available from the book's website (www.macmillanlearning.com/dunnhalonen1e).

Academic/major advisors in psychology departments (primarily faculty members) should welcome the text and its supplements as a resource to assign or to recommend to students. Advisors often find that they must answer the same set of questions over and over again. We hope that by providing a comprehensive treatment of curricular and career issues, we provide a resource that students can use to find the answers to some of these questions.

NOTE TO STUDENT ADVOCATES

We know that students who choose psychology sometimes encounter well-intentioned concern from friends and family members who suspect the choice isn't a good idea. Most of the objections rest with the belief that the degree won't adequately prepare students for employment after graduation. Concerned allies should find this book helpful in allaying fears and in assisting students in coming up with the best plan for their future.

ACKNOWLEDGMENTS

We are delighted to be a part of the Worth/Macmillan family and are grateful to our editor and good friend, Christine Cardone, for suggesting we work on this book together. Her enthusiasm for the project, coupled with her perceptive suggestions, helped us to refine our vision for the book. During the production process, we appreciated the precision and professionalism of the production team, including that of Jane O'Neill and Anna Paganelli. We thank the peer reviewers who read a first draft of the book: Suzanne C. Baker (James Madison University), Madeleine Fugère (Eastern Connecticut University), Timothy Franz (St. John Fisher University), Rachelle Cohen (Georgia State University), and Jana McCurdy (College of Western Idaho).

Dana is grateful to his children, Jake and Hannah, for their interest in and support of his work. He is also grateful to—and thankful for—Jane, whose friendship has taken him many places he never expected. He thanks the Moravian College Faculty Development and Research Committee for providing him with a summer 2014 grant that enabled him to work on the book. His colleagues in the Department of Psychology at Moravian College continue to inspire his teaching efforts and he appreciates their dedication to good pedagogy.

Jane marvels at the fact that she is about to celebrate 40 years of married life with her chief supporter and best friend. She is distinctly grateful for the APA Psychology Partnerships Project that brought Dana and her together, little realizing how intertwined their professional lives would become. It has been a fulfilling collaboration that just keeps elevating the bar. She also wants to acknowledge the support she has had from her colleagues at three different institutions—Alverno College, James Madison University, and the University of West Florida—who have fingerprints all over the ideas presented in this text.

A FINAL NOTE

This is by no means our first writing project together but it was certainly the most fun to do. Why? Simply because we got to swap stories and perspectives on the wonderful students we have taught over the years. We also had ample opportunity to rely on the wisdom of our many colleagues in psychology, including perhaps especially those who are so active in the Society for the Teaching of Psychology (Division 2 of the APA).

We welcome comments and suggestions from instructors regarding this first edition of the *Companion*. We hope you have as much fun reading the *Companion* as we did in writing it.

Dana S. Dunn
Bethlehem, Pennsylvania

Jane S. Halonen
Pensacola, Florida

CHAPTER 1

College and Psychology

If you don't know where you are going,
you might wind up someplace else.
—Yogi Berra

The most important and influential decision you will make in college is how you will find the best fit between your talents and the array of possibilities that colleges and universities have to offer. We wrote this book primarily to appeal to two types of college students: those who are already majoring in psychology and those who are thinking about doing so. We have a sneaking suspicion that another group who will benefit from reading the book are parents and loved ones who want to understand and support your selection of the psychology major.

□ □ □

Regardless of the reader group you belong to, we trust you'll find substantial help within these pages to reinforce your confidence in choosing psychology as a major, to make the most of the opportunities that lie ahead, and to prepare wisely and well for the various pathways that lie beyond graduation. We intend our comprehensive guide to the psychology major to provide friendly support (hence, to serve as your "companion") throughout your journey. It is our fondest hope that this text will help you not just to survive the work involved in completing an undergraduate degree in psychology, but to thrive as the result of the wise choices you make along the way.

We'll define just what psychology is and is not in Chapter 2; for now, we want to share some facts about the college experience and the attitudes of those heading to or already enrolled in a college or university.

THE NATURE OF THE COLLEGE EXPERIENCE

College. "College" is a familiar word. It's also an exciting word, a word full of promise and possibility. And, if nothing else, college is a powerful word—it gets people's attention. Readers who are already in college know that an undergraduate education opens many doors and sparks multiple conversations. If you haven't yet made the transition to being a college student, you may have been thinking about college for quite a while now, well before you picked up this book.

College is now a rite of passage for many people in the United States, a great opportunity to broaden personal horizons, to plan for the future, and to explore career options. A college education involves developing knowledge about a variety of areas, some familiar (e.g., English, math), some less so (e.g., philosophy, zoology). Learning in these areas provides students with new outlooks on their experiences as well as skills that are often marketable in the workplace (writing, critical thinking, public speaking).

College is not just about what happens in the classroom but what happens outside of it, too: making new friends, trying new things, working in groups, learning to be responsible for oneself, possibly holding down a part-time job in addition to studying, as well as perhaps living away from home for the first time.

And what's the difference between a college and a university? Generally, community colleges offer a 2-year degree and 4-year colleges and universities grant bachelor's degrees. A university is a large institution comprised of various colleges and schools, including those dedicated to educating graduate students (students who already hold a 4-year degree and are working toward the next level of education or training). Universities grant undergraduate and graduate degrees in many different courses of study. Whether you go to a college or a university, you will have a lot of company. Many students decide to continue their studies after they finish high school.

Heading to College: Today's Students

Who goes to college? Over 1.6 million high school graduates became first-time, full-time students in the fall of 2014, enrolling in a 4-year college or university (Eagan et al., 2014). Why do students go to college? The following seven reasons were rated as "very important" among those fall 2014 freshmen:

- to be able to get a better job,
- to gain a general education and appreciation of ideas,
- to make me a more cultured person,
- to be able to make more money,
- to learn more about things that interest me,
- to get training for a specific career, and
- to prepare myself for graduate or professional school.

What about you? Do these reasons characterize your own thoughts about going to college or do you have other reasons you might add to this list?

How did this recent group of college-bound students see themselves? They rated the following qualities as being a "somewhat strong" or "major strength" of theirs compared with the average person their age:

- openness to having their own views challenged,
- the ability to see the world from someone else's perspective,
- tolerance of others with different beliefs,
- the ability to discuss and negotiate controversial issues, and
- the ability to work cooperatively with diverse people.

How well do your views of yourself match these beliefs?

Just over 60% of these students considered it either "essential" or "very important" eventually to become an authority in their career field, while over 57% wanted to have their contributions recognized by peers in that field. In assessing their objectives in going to college, over 82% of the freshmen ranked "being very well off financially" as either "very important" or "essential," and over 72% ranked "helping others who are in difficulty" as very important or essential. Interestingly, under 45% viewed it as "essential" or "very important" to develop "a meaningful philosophy of life."

College turns out to be a very positive experience for most students. After a year of college, the majority of students—75%—report that they are satisfied or very satisfied with their experience (HERI, 2013). And 81% of students are satisfied or very satisfied with their overall academic experience.

Where does psychology fit into the mix? In fall 2014, a little under 5% of new freshmen indicated that they saw psychology as their likely major (interestingly, just shy of 2% of all freshmen that year reported that becoming a clinical psychologist was their intended occupation; Eagan et al., 2014). In fact, as a possible major, freshmen see psychology as a more popular choice than all other social science majors, including political science, sociology, and even economics.

What about 4 years later? How many students graduate with a bachelor of arts (BA) or bachelor of science (BS) degree in psychology? According to the National Center for Education Statistics (2015), in the 2012–2013 academic year, for example, 114,500 students graduated from a college or university in the United States with a degree in psychology (compare that number to the estimated 1.7 to 2 million undergraduates who enroll in introductory psychology yearly; Gurung, 2013; Steuer & Ham, 2008). Only a small percentage of those former psychology majors will go on to graduate school to continue their studies in the discipline. Most will enter the job market right away. Others will end up furthering their education by pursuing a graduate degree in some other educational area, which may or may not be related to psychology. However, the skills they acquired by pursuing a psychology major serve them well whatever professional paths they follow.

Common Concern: The Cost of College

We now know that college is many things. One other thing that college can be is expensive. Many students and their families wonder whether college is worth the cost. The short answer is that a college education remains an excellent investment—and using the word *investment* rather than *cost* is probably a good way to frame the issue. Working toward an undergraduate degree is an investment in your future.

Nearly all students considering college, in college, or fresh out of college all worry about finding a job, launching a career, and managing debt, especially student loans. It's no wonder people question whether a college degree is worth the money. An expert on college costs (Leonhardt, 2014) recently claimed that "For all the struggles that many young college graduates face, a four-year degree has probably never been more valuable" (p. A3). How so?

The evidence is actually quite clear: In 2013, Americans who are graduates of 4-year colleges and universities earned on average 98% more per hour compared to those without a degree. Other findings make the case this way: Skipping college and instead heading right into the workforce will cost you about half a million dollars across your working life—unrealized earnings that having a college degree would have provided. That's something to consider when weighing the costs of attending or not attending college.

What about the issue of incurring debt by taking out student loans? College graduates carry an average debt of about $25,000 (Leonhardt, 2014). That's not a small amount of money unless you compare it to that half-million dollars having a degree provides. In that light, borrowing money to attend college seems worth it, as the risk seems to be a modest one. However you slice it, a college education is still worth the cost.

Making the Most of College

This book is about helping you make the most of psychology as a major, but we also want to point out that attending college provides students like you with many opportunities. Studying and going to class are important parts of being a student, but so is attending to what colleges and universities refer to as "cocurricular activities," the things that occur outside of formal classes. In fact, it's a very good idea to establish some balance in your life during your college years. You should make time to study, eat as healthily as you can, and get regular exercise, of course, but also make sure to have some downtime. In other words, you might play on an athletic team, join a club or one of the numerous organizations found on your campus, pledge a fraternity or a sorority, or do volunteer work in the community. Indeed, a recent survey of first-year students revealed that more than 79% found a balance between their academic subjects and extracurricular activities (HERI, 2015). The point is to have some constructive outlet where you can renew your energy and outlook so that you always approach your studies with a positive attitude. After all, a balanced life will help you to retain what you learn in class, whether you choose psychology or another major.

BECOMING PSYCHOLOGICALLY LITERATE

There is very good news for psychology majors and would-be psychology majors: An undergraduate education in psychology provides students with a variety of skills, values, and outlooks that enable them to pursue and succeed in a variety of endeavors—in other words, it makes you literate. To be literate is to be (or become) an educated person who knows a great deal about some subject area, like psychology. Being *psychologically literate* turns out to be both personally and professionally valuable (Cranney & Dunn, 2011a). **Table 1.1** lists some traits exhibited by psychologically literate students—those who have used their time as psychology majors wisely and well.

Psychology majors acquire some distinctive skills (Hayes, 1997). Besides learning research skills, psychology majors learn how to find key information and to evaluate whether it's useful. They also become adept at "reading" people and being able to interact with them in appropriate and sensitive ways. Writing skills—being able to summarize ideas quickly and clearly—are also trademarks of an education in psychology. Compared to students who major in the natural sciences (e.g., biology, physics) or the humanities (e.g., history, art), psychology students show better reasoning about those everyday events that benefit from an understanding of research methods and quantitative skills (Lehman & Nisbett, 1990). They tend to avoid being perfectionists; they are better able than their peers to get whatever task they face done, practically and quickly (for an example, see *A Major Success Story*).

TABLE 1.1

Characteristics of Psychologically Literate Students

Solve problems in creative, amiable, and skeptical ways

Possess a well-defined vocabulary of psychological terms and concepts

Appreciate and respect diversity and diverse groups and individuals

Reflective about their own thinking processes and those of others

Good at evaluating information and using technology

Able to apply psychology principles to understanding and improving personal relationships, work issues, and things happening in the community

Act ethically, not out of self-interest

Communicate well and in different ways (writing, speaking, public presentations) to different types of people and audiences

Information from: Cranney & Dunn (2011b, p. 4). Oxford University Press.

A **Major** Success Story

The Workplace Advantage of Psychological Literacy

Dave was a full-time student who ended up majoring in psychology. During his college years, he held a part-time job at a large, upscale grocery store. He reported that majoring in psychology enabled him to develop both people and professional skills. He learned to think quickly to solve problems in the workplace, including those involving the challenges of customer service. He relied on the analytical and organizational skills he learned in class to be more efficient when restocking shelves and when making certain the produce displays were replenished. Dave maintained friendly but professional relationships with coworkers and became the "go-to person" when employees wanted advice or help—his talents as a leader were apparent. His bosses were impressed with his work ethic as well as his ability to write brief and to-the-point emails and reports.

He remained with the grocery store after graduation and worked his way into a full-time position with management responsibilities. His employers were especially pleased with his ability to listen to and solve customer problems. Dave also formally arranged a mentoring relationship with a senior executive to learn more about the organizational culture. On the strengths of his interpersonal skills with customers and coworkers and his inventive approach to solving problems, he became the head of a department in one of the grocery chain's newest stores with every possibility of rising to the top ranks of the company. Clearly, studying psychology made him a well-rounded person and allowed him to use the skills he developed in effective ways.

OUR GOALS: WHY WE WROTE THIS BOOK FOR YOU

As psychology professors, each of us has taught thousands of students, both psychology majors and nonmajors, about the discipline we love. One of the things we've noticed across our careers in higher education is that some students struggle to see how knowledge gained in the classroom can be applied to everyday work and life. In fact, an analysis published in the *Wall Street Journal* (Light, 2010) suggested that psychology majors tended to be the least satisfied with the major 6 months after graduation when compared to all other majors. Although we think there were problems in the design of the survey that produced the data driving this unhappy conclusion, we also recognize that students who don't learn to transfer their academic skills to life after graduation or who aren't proactive about forging a satisfying direction after graduation have lots of reasons to be unhappy. We want students to use mindful and intentional strategies as they pursue the psychology major. If they do so, they will be more satisfied with their choice of major both during and after graduation.

We believe that the psychology major provides students with an array of skills and habits of mind that will serve them well no matter what they do in their careers and in their personal lives. That's really the message of psychological literacy and the point of becoming psychologically literate.

We wrote this book so that students like you can use their college days well, as a launching pad for whatever comes next—career, internship, graduate school, or something altogether different. We discuss key topics, including:

- Why do students major in psychology? (Chapter 2)
- Should *you* major in psychology? Is it right for you? (Chapter 3)
- Developing psychology-related skills to enhance your career options and opportunities (Chapter 4)
- How to hit your stride as a student (Chapter 5)
- Charting your course in the major (Chapter 6)
- Tackling psychological research from start to finish (Chapter 7)
- Using psychology to improve leadership (Chapter 8)
- What career options are out there for students with a BA or BS in psychology? (Chapter 9)
- What about graduate school in psychology—what does it take and where might it take you? (Chapter 11)
- How do you apply and get in to quality graduate programs? (Chapter 10)
- Keeping connected to psychology after college (Chapter 12)
- Learning to write and format an APA-style paper (Appendix A)

Are you already a college student or are you thinking about going to college? Is college the right solution for you? Answer the questions in *Reality Check: Is College the Right Path for You?* to assess whether college is a good fit for your future.

As you read each chapter, don't forget this important fact: Among all the things that college is, it is a privilege. Census data show that as recently as 2013, only about 32% of adults in the United States had a 4-year college degree.

✔ Reality Check

Is College the Right Path for You?

Consider the following self-assessment questions:

- ☐ Do I have a clear understanding of my motives for seeking a degree?
- ☐ Does my academic record predict a successful transition to college?
- ☐ Can I set aside the time it will take to secure a diploma?
- ☐ Do I know which kind of higher education context has the greatest appeal to me?
- ☐ Have I taken steps to determine whether I would qualify for financial assistance?
- ☐ Have I considered what kind of living arrangements I'll be able to afford?
- ☐ Do I have a reasonable idea about the kind of major I want to pursue?
- ☐ Have I developed reasonable time-management strategies to keep up with multiple courses?
- ☐ Am I excited about the prospect of learning with a wide variety of people?
- ☐ Will I be able to function independently from my family?
- ☐ Will I be able to balance family and friends with school demands?
- ☐ Will I be able to cope with the debt load that will result from my degree?
- ☐ Am I prepared to seek academic advising to clarify my direction?

Review your answers. Obviously the more items to which you can respond "yes," the better prepared you will be for making the commitment to a college education.

Despite the popular hype that "college is now a necessity," most of our fellow citizens have not had the good fortune to complete a college degree. Having the opportunity to go to college is still a singular event and one that can be life changing. Coupled with choosing the right major, your college education should prove to be satisfying and fulfilling. We hope you feel this way, just as we hope that the insights we share with you about psychology will help you to make the most of your education.

THOUGHT QUESTIONS

1. What do you hope to get from a college education? Why?
2. At this point in time, what interests you about psychology? Why?
3. Do you know anyone who is already majoring in psychology? What do they like about their studies?
4. What kinds of out-of-class activities do you think you might like to pursue during college?
5. If you decided not to attend college, what would you do instead? Why?

The Nature of Psychology and the Psychology Major

Jane remembers what a struggle it was to try to help her grandmother understand what she planned to do in college. She described her excitement about what she was learning about human behavior in her psychology classes. She anticipated how interesting it would be to do research on unsolved questions about human behavior. She shared a hope that she would be able someday to use what she learned to help people with their problems as a clinical psychologist. Grandma nodded appreciatively. Later, Jane overheard her bragging to a neighbor that her granddaughter was studying to be "a brain surgeon."

□ □ □

It isn't surprising that the discipline of psychology can be a hard one to grasp. When that conversation transpired in the late 1960s, we didn't have much in the way of visible representatives who could help the unschooled come to terms with what it meant to study "psychology." Although we now have abundant examples of psychology in the media, many exemplars are narrow or misleading stereotypes that don't do much to reveal the true nature of the discipline. Despite the fact that psychology has produced some Nobel Prize winners, images of "Dr. Phil" McGraw tend to come to the minds of the public as the quintessential psychologist.

Most depictions in the entertainment media involve the noble (and sometimes flawed) clinical psychologist striving to make a difference in people's lives, often in forensic or legal settings. Such treatments tend to be great recruiting devices to students into the major but also unfortunately set prospective students up to think that the sum total of the major is about the diagnosis and treatment of

9

mental health problems. These students typically become disappointed when they learn that clinical matters actually represent a very small percentage of the under-graduate curriculum.

To set the stage for later personal explorations of fit with the psychology major (Chapter 3), in this chapter we will discuss two key topics: What exactly does the discipline of psychology entail, and what can you expect from a major in psychology?

WHAT IS PSYCHOLOGY?

In this section, we take a look at how psychology has evolved from its origins to its complex contemporary character, which involves both research and practice. We explore the difficulty the discipline has had in trying to establish a clear-cut identity for itself. We conclude this section by equipping you to dispel the myths that persist about the nature of psychology, myths that you may confront as you navigate your way through the major.

How Do We Define Psychology?

Compared to most other sciences, psychology is the new kid on the block. Most historians trace the formal beginnings of the science of psychology to 1879, when Wilhelm Wundt founded an experimental laboratory in Leipzig, Germany. This development marked a departure from the related but nonscientific discipline of philosophy. Psychology is less than 140 or so years old (by comparison, physics in some form has been around since ancient Greece, if not before). Although the discipline of psychology is fairly young, it has already undergone an evolution in character and definition.

During the earliest days of exploring psychology as a scientific endeavor, psychologists were interested in mapping the most basic functions of the human body. This version or "orientation" of psychology is referred to as *structuralism*. The label makes sense because the questions were **empirical** (that is, based on direct observation and experimentation) attempts to map human capacity. For example, the structuralists were curious about how much weight would need to be added to a standard stimulus before we could perceive it as heavier. They spent significant amounts of time testing and reporting individual perceptual experience about weights, sounds, tastes, and other dimensions of the senses through a scientific self-report process called introspection. Structuralists would be dazzled if they could see what has happened to the discipline they helped to establish.

Many other psychology orientations have emerged over time, including functionalism, **behaviorism**, and humanistic psychology, as well as psychoanalytic and cognitive approaches. It's beyond our purpose to do a systematic discussion of all of the trends and orientations in psychology. (If you are a major, you will probably have the opportunity/obligation to study that evolution in a history of psychology course.) To be fair, psychologists have not yet arrived at a shared paradigm or approach for studying behavior, which contributes to the confusion that exists about what psychology truly represents.

Most contemporary psychologists would agree with the definition of **psychology** as **the scientific study of mind and behavior in human and nonhuman animals**. Thus, psychology majors scientifically study the way living organisms behave, learn, think, and feel. An undergraduate degree doesn't qualify psychology majors to claim the title of psychologist, but psychology majors do learn to think as psychologists do by completing the major.

Let's take the definition apart because it will help to explain why the major is so easily misunderstood and might not appeal to everyone. First—and psychologists tend to be quite passionate about this point—psychology is a SCIENCE. We use scientific methods to draw conclusions about mind and behavior. Stanovich (2007) summarized that a science is not defined by any specific content area or technologies but by the general characteristics of the process used for validating conclusions. He suggested that the sciences concentrate on (a) reliance on systematic **empiricism** (direct observation); (b) commitment to making findings public to expand and build our understanding; and (c) application of key ideas in solving problems.

Psychologists like to describe behavior with a high degree of precision, carefully distinguishing descriptions of behavior from inferences drawn about behavior. We demonstrate the value of carefully defined behavior by relying on **"operational" definitions**, meaning we define behaviors through the use of observable operations. For example, if we are going to research playground aggression, we must carefully delineate what "counts" as an aggressive act. Must a punch be thrown or can mean words count as an aggressive act? Abiding by the rules of science, the psychologist is obligated to define key ideas in such a way that others could reproduce the same research protocols. Defined properly, we measure behavior and subject our measurements to statistical analyses to establish whether our experiments or research designs produce the outcomes we expect. Psychologists use a variety of strategies, from self-report measures to behavioral observations to fMRI scans—that is, all of the approaches psychologists use adhere to the scientific method.

"Mind and behavior" is an expansive way to talk about the content of what psychologists study. Over time, some subgroups in psychology have concentrated on one arena or another. For examples, behaviorists, who declared their founding principles in a historic manifesto (Watson, 1913), believed that the only valid focus of study was observable behavior. If you couldn't directly observe a phenomenon, then it had no place in their labs. In contrast, **cognitive psychology** broadened the focus to justify studying covert activity, such as dreaming and thinking. This field uses 1956—the year George Miller published a seminal article about the capacity of human information processing—as its official origin.

Psychologists don't restrict themselves to the study of humans. Contemporary psychology labs can feature primates, planaria, or pelicans, among others. Virtually any life form that engages in behavior can be the focus of a psychological investigation. Although enthusiasm has waned a bit for requiring students to work with animals as a part of their major, psychologists remain committed to conducting research on animals as long as they abide by strict rules to protect and care for those animals (Plous, 1996). Similarly, research with humans is also governed by a standard set of regulations.

Psychology's Struggle for Identity

Although the definition of psychology is fairly straightforward, the discipline has been plagued with identity problems from the outset. William James, arguably the founder of American psychology, described psychology as a "nasty little subject" (Hunt, 1961). Frustrated by the constraints of structuralism, James (1892/1961, p. 335) concluded, "This is no science, it is only the hope of a science." James was optimistic that psychology could evolve into a respectable natural science and opened the first experimental lab in America at Harvard. He later founded the orientation of **functionalism**, shifting attention to the motives behind and the purpose of behavior and away from structuralism's focus on sensory capacity.

Although many other orientations would follow over time, no one orientation has proven to be a unifying force to help strengthen psychology's identity. Contemporary critics (cf. Henriques, 2014) suggest that the proliferation of viewpoints and knowledge in the discipline reduces the coherence of psychology and may foster a deep sense of fragmentation within the discipline.

Just as a starting point, psychology operates in two distinct but related scientific spheres, as it has elements of both natural science and social science. As a natural science, psychology attempts to explain and predict natural phenomena that parallel the focus of chemistry and biology. For example, studies on the effectiveness of a new antidepressant medication clearly illustrate the natural science focus of psychology. As a social science, psychology strives to explain and predict social phenomena, using empirical methods that are similar to those used in economics, anthropology, and political science, among others. For example, a relevant social science study might explore why sports victories can sometimes result in mob violence. Any introductory course in psychology will ground students in both the natural and social dimensions of the discipline.

Another dichotomy complicates psychology's contemporary identity. Broadly speaking, professional psychology has been characterized as having two cultures (Kimble, 1984). The first culture represents the academic psychologists who create new knowledge through scientific research. The second culture includes those who apply psychological principles to solve problems. Popular culture tends to concentrate on the second culture—psychologists as helpers. Indeed, the vast majority of psychology majors initially start out in psychology in response to the impulse to "help people." However, the range of possibilities for the psychology major is not restricted to clinical concerns.

Technically, research has the potential to help people, too. And the remarkable thing about psychology is the wild diversity of options one can study. However, simply contrasting the psychology communities as "research" or "practice" doesn't capture the richness of the topics that can be studied in psychology.

The American Psychological Association (APA) maintains special interest groups that provide a great array of the special interests psychology fostered within psychology. **Table 2.1** reflects the full range of subdisciplines that constitute contemporary psychology. As you can see in Table 2.1, only some divisions (numbers 12, 17, 29, 39, 42, and 49) deal explicitly with the clinically or counseling-oriented issues most laypeople think of when they think of "psychology."

TABLE 2.1

Current Divisions in the American Psychological Association

Division 1: Society for General Psychology

Division 2: Society for the Teaching of Psychology

Division 3: Society for Experimental Psychology and Cognitive Science

[There is currently no Division 4]

Division 5: Quantitative and Qualitative Methods

Division 6: Society for Behavioral Neuroscience and Comparative Psychology

Division 7: Developmental Psychology

Division 8: Society for Personality and Social Psychology

Division 9: Society for the Psychological Study of Social Issues (SPSSI)

Division 10: Society for the Psychology of Aesthetics, Creativity and the Arts

[There is currently no Division 11]

Division 12: Society of Clinical Psychology

Division 13: Society of Consulting Psychology

Division 14: Society for Industrial and Organizational Psychology

Division 15: Educational Psychology

Division 16: School Psychology

Division 17: Society of Counseling Psychology

Division 18: Psychologists in Public Service

Division 19: Society for Military Psychology

Division 20: Adult Development and Aging

Division 21: Applied Experimental and Engineering Psychology

Division 22: Rehabilitation Psychology

Division 23: Society for Consumer Psychology

Division 24: Society for Theoretical and Philosophical Psychology

Division 25: Behavior Analysis

Division 26: Society for the History of Psychology

Continued

Division 27: Society for Community Research and Action: Division of Community Psychology

Division 28: Psychopharmacology and Substance Abuse

Division 29: Society for the Advancement of Psychotherapy

Division 30: Society of Psychological Hypnosis

Division 31: State, Provincial and Territorial Psychological Association Affairs

Division 32: Society for Humanistic Psychology

Division 33: Intellectual and Developmental Disabilities/Autism Spectrum Disorders

Division 34: Society for Environmental, Population and Conservation Psychology

Division 35: Society for the Psychology of Women

Division 36: Society for the Psychology of Religion and Spirituality

Division 37: Society for Child and Family Policy and Practice

Division 38: Society for Health Psychology

Division 39: Psychoanalysis

Division 40: Society for Clinical Neuropsychology

Division 41: American Psychology-Law Society

Division 42: Psychologists in Independent Practice

Division 43: Society for Couple and Family Psychology

Division 44: Society for the Psychological Study of Lesbian, Gay, Bisexual and Transgender Issues

Division 45: Society for the Study of Culture, Ethnicity and Race

Division 46: Society for Media Psychology and Technology

Division 47: Society for Sport, Exercise and Performance Psychology

Division 48: Society for the Study of Peace, Conflict and Violence: Peace Psychology Division

Division 49: Society of Group Psychology and Group Psychotherapy

Division 50: Society of Addiction Psychology

Division 51: Society for the Psychological Study of Men and Masculinity

Division 52: International Psychology

Division 53: Society of Clinical Child and Adolescent Psychology

Division 54: Society of Pediatric Psychology

Division 55: American Society for the Advancement of Pharmacotherapy

Division 56: Trauma Psychology

Information from: American Psychological Association (2015). http://www.apa.org/about/division/

Dispelling Myths About Psychology

There are many myths or compelling but untrue beliefs about the discipline of psychology (Lilienfeld, Lynn, Ruscio, & Beyerstein, 2010). Psychology's popularity is in part based on the ease with which all of us create on-the-spot theories about why people behave as they do. After all, most of us are steeped in our own and others' behavior (much of it ordinary, some of it downright wacky) from the moment we wake up until we go to sleep again. We can't help ourselves: Actions require explanation.

Part of the fault also lies with psychologists themselves. Collectively, we have not done a very good job of public relations in countering the falsehoods or half-truths about the discipline and the people who work in it.

If you are thinking about majoring in psychology, then you need an understanding of the most basic myths so that you not only don't fall prey to them yourself but so that you can gently but firmly counter those myths when others offer them as truths. What follows are some of the myths that surface most frequently about the nature of psychology. You may recognize some of them.

Psychology is nothing more than common sense. When people read about psychological research or hear about it—even in the classroom—they have a tendency to react as if the reported scientific findings are clear and obvious—how else could the findings have turned out? In reality, of course, the results only *seem* obvious. Psychologists refer to this as the **hindsight bias** or the "I-knew-it-all-along effect," where learning how things turned out makes great good sense once you know the outcome—however, if you examine people's expectations in advance, they often favor some other outcome (Roese & Vohs, 2012). In a classic example from 1991, psychologists Martin Bolt and John Brink asked a group of college students to forecast the outcome of whether the U.S. Senate would vote to confirm nominee Clarence Thomas to the Supreme Court (Cherry, 2014). Before the actual vote, 58% of the students predicted that Thomas would be confirmed but when they were polled after his confirmation, 78% asserted that this was the outcome they predicted in advance. Even the most thoughtful and judicious people can fall prey to this everyday bias because once we know how something has turned out, we find it very hard to entertain alternatives.

In addition, psychology contains a plethora of research findings that challenge common sense or are "counterintuitive." For example, if you are out driving and you suddenly need help with some car problems, are you better off on a low-traffic country road or a busy city street? Intuition tells you that a higher traffic volume would produce more potential helpers, but as confirmed in the classic work of Darley and Latané (1964) on "diffusion of responsibility" or "the bystander effect," your better bet is the country road; people are more likely to perform altruistic acts when they don't see others who can be counted on to intervene (see also Fischer et al., 2011).

Humans assume a lot of cause-and-effect relationships that just aren't accurate (Lilienfeld et al., 2010). For example, the right-brain (logic) versus left-brain (creative) distinction is overblown; adolescents don't necessarily demonstrate turmoil during this time of transition; and students don't necessarily learn best when teachers deliver courses designed to match their preferred styles. These are just a few of the commonsense conclusions that scientific psychology has challenged. Much of what we tacitly accept as true thrives as common sense but falters under scientific scrutiny.

Whatever it is, psychology is not a science. Psychology often doesn't get any respect as a science because many of its areas of inquiry are more familiar and accessible (love, depression) than those associated with older sciences, such as physics (black holes), biology (genetics), chemistry (covalent bonding), or some other science discipline. Laypeople generally assume that science is defined by what is being studied rather than by how the study is being done.

In actuality, a science is defined by the research methods it uses to pose and answer questions. Like other sciences, psychology relies on the **scientific method** (hypothesis testing, careful observation and experimentation, manipulation and measurement of variables, rigorous analysis, **replication**) rather than subject matter (psychologists study the behavior of organisms—everything from mice to marsupials, not just people). Psychology, then, is very much a science. If anyone still objects to this claim, as a last retort, point out that neuroscience and the study of the brain are highly technical and scientific.

Psychology is a pseudoscience. Nothing rankles a psychologist more than to have the false comparison of psychology with nonscientific behavioral explanations. Although horoscopes, numerology, and handwriting analysis can be fun and even compelling, psychologists protest the absence of scientific validation in the predictions that **pseudoscience** produces. In fact, the pseudosciences generally have no empirical data to support the claims they make about behavior (Lilienfeld, 2004).

Psychologists know how to "read minds." As psychologists, both of your authors dread getting the question, "What do you do for a living?" Answering "I'm a psychologist" is risky. Many people get nervous, begin to watch their words with care, and often inquire, "Are you going to read my mind!?" On the other hand, others see the lucky encounter as a way of getting free expert input on some psychological problem. (Saying you are a professor is almost as bad—people begin to worry you will correct their grammar.)

As should be clear, psychologists are scientists who use careful theories and research methods to study how people think, feel, and act—they don't read people's minds. If a psychologist has any particular insight into the human condition, it is likely the result of years of study, careful observation and inference, and honest hard work, not intuition or being a mentalist.

Psychologists = therapists. As you will learn later in this chapter, only some—by no means all—psychologists do counseling or therapy with people. In the popular mind, psychologists are supposed to do some form of counseling with people who are struggling with mental illness, for example, or some other psychological issue (e.g., chronic shyness). Jane, for example, fits the stereotype. She was trained as a clinical psychologist; although she does not currently have a practice, she maintained a private practice part-time as therapist for a dozen years while she established her academic career. In contrast, Dana is a social psychologist, a researcher, and has no training in clinical or counseling skills. Both of us are interested in teaching, research, and educational issues, including clarifying the nature of psychology as a science, part of which serves as a helping profession.

Because the media overrepresent clinical psychologists when portraying the discipline, many students come into psychology with the wrong idea about what the major will entail. Perhaps from an overexposure to "Dr. Phil," they eagerly anticipate courses that will be filled with case studies and fun speculations about what separates the normal from the abnormal. They are stressed when they learn the degree to which they will need to be good at mathematics to handle the demands of statistical analysis and conversely how limited their studies will be in the clinical realm. They can be horrified when confronted with the amount of biology they need to learn to understand the functioning of the brain. See *A Major Success Story* to learn about how a psychology background, coupled with mathematical skills, created a distinctive career opportunity for a psychology major.

Psychology is personally defined. No, it's not. Although some orientations in psychology are distinctly friendly to personal experience (e.g., humanism, phenomenology), the knowledge corpus of the science of psychology is carefully built from the rigorous rules of science. In addition, cognitive psychology has dramatically demonstrated how flawed personal reasoning and judgment can be. Consequently, personal experience as "proof" of a behavioral phenomenon is simply unacceptable to psychologists. A good example is the all-too-common belief that the full moon tends to induce higher levels of human craziness. No full moon effect has ever been verified (Arkowitz & Lilienfeld, 2009). A bad day as a barista during a full moon doesn't constitute solid proof of a psychological principle.

A **Major** Success Story

Data Analysis for Fun and Profit

From the outset of her major in psychology, Nikki had no intention of being a helper. She loved math and especially loved the challenges in the major that involved making sense of mounds of data. She was thrilled to discover that the research emphasis in psychology played to her strengths. She excelled in her classes and joined a research team supervised by her favorite professor. Her classmates fought to get her assigned to their team projects because they knew her persistence would help them develop and produce high-quality projects.

While she was completing her major, Nikki wasn't sure where she would end up, but after graduation she went on the job market, where a major food services corporation saw the value she demonstrated in her undergraduate major. She was able to go to work with a psychology major and a math minor in the marketing division and rapidly rose through the ranks. Not only did she secure a satisfying and profitable position, the company she worked for proposed to pay for her to continue her education to secure a master's degree as a "perk" of the job. And the food discounts weren't too shabby either!

WHAT IS THE NATURE OF THE PSYCHOLOGY MAJOR?

In this section we take a look at the process of being a psychology major, from the moment of decision on. We look at opportunities that can optimize your experience in the major. We also identify the misperceptions that abound regarding what it means to major in psychology.

Declaring the Major

Students usually end up in the psychology major in one of two pathways. Through personal experience with psychologists or imagined encounters stimulated by media, students decide that being a psychologist looks fulfilling and elect the major from the outset of their studies. Increasingly, high school students can take courses in psychology so many students come to college with experience of a psychological worldview and have a reasonable idea of what they are getting into. Dana fits this pattern; he knew from the start that psychology would be his disciplinary home.

However, often psychology represents a "found" major. That is, students start out in a different major but move to psychology when they discover the fit of the original major wasn't satisfying and something about the content of psychology was. The dynamic can grow out of taking a class with a charismatic psychology teacher or the recognition that something about the concepts and frameworks in psychology feels like home. Jane gravitated toward psychology when she found her original journalism major to be unsatisfying. Regardless of whether committed from the beginning or switched over, students can find a true comfort zone in psychological ways of thinking that will help them endure the rigors of the major.

The Typical Major Structure

Psychology departments across the country tend to offer majors that are fairly similar. For example, most students begin with an introductory psychology course. Students sometimes have the option of getting college credit in psychology in a high school dual-degree or advanced placement (AP) program. The introductory class often includes descriptions of the careers that might grow out of a psychology major and at minimum provide a broad foundation in both the natural and social science elements of psychology.

Many psychology departments offer a generic bachelor's degree, meaning that the degree addresses foundational skills and broad content areas to prepare students to be good psychological thinkers. The curriculum of such a program typically involves somewhere between 30 and 40 hours of specialized work in psychology courses that include an introduction, a research and statistics core, content courses with lab components, perhaps a history of psychology course, and electives and other classes that explore how psychology can be applied. A comprehensive study of undergraduate curricula (Stoloff et al., 2010) determined that there is no standard undergraduate program.

Many programs have incorporated the concept of a capstone course in psychology to help students pull together what they have learned over the course of the major (Dunn & McCarthy, 2010). A capstone course might be a seminar in history, an advanced introductory psychology course, a course on professional issues, or another course designed to facilitate students' integration of their learning across courses. Participation on research teams or in psychologically oriented workplace internships can also provide a fertile format for capstone-level work (see Chapters 7, 8, and 9).

Specializing Within the Major

Some educational contexts offer the option to pursue a bachelor of arts versus a bachelor of science in psychology. This distinction is not standard across colleges and universities, and individual departments can define the difference. Generally speaking, a bachelor of arts degree focuses on psychology's liberal arts side, including an emphasis on foreign language and a slightly reduced emphasis on science. The bachelor of science degree reduces the humanities influence in favor of an increase in the sciences, such as computer courses and additional math or statistics courses. Some departments have responded to the desire to make psychology more "STEM" (science, technology, engineering, and mathematics) oriented by renaming the degree as psychological science, rather than psychology.

Another trend has emerged in psychology curriculum that reflects the growth of specializations or concentrations within the major. For example, students can pursue degrees in human development, neuroscience, or neurobiology, all of which use psychology as the academic foundation for the curriculum structure. Some undergraduate programs offer certificates that can document that you have spent concentrated time in human resources, addictions, child development, or other content clusters that can add an impressive line on your resume and help set you apart from your competition.

Enriching Your Major With a Minor

Most graduation requirements leave room for students to go beyond requirements for the major and add some areas of concentration. The choices you make in filling in your education reveal a great deal about your values. For example, some students choose a particular minor because of their high level of intrinsic interest in that minor. Others purposely seek minors that will make them more fit for a specific career direction. See *Reality Check: Adding Value to the Major* to explore profitable minors, whether to enhance your career or to satisfy your soul.

✔ Reality Check

Adding Value to the Major With the Right Minor

Consider how the following minors might enrich your major and set you apart from your competition either for graduate school admission or entry into the workforce. Which choices have the greatest appeal to you for your career planning?

Minor	Graduate School Advantage	Workforce Advantage
Biology	Most graduate programs have extensive requirements in biology.	A strong background in biology can qualify you for entry in health care and pharmaceuticals.
Business	Psychologists who plan to be private practitioners also need to be good at business.	Business courses enhance your appeal in many entry-level positions.
Communications	Graduate school and the professions entail substantial speaking and writing activities.	Psychology and communications produce a great background for public relations and marketing.
Computer science	Executing research design can be enhanced using technology.	Most workforce positions have a strong intersection with information technology.
English	Concentrated practice in clear writing helps with writing one's thesis and dissertation.	Being able to write capably about psychological phenomena can open interesting entry-level job prospects.
Mathematics	Even clinicians need to complete a variety of statistics classes.	Knowing how to collect and analyze data is helpful in both the profit and nonprofit sectors of business.
Philosophy	The writing and thinking practice involved in philosophy improves intellectual capacity.	Some entry-level jobs have a lot of opportunity for deep thinking and creative problem solving.
Sociology	Sociology assists in the advocacy and community organizing components of graduate training.	Understanding both individual and group behavior can help in community organizing.
Theater	Graduate school showcases presentation skills and offers teaching opportunities.	Theater experience can build one's confidence in self-presentation.

WHAT THE PSYCHOLOGY MAJOR IS NOT

Psychology is not a very easy major. Psychology gets a bum rap as being easy for the simple reason that people are so familiar with human behavior (their own and others') that they assume they know all there is to know about it. Many students approach taking introductory psychology with the attitude that the course will be a breeze—because psychology is based on common sense—but often face a rude awakening when they get back their scores on the first exam. What sounded so plausible and obvious during class turns out to have many subtle and nuanced effects when it appears on a test.

By comparison, few students or parents will suggest that majoring in architecture, chemistry, mechanical engineering, or even German studies is "easy." People don't have as many theories about what students, let alone professionals, do in these fields (just ask someone to explain what mechanical engineers or people in German studies do—then ask about people interested in psychology). Not to put too fine a point on it, but if psychology were the "academic gut" major it is often portrayed to be, then most majors would get straight A grades (alas, they don't) and there would be legions of psychologists walking the earth (there just aren't). The scientific, mathematical, and biological components of psychology quickly prompt new majors to recognize that a psychology degree won't be effortless. If psychology courses are taught properly, the major is far from easy (Halonen, 2012).

Psychology majors cannot function as therapists. Having a bachelor's degree in psychology does not mean you are a psychologist and can counsel people or do therapy. First, a bachelor's degree is an undergraduate degree, one signifying completion of some breadth of study (what are usually called liberal arts or general education courses) coupled with study in one or more majors (like psychology). Undergraduate degrees are required before students can pursue graduate education—that is, intensive study in some area for a master's degree or a doctorate or some other advanced (also called terminal) degree. People who call themselves "psychologists" must usually have a doctorate (often a PhD or a PsyD) and must be licensed to practice. So, let's be crystal clear: Having an undergraduate degree does not entitle students to call themselves psychologists, nor can they perform professional-level therapy. As we shall see in Chapter 7, however, there are a variety of employment opportunities for students who have completed an undergraduate degree in psychology.

To do any form of professional counseling, a psychologist must have additional years of training—the average undergraduate completes a degree in 4 years, while a master's degree may require an additional 2 years and a doctorate can take 4 to 6 years or even longer, depending on the particular situation. Advanced degrees in psychology and being admitted to graduate school in psychology are topics we discuss in detail in Chapters 10 and 11, so we will postpone going into further detail until then.

Psychology majors often relish having their friends come to them with their problems. Perhaps you've been labeled a "good listener" or as someone who gives good advice. That's fine, so far as it goes. Just understand that in order to work as a professional psychologist offering guidance to people requires advanced training, a degree, and being licensed to practice. If that is your passion or goal, we encourage you to undertake the academic journey—just don't misrepresent yourself before that journey's end.

Majors choose psychology to solve their own problems. Although students who have experienced emotional setbacks may be drawn to psychology as a major, there is little in the undergraduate curriculum that focuses on the development of insights into one's personal makeup. The degree concentrates on communicating concepts, principles, and theories about human behavior from the vantage point of science. The more direct route for deep self-insight and personal change is therapy, not baccalaureate study (Halonen, 2014).

The psychology major can be a pathway to riches because psychologists are paid considerable amounts of money just for listening to people's problems. The vast majority of psychology graduates do not go on into clinical psychology or graduate school, but instead use their degree as a passport into the workforce. Unfortunately, psychology majors who move into entry-level positions do tend to garner some of the lowest salaries in the workforce (Halonen, 2012). However, entry-level salaries merely open the door to a career that may be rich in opportunities for promotion and substantial pay increases over time. **Table 2.2** lists the starting salaries of several liberal arts majors as of spring 2014. The starting salary for those employed with undergraduate psychology degrees was $37,900. The figures shown in the table are no guarantee that

TABLE 2.2

Starting Salaries for Class of 2014 Liberal Arts Majors

Major	Starting salary
Foreign languages and literatures	$46,900
English language and literature letters	$42,200
Liberal arts and sciences/General studies	$41,600
Political science/Government	$41,600
History	$40,600
Psychology	**$37,900**
Social work	$36,700
Sociology	$36,300
Visual and performing arts	$36,300
Criminal justice and corrections	$36,200

Data from: National Association of Colleges and Employers (2014).

your friend who majored in English is going to have a starting salary of $42,600 in her first job, of course, but they do indicate that students who major in the liberal arts can hold their own in workforce competition.

A still more recent salary survey published by the APA shows that the median annual salary for employees (ages 25 to 59 years) who have a bachelor's degree in psychology is $49,000. Degree recipients trained in some subfield of psychology earned more. For example, workers with training in industrial/organizational psychology earned a median salary of $66,000, while those who specialized in social psychology made $51,000. For comparison, the median salary for people with a bachelor's degree in any field, including psychology, was $61,000. Here is something else to consider: Psychology majors who go on to complete graduate degrees earn, on average, 33% more money than those who only have a bachelor's degree (American Psychological Association, 2016).

Of course, starting salaries aren't static; the potential to earn higher salaries, depending on the context, improves over time with strong performance. Psychology majors who pursue business applications, such as organizational psychology, marketing, or consumer behavior, will earn on the higher end of the scale. Those who go into social service occupations will generally make less than the average. Regardless of major, starting salaries in the human service fields are going to be somewhat disappointing when compared to salaries in business contexts, but those who opt to work in social services still can earn a respectable living.

Now, what about incomes for professional work? How much do psychologists earn? **Table 2.3** lists the average salaries for some groups of psychologists, and includes data on the average growth in salary that is related to the number of years of work experience. Note that these are averages—some psychologists have lower salaries than those reported here and others have higher salaries.

According to the National Bureau of Labor Statistics (2013), the cost of living in a particular area also has an impact on how much you earn (California and metropolitan New York are more expensive than many places in the Midwest or the South, for example). Still, a cursory examination of the numbers in Table 2.3

TABLE 2.3

Average Salaries for Psychologists

Experience	0–5 years	5–10 years	10–20 years	More than 20 years
Clinical psychologist	$65,000	$75,000	$87,000	$96,000
Counseling psychologist	$55,000	$69,000	$75,000	$70,000
Forensic psychologist	$57,000	$72,000	$85,000	$120,000
School psychologist	$51,000	$60,000	$69,000	$78,000
Industrial-organizational psychologist	$65,000	$89,000	$107,000	$109,000

Data from: Psychology Career Center (2015).

indicates that even though the typical psychologist makes a comfortable living, he or she is not rich. So, while most psychologist do fine financially, they don't necessarily make "a considerable amount of money" (National Association of Colleges and Employers, 2014).

Although a doctoral-trained psychologist may charge as much as $200 per therapy hour, that fee inspires an overestimation of income potential and fantasies of riches. At first blush, a 40-hour workweek should translate into a tidy haul of $8,000 a week. However, a full-time caseload probably represents more like 20 than 40 hours of direct service to leave time for record writing, correspondence, marketing, consultation, and meetings. In addition, fees must cover the cost of office rental, support staff, answering service, insurance, office supplies, and continuing education—and that is after taxes.

WHAT THE PSYCHOLOGY MAJOR IS

In summary, the undergraduate psychology curriculum offers a splendid opportunity to learn about the behavior of living organisms from the standpoint of science. As such, it provides a great passport into the workforce, where psychological principles can be applied to solve problems. And for high-performing and strongly motivated majors, the undergraduate degree facilitates the greatest promise for acceptance into a graduate program; from there, professional choices can be even more focused on the content and skills sets of psychology. In the next chapter, we will explore whether the psychology major is a good option for you.

THOUGHT QUESTIONS

1. Why is the discipline of psychology so frequently misunderstood?
2. In what way does psychology qualify as a science?
3. What myths complicate a layperson's understanding of psychology?
4. What are the key features of the undergraduate psychology curriculum?
5. What are some profitable minors that can enhance the value of a psychology major?
6. What are some inaccurate ideas about the nature of the psychology major?

3

Should You Major in Psychology?

Since he was a junior in high school, Dana knew that he wanted to be a psychologist and that majoring in psychology was more or less a foregone conclusion. Dana worked for his father the summer after his freshman year of college. He remembers sitting in the passenger seat of his father's car one summer afternoon, holding forth about why psychology interested him and how he was already hoping to attend graduate school. If graduate school turned out not to be in his future, he was sure that his psychology degree would provide him with lots of opportunities (though he was not sure what those might be). Dana remembers vividly how his father, a small-town businessperson, listened quietly and, never taking his eyes from the road, said pointedly, "Yes, but will you be able to support yourself?" In other words, would a degree in psychology pay the bills? Dana was speechless for a moment because he realized that he had never thought about the practical implications of majoring in psychology—he just *assumed* it would all work out, that he was following his passion, and so on. He remembers thinking, "Uh-oh."

□ □ □

Uh-oh, indeed. Although many people may applaud your choice of a psychology major, we suspect that you are likely to hear at least some concerns raised by those people who care about you about the wisdom of choosing psychology. Dana's father's concern about the economics underlying choosing to major in psychology is fairly typical and it should encourage reflection: Should you—should anyone—major in psychology? We believe the answer can be a resounding "yes," but it's important to understand the underlying issues before making any commitment.

To that end, this chapter deals with preparing you to become an effective psychology major. It makes sense to develop your rationale for choosing a psychology major from all the available options. It's inevitable. When you meet new people and they learn that you are in college, they will ask what major you have chosen and why. You will be most impressive when you can explain your choice by describing your values and your professional goals with confidence. Linking your choice to your values and goals can also be important in helping you stay steady should the going get tough.

You may also need to address the other concerns that parents, friends, and loved ones often have about choosing the psychology major. We believe you can constructively respond to such concerns but you should have a solid understanding of their origins and rationales. It's a good idea for you to engage in some self-assessment: Is your personality a good fit for psychology? What are your current skills and interests? We begin this chapter by exploring the familiar debate about whether to choose a career—really, a calling—for meaning or for money, an important issue given the typical length of most people's work lives. We close the chapter by identifying and discussing the characteristics of students who don't make particularly good psychology majors.

REFLECTING ON YOUR CHOICE OF MAJOR

Pleasing the significant people in your life matters, but it can sometimes be challenging. They want what they believe is best for you and may have their own notions about what kind of major would be most suitable for you.

Many people will be enthusiastic about your choice of major in psychology. From their own understanding of what the major entails (whether or not that understanding is accurate), they can envision psychology being a great match for your interests and talents. They will be receptive to the idea and excited that you have found an area of study that will sustain your interests over the course of your education.

Nonetheless, it's important to understand that it is not unreasonable for those who care about you to have some concern about your choice of major. Not surprisingly, the main concern often revolves around simple economics: Will a college major provide you with a reasonable salary following graduation? Will the salary also allow you to pay back any college loans, cover rent, and pay for all your other living expenses? These are real concerns that many people overlook or assume will take care of themselves once the "right" job is found. Parents' worries about their children's majors and career choices have only escalated since the onset of the so-called "Great Recession," which began in December 2007 and ended in June 2009. If you are a returning student choosing psychology as a major, chances are that you are already familiar with the challenges of a tight job market.

Many students choose majors that are practical (meaning those that ordinarily lead directly to employment) or that have a high payoff in the form of starting salary, job security, and so on. As a result, many students go to college and choose to become business or economics majors because they assume that understanding accounting, marketing, finance, and related areas will assure them of a well-paying job right out of college. Or they choose majors that lead to jobs that are in high demand, such as nursing or medical technology. Other students choose majors that have particular skills associated with them, including lab sciences like chemistry and biology as well as those in engineering or computer science. All of these majors are excellent choices as long as the students who sign up for them have both a genuine interest in them and the skills required to do well during the course of their studies. In the case of most of the majors noted above, solid quantitative skills—that is, knowledge of math and statistics—are necessary.

Although psychology is a science (recall our discussion in Chapter 1), higher education categorizes psychology as one of the traditional liberal arts majors. By *liberal arts*, we mean those areas of higher education that provide students with general knowledge (literature, mathematics, history, philosophy, as well as

✔ Reality Check

The Older Psychology Major

Some readers of this book may be *nontraditional* students, that is, some of you are older and more experienced than traditional 18- to 22-year-old college students. You are starting or returning to college after doing other things. For example, you may already have lived on your own, held one or more jobs, and even started a family. Your seasoned perspective will likely set you apart from your traditional-aged counterparts in the classroom (Weaver & Qi, 2005).

Because of life experiences, nontraditional students:

- ☐ tend to be highly motivated and want to get the most they can from their college major and their undergraduate education;
- ☐ are usually well-prepared for each class meeting;
- ☐ are very likely to participate actively in the classroom and usually don't worry about how their peers or instructors will react to their comments and ideas;
- ☐ are often confident and very likely to interact with their instructors;
- ☐ react favorably to the structured nature of college courses and enjoy learning about the course subject;
- ☐ tend to be less tolerant of classroom activity that strays from the course objectives.

If you are a nontraditional student, you have had more time to consider your options, you may be more certain about your intended career path, including your choice of psychology as a major. Although that may be true, there are still things you can learn in this chapter that will help you navigate the psychology major and college life, as well as to plan for your future.

social sciences like sociology, political science, and anthropology) rather than specific technical knowledge (like that associated with the natural sciences or the applied sciences, including engineering) or specific training needed for a profession. Studying the liberal arts effectively teaches students how to learn because it emphasizes critical thinking and reading, writing, and so on, all of which help people to develop general intellectual abilities that are transferable to a variety of situations, not to mention a variety of jobs and careers.

Liberal arts critics tend to focus on economic factors, but we must not overlook this important fact: Not everyone truly wants to commit to an academic major because it leads directly to a job. Other students are unsure of what they want to do in the near future, let alone for the rest of their lives. Many students choose a major out of intrinsic interest in or even fascination with the topic (note that we are *not* claiming that professional or technical majors are not interesting or fascinating—just that students should pursue a discipline because they are truly drawn to it). Following the recommendations or guidance of others without question is not a good idea, as you might simply settle for a major that will not be engaging or inspiring, thus making it hard to do your best work.

Making such a choice can be problematic on a variety of fronts: Would you want to work in a field for 30 or 40 years if you really had no interest in it? If nothing else, the field of **positive psychology** demonstrates unequivocally that money does not lead to happiness (Diener & Biswas-Diener, 2008). If you are not especially interested in the work demanded by some professional or technical majors, then your college grades may end up reflecting that. Will employers want to hire people with high grade point averages (GPAs) or low ones? That answer is fairly obvious.

There are the real and personal costs that result from being persuaded to major in something that does not really speak to your heart and mind. Consider this cautionary tale: Several years ago a student—let's call her Wendy—majored in education and psychology (education majors in some states are required to have a second full major). At that time, teachers in elementary, middle, and high school were in great demand and the available jobs provided solid salaries and job security, not to mention the attractive 9-month cycle of teaching, with summers off. Wendy's parents pushed her to be a teacher because they believed it was a low-risk/high-payoff career choice. Wendy did fine in her education and psychology classes. During the fall of her senior year, she did a stint of student teaching, which essentially involves being in a school classroom 5 days a week learning from a supervising teacher and doing actual teaching. This was Wendy's first and only teaching experience on the other side of the desk.

Halfway through the semester Wendy went to see her academic advisor and reported that she was miserable. She never realized what went into being a teacher and she wanted no part of it. She spent the rest of her time in college— about 5 months—trying to figure out what she did like and what she might want to do in the future. Imagine spending more than 3 years of your life pursuing someone else's dream, one that turned out not to interest you in the least? We have had dozens of students who pursued a career in teaching and ultimately thrived in their occupational choice, but they made their choices on their own because they were interested in being teachers, not because it would satisfy their parents' dreams.

What about economic and job security concerns—are they justified? Yes and no. Yes, it is reasonable for college graduates to become economically independent, buy their own homes, have good careers, start families, and so on. But no, as there is not much to be gained if students pursue majors that do not interest or motivate them, or to which they are not suited or, in some cases, for which they are not even qualified. What you need to do is to plan to work very hard to succeed in whatever major you eventually choose, whether psychology or something else.

If you do choose psychology, then you will want to develop skills that will help you do well in the job market or whatever future you plan for yourself. Let us consider your personality as well as your skills and interests and make sure you and psychology are a good match for each other.

KNOWING YOURSELF: SELF-ASSESSMENT OF YOUR PERSONALITY AND SKILLS

Industrial and organizational (I/O) psychologists argue that people's personalities—their unique and consistent behavioral traits—can be linked to the type of work they do best. In fact, there are a variety of standardized occupation interest inventories that tie people's traits to vocational possibilities and enable them to do a **self-assessment** of their personality and skills. Your college or university's career services center may make these available to you—drop by and ask.

The same argument regarding personality can be made for choosing a college major—do your own traits, your likes and dislikes, fit the major or majors you are considering? A good way to begin is to think about your particular preferences. Try answering some of the following questions before proceeding with the reading (you can come back and try some of the others later):

■ What do people tell you are your best features or skills? Do you agree?

■ Do you like interacting with people one-on-one? What about in groups?

■ What activities do you enjoy doing? Why?

■ Do you have any particular hobbies or things you do when not studying or working?

■ What would your perfect work environment be like?

■ Do you deal with interpersonal conflict well?

- What creates stress for you? Did part of any past job make you feel stressed?
- Do you like to work alone or do you prefer to be part of a team?
- Do you like to work on small details or do you prefer the "big picture"?
- How do you define success?
- Does your life have a purpose? What is your destiny?
- What would you like to be known and remembered for in the long run?
- To make the world a better place, what would you change? Why?
- What is the one word you use to describe yourself?

If you are unsure about how to answer some of these questions, think back to any jobs (including part-time or summer jobs) you have had. What aspects of the job(s) did you like? What specifically appealed to you? Was there anything that you did not like about the work? If you currently have a job, you might start keeping a journal in which you write at the end of each workday about what you like and dislike about the job. Doing so may help you to reach some conclusions about how much autonomy you like to have, if you like working alone or with others, if doing desk work is appealing, and so on. The fit between the person and the environment—the worker and the setting—matters.

Seeking a Fit Between You and a Working Environment

Psychologist John Holland (1996, 1997) developed what is known as a **trait model** of career choice, one designed to help people link their personality qualities (e.g., interests, needs, skills, values, learning styles, attitudes) to particular settings where work occurs. In his model, he categorizes individuals into one of six personal orientations and organizes occupations into one of six work environments. All else being equal, a person with a particular personality orientation should prefer to be in the linked work environment. Holland's main point is that people express their personalities, particularly their interests and values, in the work they choose to do. People who end up in educational or work environments that fit or are relatively close fits to their personalities are more likely than others to be fulfilled, successful, and determined in what they do in their major and career. In the long run, those with a good fit are apt to remain in their chosen careers longer than those who are less satisfied with their work.

Holland's (1996, 1997) six personal orientations are summarized in **Table 3.1.** Most people identify more than one orientation that could describe their personality. To begin, try to select the one type from Holland's six orientations that is the best fit for you. Then choose a second and a third, but keep in mind that these are all idealized types—no one person will fit any type or types perfectly.

TABLE 3.1

Holland's Six Personal Orientations

Realistic. The realistic personality orientation values concrete and physical tasks. Realistic people perceive themselves as possessing mechanical skills but they generally believe they lack social or interpersonal skills. They are drawn to manual and athletic activities and enjoy using tools and machines. They tend to be practical and focused on solving problems.

Investigative. Individuals with an investigative personal orientation love to solve scientific, intellectual, and mathematical puzzles and problems. They view themselves as being methodical, self-reflective, critical, curious, and highly analytical. They value their independence and enjoy taking courses in the physical and biological sciences, as well as mathematics and chemistry.

Artistic. People with an artistic personal orientation are drawn to unstructured projects that provide freedom and breadth to explore and express feeling and emotion. Such projects include painting, sculpture, music, writing, and dramatic performance. People with this orientation see themselves as independent, free-spirited, expressive, and imaginative. They like to be innovative.

Social. People with a social personal orientation are drawn toward educational, helping, and religious careers. They like to work with others, especially on teams, and to work toward achieving group goals. Such people take pleasure in socially engaging settings, such as religious communities or schools, as well as groups that involve reading, music, and theater. They tend to be cooperative, friendly, conscientious, persuasive, and insightful. Social people are sensitive to others' needs and greatly value social and educational issues.

Enterprising. People with an enterprising personal orientation like to lead, motivate, inspire, and persuade others, especially where selling material goods or convincing people to adopt particular views are involved. They value economic and political achievement, relish the chance to supervise, and enjoy exerting control as well as being recognized for their verbal expressiveness. Being powerful, wealthy, and possessing status is appealing to them. They perceive themselves to be extroverted, sociable, happy, self-confident, and popular, and they have little trouble asserting themselves.

Conventional. People with a conventional personal orientation like order and prefer to engage in systematic, concrete tasks that are prescribed and use both verbal and quantitative data. They see themselves as conformists and tend to identify with their clerical and numerical abilities. They excel at following rules and orders and typically are very detail oriented. They are drawn to straightforward rather than open-ended problems.

Information from: Holland (1996, 1997).

Now we turn to descriptions of the work environments that link to those personal orientations. **Table 3.2** has summaries of these work environments, along with a list of some representative college majors. As you review these six environments and their related majors, ask yourself whether each of the three personal orientations that most closely describe you are linked to work environments that sound plausible and pleasing to you.

The goal of reviewing these personal orientations, work settings, and majors is to get you to think about yourself by identifying—and ranking—your top three personal orientations. For example, in **Holland code**, you could be an RCE (realistic, conventional, enterprising) or an SEA (social, enterprising, artistic). Assessing your

TABLE 3.2

Holland's Six Work Environments Linked to Personal Orientations

Realistic settings. Realistic work environments are characterized by the presence of concrete, physical tasks that use mechanical skills, physical motion, and considerable persistence at tasks. Sample careers include draftsperson, automobile mechanic, law enforcement or corrections officer, electrician, engineer, cook or chef, pilot, and machine operator. Sample majors include electrical or aerospace engineering, architecture, criminal justice, and environmental studies.

Investigative settings. Work environments that are investigative include research laboratories, scientific groups or teams, and medical settings in which case conferences are held. Sample careers include computer programmer, clinical psychologist, veterinarian, dentist, marine biologist, physician, physician's assistant, and chemist. Sample majors include computer science, biology, biochemistry, astronomy, and anthropology.

Artistic settings. Artistic work environments include concert or performing halls; theaters; libraries; radio or television studios; and art, photography, design, or music studios. Sample careers include actor, painter, advertiser, sculptor, musician, author, editor, designer, photographer, interior designer, and architect. Sample majors include English, art, art history, interior design, commercial art, advertising, architecture, design, and interior design.

Social settings. Social settings include hospitals; colleges and universities; public and private schools; churches, temples, and synagogues; recreational centers; and mental health organizations, including psychiatrist's offices and social service agencies. Sample careers include counselor, teacher, professor, nurse, social worker, judge, minister, rabbi, sociologist, and psychologist. Sample majors include human development, psychology, philosophy, sociology, religious studies, education, special education, and social work.

Enterprising settings. Enterprising work settings include places like advertising companies, courtrooms, congressional offices, car sales offices, retail stores, and real estate firms. Sample careers include attorney, realtor, politician, salesperson, and manager. Sample majors include business administration, economics, broadcasting, hospitality and tourism, industrial relations, and finance.

Conventional settings. Conventional work settings are office settings generally, as well as banks, post offices, any business office, and filing rooms. Sample careers include receptionist, financial counselor, accountant, banker, bookkeeper, data processor, office clerk, and court reporter. Sample majors include accounting, finance, medical records, mathematics, and statistics.

Information from: Holland (1996, 1997).

three-letter Holland code in detail is beyond the scope of this book. Instead, we want to get you thinking on your own about your orientations, possible work settings, and potential goals for the future. You may be wondering which three-letter Holland code psychologists tend to have. It's SIA (social, investigative, artistic). Psychologists—but not *all* psychologists, of course—tend to be sociable and inquisitive and to have an appreciation for the arts.

If you selected these three letters as your Holland code, then a psychology major might be a solid choice for you. On the other hand, if you are or want to be a psychology major but did not choose all three—or even any of the three—psychologists tend toward, don't despair. All the Holland code indicates is that at this point in time you may (or may not) have interests that are similar to those of psychologists who earned their doctorates. Your code may change over time or it might not; remember, it's meant to be a guide, not a definitive diagnostic tool. This is one piece of information that you can think about along with your responses to the preference and "like/dislike" questions that are at the start of this section. You can then add these bits of data to your other responses, including those in which you identify your reasons for choosing the psychology major.

KNOW YOUR MOTIVES (MEANING VERSUS MONEY)

Being happy is a good motive for making some choices rather than others regarding education, work, and career. No one would complain about accepting a job that paid a very high salary but, as we already noted, pursuing work that pays well just for the sake of money is unlikely to lead to real happiness. Research demonstrates that once people exceed an income of about $75,000 per year, their happiness levels do not change much (Kahneman & Deaton, 2010); in effect, more money does not buy more happiness. Moreover, as people make more money, the time they need to devote to work increases substantially. Ironically, by putting in more hours to maintain or increase their income, they subsequently have less time to devote to leisure and recreation. More money generally means less fun and less time for relaxation, which tends to mean no increase in happiness (Kahneman, Krueger, Schkade, Schwarz, & Stone, 2006). Making a good living in order to cover existing expenses is important, but something is lost if happiness is sacrificed in the process. Making more money, then, is unlikely to be a worthy motive for you to pursue with abandon.

A better motive is to search for work that provides meaning and satisfaction in your life. By *meaning*, we refer to having a sense of direction in life, as well as possessing coherent values and a personal philosophy. If you see meaning in what you do—in why you are following one major and not another, one career path instead of another—then you will have a strong sense of purpose to guide you. Each day (or most days) you will approach your studies or your work with commitment, interest, and sometimes joy. In fact, doing work that is enjoyable provides a feeling of fulfillment—what we do improves us as people and makes the world we live in a much better place to be (Wrzesniewski, Rozin, & Bennett, 2003).

One way to approach the issue of meaning is to reflect on how you view your work. Professionals tend to see their work as falling into one of three categories: jobs, careers, and vocations. We've used the word "career" in a broad way in this chapter until now, when we will contrast it with these two other terms.

Jobs. A **job** is a source of income to support life outside of work. Jobs can provide financial security but the people who hold them derive little satisfaction from the work they do—it's literally just a job. For example, people who work a job would not recommend others choose their line of work (and if they themselves could do it all over again, they would do something else). Jobholders continually anticipate weekends, holidays, and vacations; most cannot wait to retire.

Careers. Having a **career** means holding a position for long enough to succeed in it before receiving a promotion and moving on to the next (higher) position. The particular work in a career is sometimes challenging or interesting, sometimes not. However, to rise higher—to get the next pay raise, the more important title, the bigger office, and so on—people with careers have to do reasonably well in their positions. Promotions indicate that someone pursuing a career is working well and is successfully competing with (and perhaps advancing past) coworkers. Careers have a competitive element so that careerists are often looking for the next opportunity.

Vocations. Having a **vocation** is like following a "calling," where work is an integral part of a person's life, providing satisfaction, pleasure, and identity. People who have a vocation love what they do, tell others about it, often socialize with peers who do the same or similar work, and belong to organizations that relate to it. People in a vocation routinely bring their work home and often take it with them on vacation (but are not usually workaholics) and do not long for retirement (many don't look forward to retiring, quite a few don't plan to stop working if they can help it). Work is more or less play, as well as a source of meaning and purpose.

Now, which would you prefer to have: a job, a career, or a vocation?

What we do know is that people who see their work as a vocation manage to blend the eagerness for what they do with the responsibilities inherent in the work (Wrzesniewski, McCauley, Rozin, & Schwartz, 1997). Quite simply, people who have a vocation are more satisfied with their work and their lives compared to those who have jobs or careers—and they devote more time to their work than those in the other groups. Very often people who have a vocation indicate that working is more satisfying than leisure, presumably because they are passionate about what they do. Those who have jobs or careers sometimes find their satisfaction in nonwork activities (e.g., hobbies) and in relationships with people who have nothing to do with their workplaces.

We are not trying to push you to seek a vocation over a job or a career; however, there are clear advantages associated with enjoying what you do on a daily basis. People who have a vocation are dedicated to what they do, so much so that others take notice. Although money, status, promotions, influence, and the like do not motivate them, many people who have a vocation acquire these things anyway because others recognize their sincere commitment to their work and to the ideals embodied within it. Bear in mind, of course, that while some callings (e.g., caring for children or older adults, running a not-for-profit organization) can lead to civic accolades, they may not provide ample salaries.

Only you can decide what your vocation, if you are to have one, will be. Perhaps psychology—and being a psychology major—represents a good start. If not, perhaps our discussion has pointed you in another direction, toward a different major that captures your imagination and motivates passion and

A **Major** Success Story ⬅

How to Stay on Campus Without Homework

Tim was not sure what kind of psychology he wanted to pursue after graduation. He just knew that thinking about behavior and predicting what people will do under various circumstances was satisfying. Tim loved his college experience and was really appreciative of how much personal development he experienced through campus life. He also knew he did not want to commit to a graduate or professional school goal. Although he viewed his desire to help people as one of his most important values, he was tired of homework and deadlines and wanted to see what kind of career options he had with his undergraduate degree.

Tim's occupational solution was ideal. He became an academic advisor at the campus he loved and was able to pursue the satisfying professional goal of helping undergraduate students reap the most benefits from their own college experiences. Tim cites the extensive experience he had in developing his communication skills in his major as essential to his success. Tim honed his listening skills, demonstrating expertise in probing students' answers to his questions. He learned how to help groups make good decisions, an ability that comes in handy in his sponsorship of a campus fraternity. His strong problem-solving skills are put to the test every day, and Tim faces the challenge with confidence.

commitment on your part. What we can do now is suggest that you think about meaning as being a more important life commodity than money (assuming the latter is available to provide you with sufficient support).

CHOOSING PSYCHOLOGY AND SHARING YOUR CHOICE

Let's imagine you do choose to be a psychology major. How will you present yourself as a student of behavior? In this chapter and in Chapter 1, we provided you with some material to support your choice. First, you are now aware of the myths that many less-informed people hold about psychology and you have evidence to dispel them. Second, you know about the economic concerns some well-meaning people (parents, friends, relatives) have about liberal arts majors and you can counter them by pointing to the fact that such majors (including psychology majors) do reasonably well in terms of their starting salaries. Third, you have done a bit of self-assessment by examining your preferences and personality while thinking about what kind of work environments appeal to you. You can tell people, for example, that there are some settings and careers that are simply better fits for you than others, and that a mismatch between who you are and where you likely work best is not going to benefit you in the job market. Finally, embracing meaning over money and vocation over job or career may be a good idea.

We can raise some other points in your favor, what we believe are some of the side benefits of majoring in psychology.

Side Benefits of Majoring in Psychology

Although a psychology major can ultimately provide meaningful career direction, there are significant secondary gains that arise from mastery of psychological content and skill at the undergraduate level (Cherry, 2014). These include:

Strengthening your self-regulation abilities. Psychology majors often learn how to manage their home and work environments to keep things running well. In other words, they are adept at **self-regulation**. They know the value of establishing goals and can implement reward strategies to improve the likelihood of meeting those goals. They are intentional in minimizing distractions and recognize that multitasking leads to poorer performance. They also learn strategies for unleashing their creativity.

Enhancing your ability to lead. Psychology majors tend to be effective at paying attention to both the outcomes of discussions and the process through which those outcomes develop. Their awareness of the quality of individual contributions to improve the caliber of the whole outcome helps them conscientiously solicit opinions from all members and deal with conflict in a way that strengthens both the solutions and the relationships among group members.

Improving your communication skills. Because the psychology curriculum promotes observation and inference skills, psychology majors can become more adept at reading people than some nonmajors. They learn that good eye contact is an important part of building trust and they carefully interpret nonverbal communications to decode nuances. They can be more adaptable in dealing with people who don't share their heritage or experiences, treading carefully and sensitively when surprised in interpersonal interactions.

Deepening your empathy and understanding. Awareness of human emotion can lead to deeper self-understanding and also undergird perspective-taking skills. Psychology majors learn to be more capable at adopting the perspective of others, which can contribute to being more effective at solving problems. Emotions are fleeting, and psychology majors recognize more readily that bad situations and unpleasant feelings are most likely temporary, not permanent.

Improving the quality of your decisions. Psychology majors learn about the array of cognitive errors that humans are inclined to make. They recognize when defense mechanisms may distort perceptions. They learn to look for disconfirming evidence to minimize confirmation biases (seeing what they expect to see) and to avoid holding onto discounted beliefs. They also learn systematic strategies for making sound decisions. Their reliance on objective evidence makes them less likely to be exploited.

Sharpening your memory skills and improve grades. Understanding how memory works can produce significant alterations in study style. Psychology majors recognize that cramming is not going to produce long-term learning and arrange their study environments to maximize their success (e.g., few or no available distractions, quiet, well lit). They are more inclined to test themselves on material until they achieve a level of mastery.

Strengthening your financial management strategies. Psychology majors understand the importance of making short-term sacrifices for long-term gains. They recognize that the fun of acquiring new shoes is temporary and pales when the cost of the shoes is invested in an account that compounds interest over time.

Engaging in healthier behavior. Psychology majors learn tools for managing healthy lifestyles. They often study the deleterious effects of poor nutrition, drug abuse, smoking, and sleep deprivation. They can implement behavior-modification strategies to make more effective choices about their health and live longer, healthier lives.

All of these are some of the side benefits of majoring in psychology, but we also recommend that you consider the possibility—even if it seems remote—that psychology might not be the best major for you.

WHAT IF PSYCHOLOGY ISN'T RIGHT FOR YOU?

Although we have worked with an abundance of talented and committed majors over time, we also know that some students who declare the major and unhappily stick it out through the bitter end probably would fare better by going in another direction. Here is a typology of students who should consider some other options.

The Premature-Foreclosure Major

Perhaps fueled by images of clinical psychologists in the media, many students commit to the psychology major, but not to the major as it really is. These **premature-foreclosure majors** envision being immersed in clinically oriented courses, solving problems with clients, and making life better for those they serve. They choose psychology because of their powerful desire to help others and tend to see a psychology major as their best or only option. Typically, these students are startled and perhaps even disgruntled by how little clinical coursework the undergraduate major involves. Similarly, they aren't thrilled by so many requirements (e.g., statistics, research) that appear to them to have nothing to do with clinical service.

We applaud students who want to devote themselves to helping others. Psychology represents just one avenue for achieving that goal and is distinctively different from other routes to the helping professions. The person who flourishes in a psychology career is one who is conversant in research and who relies heavily on existing research in picking and choosing clinical interventions. If ongoing familiarity with research is not appealing to a student, then we strongly recommend looking at social work or education, both of which are also in the helping professions. Moreover, there are many ways to enter helping or human service professions, and a major in psychology is not required for most of them.

The Antiscience Major

Declaring a science major means committing to prescribed protocols and values of science. It means learning how to exercise creativity in predicting or defining relationships among variables, demonstrating patience in working out procedural details, imposing disciplined control over extraneous matters, and executing research plans with precision. Good science majors tend to be conscientious and attentive to matters of detail.

Antiscience majors are psychology majors with no feel for science. They begin to struggle in the major when the research and statistics sequence begins. They may fret that they can't come up with appropriately creative ideas. They may select problems that are too large to explore (e.g., "I want to cure child abuse") for the timeframe of the course. They may find statistical analysis a time-consuming and even frightening burden.

Failure to embrace psychology as a science simply means the major won't be very much fun since the bulk of the major is geared toward scientific rather than clinical training. Students who struggle with the science components of psychology might want to pursue majors that emphasize social rather than scientific elements.

The Major Who Doesn't Enjoy College Reading

An unfortunate trend in college life that has been attributed to students being overly busy is a dramatic decrease in reading and studying academic material (O'Brien, 2010). Ironically, students are voracious readers when it comes to processing information from the Internet, especially in social media, but their natural enthusiasm just doesn't extend to college reading assignments.

Contemporary college students simply don't put in the time required to become masters of subjects they are pursuing. Although it may be reasonable to assume you can get by in some subject matters without doing the reading, we make the case that this is harder to do in psychology. Why? Because without doing the required reading, students have to navigate using common sense. As we discussed earlier, common sense and psychology simply don't lead to the same conclusions. Therefore, the student who doesn't do the reading will perpetually struggle with the course materials.

If you don't enjoy reading most college-level assignments, we recommend that you spend some time thinking about the kinds of reading that feel less onerous. Those content areas might help you find a major that would be a better fit. Alternatively, if no reading holds any attraction for you, you might reconsider whether a college degree is the right path for you.

The Refuge Major

One pattern we have become aware of is students' tendency to declare psychology as a major after washing out in another major. In some cases, the new declaration may work well. The first major just may not have been a good fit, and psychology fills the bill. However, many students select psychology for their second run because they think the major will be an easy one. Having failed at their first choices they think they want a major that is safe, pleasant, and unchallenging. On the surface, psychology seems to satisfy those criteria. We call these students **refuge majors**.

Before transferring to the psychology major after having had a bad experience with another major, it is a great idea to sit down with an academic advisor to talk over your plans. Describe what you expect from psychology courses and discuss your aspirations. How do you see psychology helping you to get where you want to go? It may be that other majors are better suited to the goals you have in mind.

The Driftwood Major

The vast majority of students with whom we work thrive in the major. They are energized by the challenges presented in the courses and rise to them by doing their best work. However, a substantial number of students are **driftwood majors**—they declare the major and then attempt to float their way through to graduation. Their creative ideas are uninspired. Their projects are often incompletely developed and are routinely submitted after deadline. They regularly let their project group members down. In general, they are an unexcitable lot. They graduate with the low GPAs and tend to have few ideas about how to apply what they have learned toward their future livelihood. They often show up in faculty offices two weeks before graduation and ask, "How do I get a job in psychology?"

This lack of fit is the saddest situation of all. Students possess the ability but simply never engender the kind of enthusiasm that makes the work less like work. Instead of embarking on a new path that might be more intrinsically satisfying, they rationalize that they should stay in the psychology major since they have already invested so much time in it. This situation represents the "sunk cost" scenario, in which students settle for a path that is expedient rather than pursuing a better strategic alternative.

Adrift students should analyze whether problematic fit is the primary reason for their lackluster performance. Overscheduling, learning disabilities, emotional challenges, problematic study habits, and an absence of motivation or drive can all contribute to performance that will fail to earn good grades. These traits will also potentially alienate their professors, the very people on whom they might be counting for a strong letter of reference. Student services usually provide access to skilled counselors who can evaluate whether another pathway might lead in a different direction, one in which the student might perform better.

YOU ARE WHAT YOU DO: WHY NOT MAJOR IN PSYCHOLOGY?

Choosing a college major is an important decision, one of the most important ones you will make in your life—so why not select a course of study that you can be enthusiastic about? Why not choose psychology? Psychology is a wonderful, exciting, and ever-expanding area of study. What could be more interesting or revealing than learning about why people—including you—behave as they do? You will quickly learn that you get out of psychology as much as you put into it. Although it's possible to muddle through almost any academic major, why would you want to? Choose a major that satisfies your heart, soul, and mind. We think psychology might just be the right choice for you.

THOUGHT QUESTIONS

1. Do you know another myth about psychology? Can the material in this chapter help you to dispel it?

2. What concerns, if any, do you have about choosing to major in psychology?

3. Are there any other majors you are considering? Are they similar to or different from psychology?

4. Besides those we discussed in this chapter, do you have any other motives for choosing to major in psychology?

5. What goals and values underlie your rationale for choosing a psychology major?

6. What will you say to well-meaning people who try to dissuade you from pursuing a major in psychology?

7. What are some options you can pursue if psychology turns out not to be a good fit?

8. How will you embrace psychology? List some reasons that psychology is apt to be the right choice for you.

4

Building Psychology-Related Skills

In your journey to complete a psychology major, you will probably end up taking somewhere between 12 and 15 courses. Typically, lower-level psychology courses provide a general introduction to a broad array of concepts and theories in psychology. At advanced levels, you will explore specialized areas of psychology in greater depth. Although there is no standard curriculum for psychology (Stoloff et al., 2010), there are standard expectations for what kinds of skills you should acquire or refine during your pursuit of the major.

□ □ □

Jane and Dana both have regular opportunities to serve as psychology program reviewers. As a routine part of our visits to other departments, we interview students who are just about to graduate and ask, "Now that you are almost ready to go, what have you learned to do as the result of your study of psychology?" Sometimes students react with a wide-eyed speechless pause. They can often readily tell us their GPA and list the courses they have taken, but they haven't yet focused on how their skills have changed as a result of pursuing the psychology major. How can this be?

There is a simple explanation. Historically, higher education concentrated on transmitting the content of the various disciplines in college. Professors tended to frame their jobs as lecturing, assuming that students' relevant skills would change implicitly as the result of learning about the discipline and completing the requirements of their courses. In more recent years, however, professors have come to recognize that students do not necessarily have a thorough understanding about how their thinking will change based on their learning. Without any informal assessment or even acknowledgment of what changes are expected, it is no wonder that so many students fail to grasp or feel conversant in describing the cognitive changes that they may have undergone because of what they gained from their majors.

In 1995, Barr and Tagg proposed that it was time for a new paradigm in higher education. They characterized the traditional approach to classes in higher education as a **content-centered approach** and described many problems involved with using this strategy. Chief among the concerns was that the learning that students did in a content-centered approach tended to be geared toward passing content tests and didn't produce the type of learning that endures. They argued that a new **learning-centered approach**, in which the professor's job moves beyond sharing content to an explicit focus on skill development, would produce much longer-lasting learning.

The implications of the paradigm shift are huge. First, faculty members now experience some pressure to make learning goals explicit and to provide assignments that give students ample opportunity to achieve those goals. Students should also receive feedback about how effective they are in demonstrating the skills. Learning-centered courses move the teacher from the **"sage on the stage"** to the **"guide on the side"** (King, 1993), which often promotes substantially greater student engagement in the process.

Many important stakeholders in higher education have embraced the idea that an undergraduate degree should produce transformative effects not just in what student know but in how they think. Accrediting bodies that oversee and validate the quality of academic programming across the country typically require that programs articulate specific observable student learning outcomes that drive the design of courses in the program. Mature programs also have strategies for collecting data on how well students are learning the content and how well they exhibit the expected learning skills. This practice helps the programs move toward continuous improvement (Stanny & Halonen, 2011).

In this chapter, we assist you in answering the question "What are you learning to do in your major?" First, we look at the popularity of the psychology major and examine the emerging concept of "psychological literacy." Next, we explore the American Psychological Association's (2013) *Guidelines for the Undergraduate Psychology Major*. We correlate undergraduate student learning outcomes to the workforce skills that employers appreciate. We conclude the chapter with a discussion of the metacognitive changes—in effect, how you think about your thinking—that are likely to happen in your outlook and attitude as the result of studying psychology.

THE STATUS OF THE UNDERGRADUATE PSYCHOLOGY MAJOR

Psychology is a wildly popular undergraduate degree. It is typically among the top five majors on any campus and in some schools, it is the most popular major. Consider this: Out of the 1.84 million bachelor's degrees that were conferred in the 2012–2013 academic year, 114,080 (6.2%) were awarded to psychology majors (American Psychological Association, 2016). Nationally, that percentage made psychology the fourth most popular college major after business, health professions and related programs, and social science and history. See **Figure 4.1** to understand the substantial growth that has taken place in psychology at all levels, but particularly note the dramatic growth in psychology at the bachelor's level.

Speculations abound as to why the major is so popular (Halonen, 2011). On the negative side, the perceptions that the major may be an easy one can channel substantial numbers of students into the major who may be expecting a less-than-rigorous experience. Students usually get disabused of this perception with the return of their first exams. On the other hand, more positive critics point to psychology as providing a distinct "added value" to a liberals arts degree. For example, McGovern et al. (2010, p. 25) effused, "Undergraduate psychology—whether one course, several, or a full major—offers the very best potential of liberal learning. It is at the juncture of the humanities and the sciences where students gain the human-focused values and the scientific tools necessary to see and to care about the human condition and to improve it." A somewhat more succinct description of the value of studying

FIGURE 4–1 Growth of psychology degrees from 1950–2014.

Data from: Norcross, J. C. (2015, August 7). Undergraduate study in psychology: What APA's national survey tells and warns. American Psychological Association convention. Toronto, Canada.

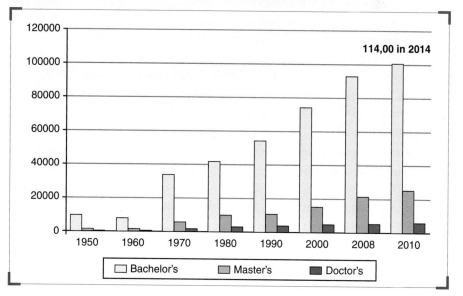

psychology comes from one of our colleagues, who suggests that you should "study psychology so you won't be a jerk!" Both approaches point to the practical value of the major in navigating increasingly complex contemporary life.

The Emergence of Psychological Literacy

We introduced the concept of psychological literacy in Chapter 1. Boneau first coined the term "psychological literacy" in a classic survey published in 1990 in the *American Psychologist*. Boneau surveyed textbook authors to determine if he could identify the "top 100" psychology concepts that were important to an undergraduate education. (Note that this research represents a perfect example of the idea that the curriculum is primarily about content.) More recent discussions of psychological literacy reflect the broadening of the paradigm, which now takes into account what students learn to do and how they learn to think in the major (e.g., Cranney et al., 2014).

At a recent APA-sponsored conference, informally referred to as the Puget Sound Conference on Undergraduate Education, psychologists worked on developing a blueprint for an undergraduate curriculum that would effectively train students to become psychologically literate (Halpern, 2010). Newer views of psychological literacy move beyond Boneau's conception of a well-defined collection of psychological concepts and theories to emphasize building students' critical thinking skills (Cranney et al., 2014). Cranney and Dunn (2011a) defined **psychological literacy** as entailing an adaptive and intentional application of psychology to meet personal, professional, and societal needs.

McGovern et al. (2010, p. 11) articulated the contemporary components of psychological literacy, including:

- having a well-defined vocabulary and basic knowledge of the critical subject matter of psychology;
- valuing the intellectual challenges required to use scientific thinking and the disciplined analysis of information to evaluate alternative courses of action;
- taking a creative and amiably skeptical approach to problem solving;
- applying psychological principles to personal, social, and organizational issues in work, relationships, and the broader community;
- acting ethically;
- being competent in using and evaluating information and technology;
- communicating effectively in different modes and with many different audiences;
- recognizing, understanding, and fostering respect for diversity; and
- being insightful and reflective about one's own and others' behavior and mental processes.

An individual who develops the knowledge base and capacities described in the list certainly fulfills the goals of the Puget Sound Conference of fostering

---

A **Major** Success Story

A Daily Dose of a Psychology Major

Former psychology major Jon Stewart, who was both the host of and a writer for the very popular *Daily Show*, managed to revolutionize the way people stay current with contemporary events. Jon provides a superb example of the characteristics of the psychologically literate citizen and how those characteristics prepare people for workforce success. Critics have called Jon "the most trusted name in fake news." His satirical approach to the news has helped him capture a shelf full of Emmys and several Peabody Awards for excellence in broadcasting.

After graduating from the University of William and Mary, Jon held numerous jobs. He was a contingency planner for the New Jersey Department of Human Services, a contract administrator for the City University of New York, a puppeteer campaigning to sensitize people about learning disabilities, a high school soccer coach, a Woolworth's shelf stocker, a bartender, and a busboy. Jon mustered his courage and tried stand-up comedy, earning the 2 A.M. slot in a New York comedy club. From his 7 years in stand-up, he branched into other entertainment ventures, including acting in movies and televisions shows and authoring best-selling books.

Despite the fact that Jon tends not to give much credit to his psychology major, many critics of his interview style see clear evidence of a background in psychology. His self-deprecating style puts his guests at ease. He is a careful listener and exercises expert interviewing strategies. He is insightful about motives, both those of other people and his own.

Information from: Columbia Journalism Review guide. New York, NY: Routledge.

---

psychologically literate citizens. A person who personifies psychological literacy is discussed in *A Major Success Story: A Daily Dose of a Psychology Major*.

National Guidelines on Undergraduate Psychology

The American Psychological Association recently revised their notions about what the appropriate learning goals should be for undergraduate psychology programs (Halonen, 2014). Their first version, developed in 2002 and approved in 2007, examined the contributions of undergraduate psychology programs to the development of liberal arts skills as well as to the foundation of effective psychological thinking. However, their original architecture of 10 learning goals proved somewhat overwhelming to psychology faculty, which prompted the revision group to make some important changes. They collapsed the original 10 goals into five:

- Knowledge Base in Psychology
- Critical Thinking and Scientific Inquiry
- Communication
- Ethical and Social Responsibility in a Diverse World
- Professional Development

The task force identified relevant student learning outcomes for each of the goals and made suggestions about how the outcomes differ between 2- and 4-year programs. The goals of the *APA Guidelines for the Undergraduate Psychology Major* and their corresponding learning outcomes can be found in **Table 4.1**.

TABLE 4.1

APA Guidelines for the Undergraduate Psychology Major: Version 2.0

Goal 1: Knowledge Base in Psychology

Students should demonstrate fundamental knowledge and comprehension of the major concepts, theoretical perspectives, historical trends, and empirical findings to discuss how psychological principles apply to behavioral problems. Students completing foundation courses should demonstrate breadth of their knowledge and application of psychological ideas to simple problems; students completing a baccalaureate degree should show depth in their knowledge and application of psychological concepts and frameworks to problems of greater complexity.

1.1 Describe key concepts, principles, and overarching themes in psychology

1.2 Develop a working knowledge of psychology's content domains

1.3 Describe applications of psychology

Goal 2: Scientific Inquiry and Critical Thinking

The skills in this domain involve the development of scientific reasoning and problem solving, including effective research methods. Students completing foundation-level courses should learn basic skills and concepts in interpreting behavior, studying research, and applying research design principles to drawing conclusions about psychological phenomena; students completing a baccalaureate degree should focus on theory use as well as designing and executing research plans.

2.1 Use scientific reasoning to interpret psychological phenomena

2.2 Demonstrate psychology information literacy

2.3 Engage in innovative and integrative thinking and problem solving

2.4 Interpret, design, and conduct basic psychological research

2.5 Incorporate sociocultural factors in scientific inquiry

Goal 3: Ethical and Social Responsibility in a Diverse World

The skills in this domain involve the development of ethically and socially responsible behaviors for professional and personal settings in a landscape that involves increasing diversity. Students completing foundation-level courses should become familiar with the formal regulations that govern professional ethics in psychology and begin to embrace the values that will contribute to positive outcomes in work settings and in building a society responsive to multicultural and global concerns. Students completing a baccalaureate degree should have more direct opportunities to demonstrate adherence to professional values that will help them optimize their contributions and work effectively, even with those who do not share their heritage and traditions. This domain also promotes the adoption of personal and professional values that can strengthen community relationships and contributions.

3.1 Apply ethical standards to evaluate psychological science and practice

3.2 Build and enhance interpersonal relationships

3.3 Adopt values that build community at local, national, and global levels

Goal 4: Communication

Students should demonstrate competence in writing and in oral and interpersonal communication skills. Students completing foundation-level courses should write a cogent scientific

Continued

argument, present information using a scientific approach, engage in discussion of psychological concepts, explain the ideas of others, and express their own ideas with clarity. Students completing a baccalaureate degree should produce a research study or other psychological project, explain scientific results, and present information to a professional audience. They should also develop flexible interpersonal approaches that optimize information exchange and relationship development.

4.1 Demonstrate effective writing for different purposes

4.2 Exhibit effective presentation skills for different purposes

4.3 Interact effectively with others

Goal 5: Professional Development

The emphasis in this goal is on application of psychology-specific content and skills, effective self-reflection, project-management skills, teamwork skills, and career preparation. Foundation-level outcomes concentrate on the development of work habits and ethics to succeed in academic settings. The skills in this goal at the baccalaureate level refer to abilities that sharpen student readiness for postbaccalaureate employment, graduate school, or professional school. These skills can be developed and refined both in traditional academic settings and in extracurricular involvement. In addition, career professionals can be enlisted to support occupational planning and pursuit. This emerging emphasis should not be construed as obligating psychology programs to obtain employment for their graduates but instead as encouraging programs to optimize the competitiveness of their graduates for securing places in the workforce.

5.1 Apply psychological content and skills to career goals

5.2 Exhibit self-efficacy and self-regulation

5.3 Refine project-management skills

5.4 Enhance teamwork capacity

5.5 Develop meaningful professional direction for life after graduation

Keep in mind that the *Guidelines 2.0* (APA, 2013) expressed what you should know and be able to do upon graduation. Some psychology programs may adopt the *Guidelines 2.0* outcomes to guide their evaluation of students who are completing the degree. But otherwise, the *Guidelines* provide a framework that faculty need to use to determine which skills each individual course should contribute to the overall program. Most undergraduate syllabi stipulate the skills that the course should foster; however, these are not always laid out systematically using the APA framework. **Table 4.2** shows an example of how using the program outcomes as a guide can help departments develop outcomes for individual courses; this example addresses outcomes in introductory psychology.

Not all faculty focus on skill development in the design and delivery of their courses. However, students who don't get a skills infrastructure in their courses can examine *Guidelines 2.0* and begin to describe the ways in which a course might be having an impact on how they are learning to think. Using *Guidelines 2.0* to shape how you characterize your own learning can dramatically improve your answer to the question "What are you learning to do in your major?" This ability will become especially important as you near graduation and contemplate job interviews.

TABLE 4.2

Introductory Psychology Student Learning Outcomes Based on the *APA Guidelines 2.0*

Introductory Psychology Course Goals

All students in an introductory psychology course should be able to do the following upon completion of the course, consistent with the department's assessment plan and coherent with the *APA Guidelines 2.0*.

Content

Acquire basic knowledge of theories, concepts, and principles in psychology

■ Characterize the development of psychology as a scientific enterprise

■ Discuss classic research in psychology, including its historical and cultural contexts

■ Explain the principles of psychological literacy

Critical Thinking

Apply knowledge of sound research procedures to solve problems

■ Use evidence to develop and evaluate claims about behavior

■ Evaluate the quality of research designs and the validity of research claims

■ Look for alternative explanations in evaluating the validity of claims

Communication Skills

Refine communication skills related to psychological science

■ Begin using APA conventions in scientific writing

■ Verbally express ideas precisely and persuasively in multiple formats

■ Assess the strengths and weaknesses of their collaborative style as a group member

Ethical and Social Responsibilities in a Diverse World

Discuss the role of ethical practices in psychology

■ Identify relevant ethical issues involved in psychological research and practice

■ Discriminate ethical from unethical practices

■ Describe why ethics matters in psychology

Professional Development

Refine skills to complete projects

■ Develop strategies for completing assignments in a timely fashion

■ Evaluate the strengths and weaknesses of their performance

■ Identify applications of psychology that produce career opportunities

LINKING UNDERGRADUATE GOALS TO WORKPLACE OBJECTIVES

Any effective liberal arts major should provide a passport into the professional work world. We believe that psychology provides one of the strongest and most adaptable majors that higher education has to offer. The content of much of the undergraduate curriculum is uniquely suited to supporting strong performance in the professional world. The skill set of the psychology major also readily translates into workforce demands. As such, the undergraduate major confers a **psychological advantage** in the workforce over other liberal arts programs. The psychological advantage should also confer positive effects for those headed to graduate school.

A standard undergraduate psychology curriculum offers workplace-related content that can't be found in other disciplines (cf. Landrum et al., 2010):

■ How are attitudes formed, and how can they be changed? (social psychology)

■ What strategies are best for selecting and developing employees? (industrial psychology)

■ What factors make people more or less effective in processing information? (cognitive psychology)

■ What variables motivate top performance? (psychology of motivation)

■ What are the best ways to promote learning new skills? (psychology of learning)

■ What environmental designs help people do their best work? (environmental psychology)

■ What stress levels are optimal for effective performance? (psychology of emotion)

In addition to the content of the courses in the major, psychology students gain skills that give them a competitive advantage as they enter the workforce (Halonen, 2011). Workplace-related skills refined by the psychology major could include:

■ accurately describing and predicting individual and group behavior;

■ understanding and using data to support an argument;

■ interpreting research data and graphs accurately;

■ evaluating the legitimacy of claims about behavior;

■ synthesizing information from diverse sources;

■ having insight into problematic behaviors;

■ demonstrating the capacity to adapt to change;

■ operating effectively in informal and formal channels of an organization;

- managing difficult situations and high stress environments;
- communicating effectively in oral and written modes;
- starting and executing projects with limited information and experience;
- exhibiting persistence in challenging situations;
- working effectively in teams that include people with diverse backgrounds;
- engendering trust through personal integrity; and
- writing reports that follow directions and use appropriate conventions.

To help you think more about what you have learned to do in the psychology major, take a look at *Reality Check: If They Could See Me Now*.

✔ Reality Check

If They Could See Me Now

Assume you are applying for a tutoring job on campus. Actually, this idea is a good one since research suggests that working on campus appears to help contribute to academic success (Kuh, Kinzie, Schuh, Whitt, & Associates, 2010). Pretend you are preparing for an in-person interview by making an inventory of the skills you think you have gained from your major. List 10 skills that you think would help you make a persuasive case about your ability to be a high-quality on-campus tutor. You can use any framework described in this chapter (e.g., psychological literacy, APA learning outcomes, or workplace abilities) to frame your analysis. To help reinforce the specific contributions of your major to your skill development, describe the context in which the psychology major helped you to acquire or refine that skill.

No.	Skill	Psychology context
1		
2		
3		
4		
5		
6		
7		
8		
9		
10		

Metacognitive Changes

Some changes that will happen to you in the course of the major will be "metacognitive," meaning that your understanding of your own thoughts and attitudes will change. Successful psychology majors take on the characteristics of those who value a psychological perspective on the world. These characteristics include the following:

Intellectual curiosity. Psychological thinkers relish the opportunity to think deeply about behavior. They enjoy asking questions to get to a deeper understanding of behavioral motives. They like being able to predict outcomes. They enjoy solving puzzles.

Expectation of complexity about the origins of behaviors. Psychological thinkers surrender the notion that the world is simple. They don't just settle for one simple causal agent when a host of influences may be at play in explaining behavior. They enjoying teasing out the variables that may explain behavior and find research on such questions to be a satisfying way to address the complexity.

Tolerance of ambiguity. Psychological thinkers understand that behavior is complex and embrace the fact that we may never account for all the factors that influence some behaviors. They are not daunted by complexity, but are inspired by it. Consequently, they can also tolerate very high levels of frustration and tend to be patient when answers aren't easily forthcoming.

Amiable skepticism. Psychological thinkers can be hard to persuade. They are aware that anecdotal evidence represents a flimsy form of justification. At the very least, they are likely to consider simplistic explanations about particular behaviors with the question, "What's your evidence?" They are comfortable adopting a skeptical stance until they can generate persuasive evidence.

Enthusiasm for the value of human diversity. Social psychology fosters an appreciation for the value of group problem-solving. Consequently, when group members bring perspectives that reflect differences in sociocultural background (e.g., race, gender, ethnicity, nationality, regional affiliation), the caliber of problem solving is likely to improve. Psychological thinkers don't just respect human diversity, they welcome it.

Recognition of the value of ethics and integrity. Doing the right thing for the right reason is not always an easy course of action. Psychological thinkers understand the importance of building trustworthy relationships with others. They resist temptations to take questionable or inappropriate shortcuts. They enjoy doing the right thing for the right reason, even when people aren't observing their actions.

Engagement in civic and social responsibilities. Psychological thinkers tend to consider the broad impact of their actions. They recognize the satisfaction that comes from making constructive contributions to others. They tend to be particularly sensitive to individuals who function at some disadvantage, which explains the inclination of some psychological thinkers to work in a service-oriented capacity. Regardless of their occupations, they enjoy feeling a part of something bigger than themselves.

Humility. Psychological thinkers tend to be humble about the limitations of what they know. We may never know all the answers to some complex behaviors; some phenomena can never be put to an empirical test. Therefore, we often must make decisions using incomplete information. Psychological thinkers do the best they can and are not surprised when new information emerges that changes how we think about a phenomenon.

IN CONCLUSION

When it comes time for a letter of recommendation to help you with your career goals, your professors are likely to draw their descriptions of who you are and what you can do from among the lists addressed in this chapter. The more conversant you are about what constitutes the skills of the psychology major, the more likely those letters from your professors will be persuasive.

Even if a professor may not hold you to any performance standards for skill development in your courses, it's a good idea to analyze the psychology course you are completing to compare how satisfied you are with how you are changing as the result of taking the course. Did the professor promise that your skills would grow as a result of the class? Can you think through the various experiences you had in the class that supported that growth? How did you do in the course from the standpoint of changing your skill set? What can you extract from the experience that may help you in your next psychology course? With a little practice, chances are good you won't ever be confused or tongue-tied if someone were to ask you, "What have you learned to do in your psychology major?"

THOUGHT QUESTIONS

1. What is the difference between a learning-centered approach and a content-centered approach to course delivery?

2. How popular is the psychology major in contemporary higher education?

3. How would you describe the characteristics of the psychologically literate citizen?

4. What are the five major learning goals of the *APA Guidelines for the Undergraduate Psychology Major 2.0*?

5. What should you be able to do as the result of completing an undergraduate major in psychology that would have appeal for future employers or would help you to be admitted to graduate or professional school?

5

Hitting Your Stride as a Student

To succeed academically, you need to refine skills, develop routines, be persistent, and avoid being discouraged when you have a setback. Approaching challenges with an open mind and a good sense of humor helps, too. The goal is to hit your stride as a student. Let's turn to practices that work, beginning with the one that mystifies most people: time management.

MANAGING YOUR TIME

When Dana was in college, he noticed a couple things about his fellow students. Those who did well in the courses for their major seemed to be interested in what they were studying (recall Chapter 2). Those who did less well often didn't like what they were studying and seemed overwhelmed by their workload. His friends who left before completing their degree tended to do so not because they couldn't do the work, but because they did not fit into the rhythms, requirements, and social norms at that particular university. They either transferred to other colleges or universities that were better suited to their goals (or had the major they wanted), or they took time off from college to regroup and figure out their next moves. Few "flunked out" calamitously or completely.

No matter how smart they are, college students are not immune to the cognitive biases that make it easy to mismanage time. For example, humans regularly suffer from *the planning fallacy*, a process that entails underestimating how much time really must be devoted to a task to complete it successfully (Buehler, Griffin, & Ross, 1994). They may not understand the true complexity of the demand or they forget relevant experiences from the past that would have helped provide more accurate targets.

In general, people also tend to exhibit *positive illusions* (Taylor & Brown, 1994). They optimistically evaluate themselves more favorably than they truly deserve. This optimistic bias can contribute to an expectation that tasks are going to be easier than they really are simply because good outcomes will naturally follow when people believe in themselves.

Finally, the *overconfidence effect* (Kahneman, 2011) contributes to poor planning. Sometimes people tend to exhibit strong beliefs that things will work out in their favor, regardless of indicators that they might be wrong.

Those who succeed in college learn to manage their time wisely and well—they are time savvy. They know which assignments require lots of time and which need less time. They learn how much time, for example, to "budget" to write a paper or to study for an exam. They keep up with the work in their most challenging courses while knowing what is happening in their less demanding classes. They do their reading before class meets so that they are prepared for discussion or a pop quiz. Students who fare less well miss deadlines, submit work late or not at all, fail to prepare for exams, and routinely pull draining all-nighters to stay afloat. Many suffer sleep deprivation and end up receiving poor grades despite their academic abilities. Success in college does not depend on what you know or don't know but on how well you juggle all your course responsibilities and your extracurricular life—how well you manage your time.

Even bright and interested students can fail if they never learn to manage their time well. They may never learn to make the transition from high school demands to college-level demands, which are steeper: more reading, more writing, more tests and papers, and more self-reliance. Today's students often have competing responsibilities, too, including jobs. Many value their social activities a great deal and spend a considerable amount of time with their peers. And then, of course, they have the constant lure of online life and social media—they are connected to friends and family so much so that they communicate with both groups several times a day.

How do students tend to divide their time in a typical college week? **Table 5.1** shows how students in one noted research project on the challenges of the first 2 years of college life spent their typical week (Arum & Roksa, 2011). Drawing conclusions is easy: Students in this sample spent the majority of their time engaging in leisure pursuits (partying, playing video games) and the least amount of time studying (and they spent almost *twice* as much time relaxing as they did sleeping!). This report represents only one study, but it did include a variety of students from a mix of colleges and universities.

Take a few minutes to figure out how you divide your time, using the activities list in Table 5.1. Feel free to add any activity you routinely do that is not included there. The main questions for you are these: Are you spending a sufficient amount of time studying to do well academically? Are you managing your time well?

What kind of a time manager are you? Time for a reality check.

What if you are still having a hard time managing your time? Consider keeping a time diary.

TABLE 5.1
_____

College Student Use of Time in a 7-Day Week (168 hours)

Activity	Percent of students' time
Attending classes or lab sessions	9
Studying	7
Work/volunteer work/club participation	9
Sleep (estimated)	24
Socializing and recreation	51

Data from: Arum & Roksa (2011).

✔ Reality Check

Managing Time Like a Pro

Which of the following recommendations can you claim as part of your time-management routine?

- ☐ I do not miss class unless I am ill.
- ☐ I prioritize my studies by doing the most challenging work first.
- ☐ I allocate time across my classes rather than studying just one class per day.
- ☐ I start planning projects and assignments when they are assigned, not at the last minute.
- ☐ I stay current in my reading and meet the due dates for my assignments.
- ☐ I work backward from due dates to identify reasonable blocks of time in which to complete my projects.
- ☐ I devote more time management to online than face-to-face classes because online courses require more self-direction to complete the work.
- ☐ I schedule classes over the length of the school day to increase study time between classes. (I don't sleep in!)
- ☐ I concentrate my studying during daylight hours to avoid late-night distractions.
- ☐ I study in quiet places that provide little interruption.
- ☐ I shut off my phone and don't constantly check social media.
- ☐ I never study on my bed.
- ☐ I take short breaks to stay attentive and engaged.
- ☐ I adhere to an established routine whenever possible.

Which recommendations do you need to explore to improve your time-management strategies? Which recommendations do you reject with a reasonable rationale?

Keep a Time Diary

A **time diary** is basically a record of how you spent your time during a typical week. Keeping one requires that you log the start and stop times for whatever you are doing (e.g., eating breakfast, attending your first class, checking Twitter, going for a run, meeting a friend for lunch, writing your history paper) so that you account for all of your awake time each day. When the week is over, you can review your diary to see what activities took most of your time and whether they are the ones that are going to help you do well in school. For example, if you are spending more time in the gym each week than you are studying for your classes, then something is wrong. If lunch with your friend always stretches to 2 hours, you might want to arrange another time—say, a weekend evening—to catch up. For the time diary to be effective, you have to be completely honest with yourself and then commit to creating a more workable (efficient) schedule that allows you to maximize how much you study, so that when you do socialize with friends, you don't feel anxious or guilty about it.

We now turn to a common problem shared by many students: They don't get enough sleep.

Don't Forget Sleep

How much sleep do you usually get each night? How much sleep do you need?

For some reason, many students like to brag about how little sleep they get, as if going without is a badge of honor or an indication of their fortitude (less rest makes me the best!). But the fact is that most people need between 6 and 8 hours of sleep per night to do their best thinking. All-nighters tend to produce very fragile learning that may not be easy to retrieve under stressful testing circumstances.

Ample research shows that when we do not get sufficient sleep, our work suffers (Dement & Vaughn, 2000; Maas & Robbins, 2011). People—students as well as working adults—who get enough sleep accomplish many more tasks quickly and efficiently while feeling less stressed, less harried, and less tired. Getting reasonable amounts of sleep also turns out to be associated with better health. Ask yourself this: How many people do you know who routinely get sick when midterms, final exams, and holiday breaks roll around? Are you likely to "crash and burn" as stress and work mounts across the semester? One psychologist who studies sleep, James Maas, suggests that sleep is like a bank account: The less you get, the more you suffer a **"sleep deficit,"** which undermines your performance, your well-being, and your health (Maas & Robbins, 2011). So, try to avoid having a low sleep balance in your "account" by aiming to get as close to 7 or 8 hours of sleep per night as you can.

Of course, you might not find it possible to get that many hours each night. You may have a noisy roommate, early classes, late work hours, or child-care issues, among other possible challenges. One helpful technique is to try to fit in a nap at some point during the day—say, between classes. Short naps (about 20 to 30 minutes) can improve your alertness, enhance your task performance, and reduce mistakes without causing you to feel groggy or adversely affecting your nighttime sleep (National Sleep Foundation, 2015). A well-timed nap can leave you refreshed and ready to go.

Oh, one last point: Too much sleep (that is, far more than 8 hours—some students sleep 12 hours or more in a night) is just as counterproductive to your efficiency and success. A routine, moderate amount of sleep in a very dark and quiet place will produce optimal results.

We now turn to ways to improve study skills.

IMPROVING SPECIFIC STUDY SKILLS

Jeanie was enrolled in a psychology of adjustment class. The material was engaging because it covered a lot of ups and downs she was experiencing in her academic, social, and personal life. She never missed class and was an active participant, asking and answering questions. She took the first exam with confidence and thought she did pretty well—until she received her exam grade in the next class. It was well below the class average and one of the worst test grades she'd ever earned. How could she do so poorly on material that "spoke to her"? She went to see her professor, who asked some questions about how she studied. After a few minutes, it became clear that while she did the reading and reviewed the course material, she didn't read strategically. She just assumed that if she read the chapters and the section summaries that she would do well. The professor suggested some ways to prepare for the next exam and Jeanie followed them. When she took the next test, she received a much higher grade than on the first. She decided to use the techniques the professor suggested when studying for her other classes and soon noticed her grades improving in those as well.

By the time students get to college, most are confident—probably too confident—that they know how to study. Many students rely on the system they have always used. Some end up succeeding. But many others do not. They discover that college-level work is more rigorous and detailed, that courses cover material more quickly, and that the competition among students—whether obvious or not—is more pronounced. In this section, we review some techniques and offer suggestions to help you study more efficiently and effectively so that you retain more of what you learn.

Reading

Technology has certainly made our lives easier and more entertaining, but the emphasis on short messages—texting or tweeting—may have a cost. Students become used to reading shorter, briefer bits of writing. Fewer students seem to be reading for pleasure these days, which means that college-level reading seems much more like work than perhaps it used to. Reading chapters in textbooks, especially densely written technical material or highly detailed introductory

TABLE 5.2	

The SQ3R Method for Effective Reading

Survey: Before you begin to read, get a feel for what's to come. Look over the chapter or section headings to get a sense of the material. Once you begin to read, you will know where the chapter is headed.

Question: Examine the headings in the chapter or section. Turn them into questions ("Conformity" becomes "What is conformity?") that you can later answer when you complete the reading.

Read: Get started reading the chapter or section. Answer the questions you just asked *as you read* and *after you finish reading.* If you finish and still aren't sure your answers are correct, go back and reread sections as needed.

Recite: With the answers in hand to the questions you posed, recite them—that is, say them *out loud* and in *your own words.* You want to "own" the concepts by putting them in your own words, which will make them easier to recall later for a quiz or test. After you've said them out loud, *write them down* in your notes.

Review: After you finish the chapter or section, do a memory check by asking yourself about the key questions you posed earlier. Try not to look at your written answers unless you absolutely must.

Information from: Robinson (1970).

texts, becomes a real challenge for some students. Some students do **"drive-by" reading**, which means that they read too fast at too shallow a level. By disallowing any reflection time, they cannot create personal meaning about the assigned content. Developing that personal meaning makes it easier to learn.

How should you approach reading to retain information? The best way to read entails using your time effectively by actively thinking about what you are reading. To do so, don't try to read an entire chapter (or book) in one sitting. Divide the chapter into segments and read one per study session. Don't try to do them all at once or you will risk getting tired or bored.

As you read a section, use the **SQ3R method** (Robinson, 1970), which you may have learned sometime in your past. This acronym stands for the key steps in reading for meaning and retention: **s**urvey, **q**uestion, **r**ead, **r**ecite, and **r**eview. Each step is summarized in **Table 5.2**. The steps are easy, straightforward, and surprisingly effective. Once SQ3R becomes routine to you, you will be able to approach all of your reading systematically.

Nota Bene: Highlighting Doesn't Work So Well

"Nota bene" is Latin for "note well" or "take note of this important point." Take careful note of this important fact about highlighting and underlining as you read: It does not promote learning. That's right, it doesn't work. Generations of students who have relied on yellow or pink highlighters to mark up their texts and notes and whatever else have lulled themselves into a false sense of security. Controlled research demonstrates that highlighting does not work, largely because it prevents students from adopting other, more practical techniques that actually help people learn (Dunlosky, Rawson, Marsh, Nathan, & Willingham, 2013). Highlighting has been shown to be an empirically ineffective study tool. "Say it isn't so," we hear you cry; alas, all those thick, colored markers you bought in the college bookstore will have to find some other purpose.

Note Taking

The availability of portable devices like smartphones, tablets, and laptops are changing the face of the college classroom. Many students no longer tote traditional paper notebooks to class. Instead, they type their notes into whatever device they prefer, which not only saves space and paper, but seems to be easier than using a pen or pencil. Unfortunately, what seems like a great solution may present problems for learning.

Let's begin with handwriting or, rather, how it is slowly but inexorably being replaced by typing on a keyboard. Is moving a pen across paper really so different than tapping keys? According to some psychologists and neuroscientists, the answer is yes—compared to typing, handwriting is intimately tied to deeper learning, the generation of ideas, and information retention (Konnikova, 2014).

Two researchers wondered whether relying on electronic devices might lead to more shallow information processing and subsequent learning than the pencil on paper approach (Mueller & Oppenheimer, 2014). They conducted a series of studies, most of which followed the same structure: Researchers assigned students to classrooms and had the students take notes using either laptops or traditional notebooks. The researchers presented the same lectures to both groups, who were told to use their usual approach to note taking. Half an hour or so after the lectures, the students took an in-class exam on what they heard. The questions were both factual ("Who was shot in Ford's Theatre?") and conceptual ("Explain how a true democracy differs from a representational democracy").

Although the students who used the laptops took more copious notes, the notes were usually **verbatim**—that is, the students recorded exactly what they heard. By failing to put the ideas into their own words, they acted like stenographers. In contrast, the notebook group changed the lecture content, turning it into information that was meaningful to the individual note takers. Not surprisingly, the laptop group did much worse on the recall test compared to the traditional notebook group. Despite the fact that the traditional notebook group wrote fewer notes, they engaged in higher-order thinking and deeper processing than the laptop group because they wrestled with the concepts instead of just transcribing them.

The bottom line is clear: Writing—not typing—is linked with better information retention. To maximize your learning, take a traditional notebook to class with you. If you have virtually illegible handwriting, then transcribe your notes into digital form later. Your initial learning—wrestling with key concepts via handwriting—will already have occurred. Subsequently translating your written text into a more readable (typed) form might help you rethink and further clarify what you wrote earlier.

How to Study

During high school, Randy routinely waited until the night before any big test to prepare. Usually, he spent a couple of hours memorizing his notes and flipping through whichever chapters were going to be on the test. This method worked pretty well, as Randy usually earned A's and B's. When he got to college, he decided he would continue to rely on this approach. When he got back his grades from the first exams in each of his classes, he was shocked at how low his test grades were. He didn't fail any exams, but his scores were mediocre at best. Randy also realized that the volume of material and detail associated with each class was greater than anything he had encountered in high school. He needed to find a better way than "cramming and jamming" the night before tests to succeed in his classes.

Students like Randy use what we might call the **binge method**: They spend several hours reading, rereading, and reviewing notes—often trying to memorize terms or concepts—the day before an exam. This practice is ineffective for several reasons. Studying the same material for hours and hours at a stretch gets dull. Ironically, it is also anxiety provoking to learn under last-minute pressure. Doing so means that you might neglect studying or keeping up with what's happening in your other classes. Isn't there a better system?

Psychologists have long suggested using an evidence-based approach to studying (Dunn, Saville, Baker, & Marek, 2013). One of the most thoroughly researched findings concerns what is known as **spaced learning** or the *spacing effect*. Students who distribute their studying of particular material across some period of time—say, studying a set interval of time (30 minutes to 2 hours or so) every day for an exam that is 2 weeks away—learn and retain more information than those who cram just before the exam. Space your learning and make it a routine to perform better than you would from last-minute cramming. Students who adopt this strategy also tend to be less stressed about their coursework because they are almost always caught up.

A related finding on study efficiency deals with where people study, or **contextual cues**. Research shows that people who study to-be-learned material in different venues have an easier time recalling what they need to know during exams than those who always study in the same place (Smith, Glenberg, & Bjork, 1978). Mixing up where you study allows you to develop what psychologists call **multiple retrieval cues**; if you always study in the same place (your desk, a carrel in the library, or the same table in a coffee shop), you will develop cues associated only with that place. Study your course material in different places to make your learning sturdier. Being flexible about where you study is apt to pay a variety of academic dividends. Studying will be easier to initiate and you will be less dependent on particular contextual cues. **Table 5.3** lists some additional steps you can take to improve how you study. Consider trying one or more of them.

TABLE 5.3

Steps to Improve How You Study

Always attend class: Sit where you can get to know the instructor and other students. Avoid sitting in the back row.

Schedule time to study for each of your classes: Set aside two 3-hour blocks per class, twice a week, for doing reading and homework.

Write down important dates: Know when your homework and papers are due and the dates of your exams. Put this information in your phone, calendar, or planner.

Start assignments, including reading, early: Working ahead allows you to pace yourself and to avoid "cramming" or doing everything at the last minute.

When you get tired, take a break: Go outside for a brief walk, check your email, get a drink, whatever. You can also switch your study to a different subject to avoid fatigue or boredom.

Review any key terms and complete any practice tests in your reading: Such end-of-chapter exercises can give you a sense of what you know and don't know.

Celebrate your achievements: Reflect on what you are learning as well as your progress toward meeting your academic and professional goals.

TEST-TAKING 101

We now turn to the main event of most students' academic careers—test-taking. As you likely know, tests are a big part of college life. You can use some of these straightforward strategies, in addition to studying for your exams consistently and in advance, to increase your chances of doing well.

Look over your exam before beginning it. Too many students just write their names on the exam and then plunge in without knowing what will come later in the test. Take a couple of minutes to flip through the exam so you know what kinds of questions or problems there are, how many points they are worth, and if there are any questions that are going to require much more time than the others. Doing so allows you to budget your time better. You might want to start by answering longer questions first, saving the quicker ones (often multiple-choice questions) for last. If nothing else, looking through the exam will reduce your anxiety—there won't be any surprises or, if there are, you will have time to think about how to handle them.

Do well on multiple-choice questions. The basic strategies for answering multiple-choice questions—test questions that require the test-taker to select the best possible answer from an array of possibilities (usually 4 or 5)—are as follows. First, make sure you read the entire question. It is easy to get tripped up on a question if you stop with answer A only to find out that the options you didn't read were also right and the correct answer was "All of the above."

Once you have read all the alternatives and you know the answer to a question, mark the answer right away and move on to the next question. When you come to a question you don't know, skip to the next one and answer it and any remaining questions. You can answer those multiple-choice items you don't know last—just don't forget to come back to them! When you come back to a question you initially could not answer, try to identify which of the answers are not at all plausible. Doing so will often narrow your choices from 4 or 5 options to 2 or 3. If you still cannot reason out the answer, choose the one that "feels" best—and then move on.

If you have time at the end of the exam to review your answers, you can circle back to check those challenging multiple-choice items. It is quite all right to change answers, as research shows that review often motivates students to alter incorrect answers to correct ones (Benjamin, Cavell, & Shallenberger, 1984).

Answer essay questions effectively. The best approach to answering essay and open-ended questions starts with putting your pen down for a moment. Think about what the essay question entails. Then, pick up your pen and jot down a brief outline of the points you want to make. (You can write this on the test itself or on the exam booklet.) The outline keeps you from forgetting key issues as you write your answers and prevents you from writing too much. Avoid the "regurgitation" method of essay writing. There is no need to tell the instructor everything you know about a topic; just answer the question being asked. Whenever possible, use concrete examples to illustrate the points or argument you are making in your essay. Being specific is almost always better than being general or, worse, vague. Once you finish an essay, look over the question prompt one more time and go back through what you wrote to make sure that you responded to all parts of the question.

Check how much time has passed and how much is left to complete your exam. Pace yourself during an exam. Don't rush, but don't work at a leisurely pace, either. When half the test period is past, for example, you need to be more than halfway through the test so you can allow some time to review.

Never, ever leave a question blank. Even if you have no idea what an answer might be, write something. Just don't be obnoxious or silly in your answers because that will produce a toxic effect on your professor's judgment of you. Return to a blank question after you've completed the rest of the test. The answer to the question—or a possible answer—may come to you as you answer other questions, or you might see a cue or a clue in another question. Remember, if you leave a question blank, there is no opportunity at all for the instructor to give you partial credit for what you do write. Always write something.

Don't leave an exam early unless you have thoroughly reviewed your answers. Far too many students race through their exams to finish them as quickly as possible. Such speed can lead to skipped items (forgetting to come back to that multiple-choice question, for instance), incomplete answers (forgetting to address one of the points in an essay question), and flat-out wrong answers. If you finish before time is called, go back through your exam to make sure you have answered all the questions and have done so to the best of your ability—there is no prize for being the first one done and certainly no problem with being the last person to finish a test. Use your time wisely to make certain that you have answered the questions to the best of your ability.

Anxious about math? Many students (even psychology majors) become anxious when they are confronted with math problems. Statistics and data analysis, both of which are important aspects of understanding and carrying out research methods, are integral to psychology. Psychologists of all types need to be comfortable with the language of mathematics; so do students of psychology.

If you have math anxieties, you may shy away from completing your math and statistics requirements by postponing taking them until late in your college career. Doing so is a mistake for several reasons. First, math skills (particularly the logic required to do math and the step-by-step nature of solving problems) are useful in a variety of courses, not just those that are explicitly quantitative. Second, the longer you wait to complete even basic math requirements, the rustier your high school math foundation will be. Third, if you know you get anxious about quantitative work, you need to try to overcome your fears sooner rather than later. Many math and statistics departments offer problem-solving sessions or tutoring. Taking advantage of these resources will help, as will always completing your homework assignments and regularly meeting with instructors or teaching assistants during their office hours. Once students who are anxious about math or statistics "break through" their fear and concern, they approach the course material with a fresh and open attitude, one that makes it easier to understand and learn new skills.

If at first you don't succeed, seek help. If you are struggling with one of your courses, ask your instructor if any tutoring services are available. Many colleges and universities offer a variety of tutoring options to help students. Among psychology students, for example, seeking tutoring for learning statistics is popular, and many psychology departments have "stats" tutors—often senior majors who did well in the class—available to help. Many schools also have writing centers that can offer assistance with writing papers or learning to effectively answer essay questions.

Suggestions for students with disabilities. If you have a documented disability that might influence your test performance, you should inform your professors at the start of the semester. Generally, students with disabilities are entitled to extra time to complete exams or access to specific testing conditions (e.g., a non-distracting space). Find out whether your college or university has a disability resource center. If it does, you can use the center to learn about your school's resources and policies. If your school doesn't have a resource center, it will likely have policies to help students with disabilities. Be sure to follow university policies in order to secure accommodations.

Having a disability doesn't limit the professional success you can have in a psychology-based career. See *A Major Success Story* for a great example.

A **Major** Success Story ⬅

Applying Psychology to Customer Service

Not many people would think of a learning disability as a blessing, but Julian's life story demonstrates just how far one can go with a great education in psychology, a plucky spirit, and a different point of view. Diagnosed with attention deficit disorder later in life—coincidentally, at the same time his daughter received a similar diagnosis—Julian came to recognize that the condition actually allowed him to make new and interesting connections that might elude someone with more typical processing skills. His capacity for "thinking outside the box" gave him significant advantages in solving problems and he found the perfect outlet—hotel management—for his unique talents.

Even before he had started college, Julian had begun working with a local chef in a beach resort. His character and work ethic were so impressive that by the time he graduated from college, he had 8 years of experience in hotel management. He was mentored by a successful hotelier and absorbed the information he learned. He was able to parlay his knowledge and energy into building a thriving hotel management and marketing company with more than 1,800 employees.

What advantages did his psychology major contribute to his professional success? Julian has been surprised by how much his psychology background has helped to set him apart. Understanding people provides a real advantage in his competitive industry. He credits psychology with enhancing his listening skills and his power of intuition. He is tickled when people describe him as being able to "see around corners." He also believes that the compensating strategies he developed to help him focus despite the distractions of ADD helped him become a better problem solver.

What advice does he have to offer undergraduate students? "Be willing to be wrong and to laugh at yourself. Expect answers from the most unlikely places, and open yourself up to the infinite possibilities around you. Recognize that you can't control the world. It's how you react to it that's going to define you."

Information from: Salley (2014).

ABOUT GRADES: REVIEW YOUR SUCCESSES AND STRUGGLES

When one of our colleagues returns graded material to her students, she always tells them they are permitted 15 minutes of joy, ambivalence, or self-pity—and no more. In other words, if they get a good grade, they are only allowed to revel in the success for a short while, and if they do poorly, they can only feel sorry for themselves for a brief time. If their grade is just okay—not great, not bad— they should not spend too much time being distracted by it.

Why does she impose this limit? Because students are apt to focus exclusively on their grade or score. In so doing, they ignore important information, such as what material they knew well and what they knew less well. Learning from successes and mistakes is important. You should always conduct a "postmortem" on your quizzes, tests, papers, and the like. By reviewing the answers you got wrong, for example, you have a second chance to learn the material, which will likely appear in some form on a later exam or other assignment. The questions you answered correctly tell you what you know well. All too often students only look at their grades and ignore all other comments from the instructor. Don't do that! Take the time to read and learn from them. Whatever you do, don't throw graded materials away—save them and review them before the next such assignment or test so that you avoid making the same errors (e.g., writing a too brief conclusion to a paper, forgetting to answer all parts of an essay question).

It is a very good idea to get into the habit of doing "exam wrappers" every time you get back a test. **Exam wrappers** are questions aimed at getting you to review your performance and on any comments from instructors on a test (Lovett, 2013). By answering these questions and examining the test, you can see what worked and what didn't so that you can adjust your study habits and approach to test taking for the next time:

- How did you prepare for the exam? Are there things you might want to do differently next time?
- What sorts of errors did you make on the exam? Is there any pattern or commonality among them?
- What can you do differently to prepare for the next exam?

PERSONAL ETHICS

You are a professional in training, and part of that training is building trustworthy character. The habits you adopt now will affect you and how you act in the future. Part of your responsibility as a student is to be ethical, that is, to follow a moral code. In the context of college and university life, this code generally reflects three areas of emphasis:

1. **Do your own work**. As a student, you are responsible for undertaking and completing your own assignments, taking your own tests, writing your own papers, and so on. "Do your own work" means that you do not submit other people's work as your own to receive academic credit for it. To do otherwise is to lie and to cheat.

   No doubt your school has clear rules about what constitutes academic lies and cheating, and you should familiarize yourself with them. Your school's student handbook is a good place to begin. For example, quite a few handbooks specify an honor code that requires students to turn in fellow classmates whom they believe have cheated on a test or an assignment. If this requirement makes you uncomfortable, you might consider submitting the offender's name anonymously.

2. **Do not plagiarize**. **Plagiarism** is the act of taking another person's ideas—usually in written form—and passing them off as your own without properly attributing the ideas to their original authors (that is, without citing supporting references). Plagiarizing the work of others is a form of academic theft. Some people intentionally plagiarize by

knowingly copying phrases, sentences, and even whole paragraphs from published works or sites on the Internet. This is known as *intentional* plagiarism. In *unintentional* or accidental plagiarism, the perpetrator is often unaware of having plagiarized. When summarizing some set of ideas, for example, they may incorporate quite a bit of the original language into their writing without using proper supporting citations. It sounds right because it turns out to be more or less verbatim from the original source.

The facts are these: College students don't write like psychology professionals. Professors easily spot plagiarized writing because the voice in the writing doesn't correspond to the way most undergraduates speak or write. In addition, most professors have access to technology that can provide formal estimates of unoriginal writing in submitted assignments and direct the professor to the actual lifted material. Although the risk of getting caught and penalized should deter plagiarism, a more important reason to do your own work is to maximize your learning and the development of your communication skills. **Table 5.4** provides some concrete steps for avoiding plagiarizing textual materials.

TABLE 5.4

Simple Steps for Avoiding Committing Plagiarism

1. Review the material you intend to *paraphrase*, that is, rephrase and summarize in different words.
2. Put the text away where you cannot see it, or close your document or web browser.
3. Draft a summary in *your own words*.
4. Compare your summary with the original text to make certain you are conveying the main message.
5. Repeat the above steps as needed.

Other suggestions

- Never cut and paste material into your writing from online sources; instead, paraphrase it using the above instructions.
- Rely on *your own* ideas as much as possible; use the ideas of others to support *your* arguments or observations.
- Keep a detailed list of any references you are using (as a psychology student, your citations should be written in APA style).
- Cite these references by author last name and the date of publication—for example, (Jones, 2014)—in your writing so your instructor knows the source of an idea and can consult it as needed.
- Use quotes sparingly. Selecting only high-impact quotations will force you to develop your paraphrasing skills.

One last thing: If you must quote from an article, chapter, book, or other source, select a brief quote, use quotation marks, and indicate the source in the text and in a list of APA-style references.

Like most adults, college students feel harried, so they often rush to complete their tasks, including their assignments. Unfortunately, such hurrying often leads to academically dishonest behavior. Developing time-management skills is a good way to avoid committing plagiarism. Some students end up justifying plagiarizing material when they are rushing to finish a paper or other assignment. They assume no one will notice, that they will only do it "this one time," and thus believe (hope) they can get away with it. Managing your time—planning how and when you will do your course work—reduces your risk of plagiarizing. And remember, it's always better to turn in a late assignment, even with late penalties, than it is to plagiarize the work of others.

3. *Avoid behaviors that will tarnish your honorable reputation.* Appleby (2011) recommends that college students be aware of the full range of academically dishonest behaviors, including:

Cheating. Some forms of cheating are using another's work with or without the student's consent, such as copying answers from a test or homework assignment; sending a substitute to take an exam; collaborating on projects that are supposed to be independently created; or altering grades assigned by instructors.

Submitting the same work to multiple classes. Some students will submit the same assignment, often a paper, to more than one class. It's fine to write two different papers on the same topic for two different classes, but it is unethical to turn in the same paper twice.

Fabricating. **Fabricating** is falsifying or inventing information in order to appear to have done library or other scholarly research. Making up a source is foolhardy because faculty members can often detect the deceit—and what will happen when an instructor looks for the reference or asks for it?

Misusing materials. Although this may not happen very often, sometimes students obtain advance copies of quizzes or exams, or they use a calculator when it is against the rules. Using unauthorized materials is cheating, plain and simple. Not only does it represent an unfair and unearned advantage over other students, it is a clear lapse in personal **integrity**.

Interfering. Any actions you take that obstruct a fair assessment of another student's work constitute a violation of integrity. Similarly, attempting to influence your teacher through bribes or threats is unethical.

Facilitating academic dishonesty. **Academic dishonesty** includes any attempt to help another person violate standards of academic integrity. You may believe you are being a good friend by letting a peer copy your homework, but what you are doing is enabling cheating. Doing so makes you as culpable for the dishonest act as the person who engages in the actual cheating.

Rendering false excuses. One final area deserves some attention: **misrepresentation**. Many students feel overwhelmed by their workload at times, but only a minority of them choose to deal with this by telling what they believe to be "little white lies" to their instructors ("I had to miss the exam because I woke up with a fever" or "I couldn't submit the paper to you during the last class because my car broke down on the way to school" or—the perennial favorite—"My grandmother died"). Using any form of deception or misrepresentation to postpone, delay, or otherwise avoid completing your schoolwork is academic dishonesty. Don't be surprised if your professor asks for some form of evidence (e.g., a car repair bill, a note from your physician, even an obituary) as a means of discouraging deception before they accept your explanation for your failure to deliver your work on time.

Getting into the habit of doing the right thing for the right reason helps to build positive character. You can take pride in being someone who can be trusted. Later you will find that your professors are more enthusiastic about writing letters of recommendation for you if your character is unblemished.

NAVIGATING CYBERSPACE

We now want to focus on a very important and sometimes overlooked topic: your **cyberidentity**—how you present yourself effectively to other students and to professionals (including your instructors and academic advisor) in the online world. We believe this is important because so much of our lives now revolve around social media (e.g., Facebook and Twitter) and our individual online presence.

Here are some rules for the (virtual) road:

Whatever you put on the Internet is there FOREVER. Anything you post on a website—a comment, a picture, whatever—is permanent. The website may shut down, but it's quite likely there is a copy of your post elsewhere, possibly many other places. Think very carefully about what you share with others because it could come back to haunt you. Off-color language or jokes, snarky or rude comments, and inappropriate photos of yourself or others have the potential for time-release embarrassment. Important people in your life (friends, family, college faculty, current or potential future employers) may not appreciate or understand your post.

Do not leave your social media accounts open to everyone. If you use Facebook, Snapchat, or other social media, be sure to set your security settings appropriately. For example, you might only want your friends but not strangers seeing all of your posts. Would you want a potential employer or a graduate school admissions committee to see everything you have posted, including the comments and links that your friends have added? If your answer is "no," then you may want to make some changes to the kind of information you allow to be seen.

Appropriate communications. Many faculty members have received email messages from students like this one:

> Hey, are you in your office? When are your office hours? Please respond immediately. Dude, I need to see you like right now! (From beefcake69).

The level of presumed familiarity and informality in this sort of message is not appropriate for a message sent from a student to a faculty member. Such messages inevitably create a negative impression.

Think before you send that email. For example, look at the course syllabus to see when the professor holds office hours. That saves you writing an email and avoids wasting your professor's time. However, if that doesn't work, a better email would be:

> Dear Professor Hanson:
> Do you have any office hours today? If not, would you be able to meet with me another day this week? I'd like to talk about my grade in your Social Psychology class. I probably need about 5 minutes of your time. Thank you.
> Judy Jensen

Naturally, pay attention to the content of email messages you send not just to your professors; you should carefully construct and vet any communication you send, whether to peers or professionals. A colleague suggests to her students that they write any email message as if they were contacting the boss of the job they hope to obtain after graduation. Developing good email habits now will serve you well once you leave college.

CLOSING THE LOOP

This chapter has provided guidance aimed at helping you to develop into a solid and confident student of psychology. We've covered key issues—from how to get the most from your reading, to study skills, test-taking strategies, and the importance of being an ethical student and managing your presence in cyberspace. We want to close our discussion of student skills by offering a few final suggestions.

Learn from your mistakes. No one goes through college without a few mishaps. Even a spectacular blunder can be informative. When you make a mistake, allow yourself to learn from it. React with grace rather than with anger, upset, or regret. Then move on to the next challenge. One of the great things about life during college is that you get to reinvent yourself at the start of each semester. If you did not like how things turned out in the fall term, you have the opportunity to redeem yourself, to change your ways, to study harder, or whatever, come the next term. Resolve to learn from your mishaps or mistakes instead of trying to forget about them.

Overcome wishful thinking. A mark of a maturing mind is the wisdom to recognize that imagined or desired outcomes—our hopes and dreams—don't always turn out as we planned. We have to learn to face those facts with understanding and good humor. It can take some time, effort, and experience to reach such a point.

One common delusion that students express, driven by **wishful thinking**, is that they will still be able to achieve an "A" in the class by doing well on the final when their prior work was clearly unsatisfactory. They may assume that a strong final performance will impress their professor, or they predict that a professor is just too nice to flunk someone who tries hard. Such thinking is called wishful thinking for a reason. Just because we want a certain outcome doesn't mean it will—or even can—happen. Being positive is important, yes, but you cannot ignore concrete performance indicators like grades. Working hard while moderating your expectations is usually wiser than assuming that things will simply fall into place for you. For the future to turn out as you hope, you need to work hard and to be responsible in the present.

Always do your best work. It is very easy to convince yourself that "next time" you will do better on whatever academic task presents itself, from getting a higher score on an exam to writing an "A" paper. But what if next time never comes? Too often we promise ourselves we will fix our problematic behaviors, only to engage in them again later. Our final suggestion is not divinely inspired but based on common sense: Always try to do your best work. Treat each responsibility, whether great or small, as if it is worth doing well. If you do your best, you can avoid feelings of regret when things don't go quite as planned, just as you can relish your little victories when things go well.

THOUGHT QUESTIONS

1. How can you manage your time more effectively? Identify three changes you can make and try them out.

2. Are you getting enough sleep? If not, what can you do to ensure you get a sufficient amount of sleep each night?

3. Have you always relied on the same study techniques? Are you sure they are effective?

4. Do you always study in the same place? If yes, can you try to study in a few other places in order to develop more retrieval cues?

5. What test-taking strategy would you like to try?

6. How can you become a stronger student and hit your academic stride? List some concrete steps you can take.

7. What is your current cyberidentity like? Should you make any changes to it?

6

Charting Your Course in the Major

The objective of an undergraduate psychology degree is not to produce professional psychologists but to educate people so that they can think like psychologists. That goal should be manageable in a 4-year undergraduate program (Stoloff et al., 2010). This time frame should also work for students who begin their major at a community college and transfer to a college or university to finish. However, 4 years in college can go by fast, unless the 4 years stretch into 5 or 6 due to a variety of challenges, including lack of access to needed classes, funding shortfalls, or others. Some delays can be caused by bad decisions you make as a major, particularly when you may not see the long-term consequences of decisions that will impede your progress.

□ □ □

The goal of this chapter is to help you become more intentional in your decisions and actions so that you can get the most out of the major. We provide a map of the terrain that must be navigated during your years as a major. We offer some guidance to help you optimize both your enjoyment of and your efficiency in the experience. First, we examine the common stages of the undergraduate degree program, highlighting the cognitive changes you are likely to undergo. We recommend strategies for achieving optimal outcomes to facilitate your best options after graduation. We conclude by addressing some of the advising questions that frequently emerge in the process of meeting program requirements.

STAGES IN THE PSYCHOLOGY MAJOR

Students often tend to think about their courses in a compartmentalized fashion; they take school one course or term at a time and don't always look at their academic career as a whole. From our vantage point as professors, we see some predictable stages in how students change over time that are not necessarily linked to the completion of any given term (Halonen et al., 2003). In this portion of the chapter, we take a look at those stages.

The Novice Stage

The **novice** or first stage involves students who are new to the discipline. Although our comments focus on the changes that transpire in students when they take introductory psychology, the characteristics of the novice learner tend to apply to those in other classes early on in their coursework, when they are just learning about the nature of the discipline.

Years ago, students could not take psychology until they reached a college campus, but with the advent of Advanced Placement (AP) and dual-listed psychology classes, many students now arrive at college having already taken their first psychology class. Regardless of where the novice student initially encounters psychology, the experience in the first course can have a profound impact. For example, on the strength of her Introduction to Psychology course, Jane switched from journalism to psychology and never looked back.

Characteristics of the novice learner. We love working with beginning students. They show enthusiasm for acquiring new concepts and theories that help explain behavior, but even the best students are surprised by how much of psychology doesn't fit readily with what they think they already know about psychology. Novice students typically need to overcome the misconceptions they have about psychology, including the belief they may have that psychology is purely a clinical enterprise. They struggle to understand why psychologists insist on **objectivity** in describing behavior and often confuse behavioral description with far more elaborate inferences about the behavior. They aren't particularly interested in evidence to support claims about behavior, but tend to trust their own experience and believe the testimony of trusted others. They are often big fans of **pseudoscientific explanations** (e.g., astrology, handwriting analysis) and actively resist having those beliefs challenged (Lilienfeld, 2004).

Novice learners wrestle with accepting the trappings of science as part of the discipline they are learning to explore. They find having to adopt the conventions of APA format in their writing and speaking projects to be cumbersome, bewildering, and even tedious. They struggle to distinguish independent from dependent variables in simple research designs and often aren't too excited to learn the significance of the difference of those terms.

Students who are just starting out in psychology show many of the characteristics of the **dualistic learner**, a concept developed by William Perry (1970). Beginners tend to dislike **ambiguity**, prefer simple answers for complex questions, and expect their professors to have all the answers. There is very little gray area in how they think about problems. They can be easily frustrated by questions that don't yield easy or quick answers, but through their study of psychology, they begin to recognize nuances and to understand that the causes of behavior are often subtle.

Recommendations for the novice learner.
Several tips can help novice psychology students settle into the major and distinguish themselves as serious, intentional students. Our goal in this section is to help students move away from the mentality of merely "getting through" their courses. Instead, we advocate strategies that will enrich experiences drawn from courses and lead to longer-lasting learning.

1. *Actively look for ways to apply what you learn.* Not only will your learning stay with you better, but considering the material in a personal way may help you identify areas that you might be interested in pursuing later in independent studies and projects.

2. *Start to winnow the broad subtopics in psychology to the ones that you are most enthusiastic about studying.* Knowing that you prefer "social" topics over "perception" topics can shape your choice of future courses. You can also develop your personal collection of resources that will support project work across courses that more closely reflect your individual interests.

3. *Invest yourself in class discussion.* If you aren't participating at all when you have the opportunity, take a deep breath and then take the risk of speaking up. It is rare that bad things will happen if you try to contribute. You simply will get more out of the class if you can share your ideas and perspectives because expressing your ideas facilitates your understanding and retention. Talking about course ideas will help consolidate your learning. You will also have more to say if you come to class prepared to engage in discussion.

4. *Be careful about self-disclosing excessively in class.* The content of psychology classes may tempt you to say too much about yourself that may be inappropriate or off topic. Participate, but exercise careful self-monitoring both about the frequency and the depth of your disclosures in class. If you often volunteer to answer questions but your professor avoids or delays calling on you, take that as a subtle signal that you might need to "sit on your hands" and let other people carry some of the responsibility.

5. *Visit your professor during office hours.* Very few students take advantage of this resource (i.e., individual professor attention) already paid for

in their tuition. The visit will set you apart and add to your comfort in the class. See *Reality Check: Finding an Academic Mentor* for some additional pointers that can lead to a profitable mentoring relationship.

6. *Get comfortable with conceptual messiness.* Not much about psychology is tidy. The sooner you can begin to construe ambiguity as interesting rather than frustrating, the more fun you'll have in the discipline.

7. *Hang out in the psychology department or wherever students gather.* Some of your lifelong friendships may be waiting for you in the student lounge. Informal connections can also help you identify faculty who may be looking for additional hardworking student volunteers.

8. *Seek opportunities to get to know the faculty and other people in the major through attending student events.* Many departments host a psychology club that schedules social and service activities to enhance student experience. Students who develop strong academic records may also be invited to join the national honorary, Psi Chi or Psi Beta, if their department sponsors a chapter. Volunteer for committee work in psychology-related interest groups to help refine your leadership skills. Be sure to follow through on any commitments you make so that faculty and your peers know that you are reliable.

The Developing Stage

In the middle stage, which we refer to as the "developing" stage, students focus on how to think about behavior as a scientist. At the outset of this stage you should be taking the courses that serve as the backbone for scientific inquiry— research methods and statistics. Departments exercise different strategies about how best to address the development of research skills. In a typical sequence, students take a statistics class, sometimes taught by the mathematics department, before taking a class in research design. However, some programs have a two-semester research skills sequence that combines methods and statistics. Ideally, you should finish your statistics and research methods courses before taking higher-level core classes (e.g., cognition, social, developmental, neuroscience) and advanced courses so that you have a framework for thinking empirically (Dunn et al., 2010). Indeed, students learn more rapidly in advanced classes in specialized topics of psychology when they already have a thorough background in research methods.

Characteristics of developing learners. Developing learners become more sophisticated in describing behavior and inferring meaning or motivation as they go along. They start to become comfortable with measurement and precision as necessary elements of good science. Developing learners begin to explore theoretical frameworks, including recognizing that any theory has strengths and weaknesses. They can manage small-scale research projects and

✔ Reality Check

Finding an Academic Mentor

Some students are more likely to be successful in academia if they can develop a special relationship with a professor. A student may be drawn to a faculty member because of the faculty member's personal charisma or a shared passion for particular ideas; regardless, having a professor who is accessible and supportive can make all the difference in helping students stay the course through to graduation. Mentors can also be instrumental in helping students achieve their goals following graduation.

How do you know a faculty member might be open to taking on a mentoring relationship? It helps to do some observational research. Size up the student traffic in the professor's office. If students are regularly present during office hours, the faculty member welcomes the presence of students and probably has some mentoring relationships underway. On the other hand, if no one is visiting a faculty member during office hours, that faculty member might be more available to be a mentor. Most faculty members genuinely enjoy working with students, which is why they got into teaching in the first place.

What's the best way to engage a faculty mentor? Visit your professor during office hours and ask for a few minutes of his or her time. Mentoring relationships tend to grow out of positive interactions. Which of the following topics would you feel comfortable exploring with a prospective mentor?

- ☐ Clarifying something confusing in the professor's lecture
- ☐ Getting specific recommendations on next semester's courses
- ☐ Asking your professor to look over your notes to see if you are capturing the key information
- ☐ Requesting test-preparation tips
- ☐ Inquiring about the professor's academic background
- ☐ Asking how the professor balances work and family life
- ☐ Determining whether the professor collaborates with students on research
- ☐ Volunteering to be part of the professor's research team
- ☐ Seeking advice on potential career options

What's the best way to nurture the relationship once it has been established? Be completely reliable in performing any tasks you have agreed to take on for the professor. Demonstrating strong work ethics in completing your obligations not only solidifies the relationship, but it makes it much easier for your mentor to write a glowing letter of recommendation when the time comes.

---

also select and properly apply statistical analysis to determine whether their hypotheses were successful. They begin to develop some vigilance regarding the ethical constraints that characterize well-designed research.

Developing learners begin to have major changes in attitude during this stage that help them move in the direction of becoming apprentice psychological thinkers. In Perry's (1970) framework, they become **relativistic learners**, recognizing that hard and fast truths are fairly elusive. They start to grasp how two individuals can share the same space but not experience the same subjective reality. They show more appreciation for precise definitions and crisp procedures because of the degree of control these practices provide in determining valid research conclusions. Although they still prefer simpler over more complex answers, they begin to show enthusiasm for targeting as many variables as possible that might be influential in explaining behavior. The "amiable skeptic" (someone who challenges conclusions from a collaborative stance) begins to emerge in this stage, but this approach may be driven by seeking professor approval rather than by a deeply held value.

As developing learners face demands for becoming more sophisticated in their use of APA format, their communication skills grow. When seeking information, they initially want to use every reference they spend time examining rather than recognizing that being selective ultimately helps them produce a stronger argument. They haven't yet mastered writing for a psychology-oriented audience but no longer protest about using APA conventions to do so effectively. As project managers, they can take on more complex tasks and feel more comfort in sharing the workload even with people they wouldn't have chosen for their team. They can give and take criticism but tend to be satisfied with superficial ("That was really great!") rather than in-depth reviews, even though a deeper approach to feedback will be more helpful and promote better learning.

Recommendations for developing learners. During this stage, developing learners become even more intentional about getting the most from their learning and serious students begin to set themselves apart from majors who are just slogging through. They are striving to master the conceptual frameworks of many subspecialties in psychology. They should be actively identifying the specific kinds of psychology that they find most appealing, upon which they can build future plans.

Here are some tips about this stage for the developing learner:

1. *Follow the recommended sequences of courses.* Course curricula, whether comprised of general education requirements or those for a major in psychology, are usually laid out in a particular manner for specific reasons. Generally, introductory requirements should be completed before intermediate courses, which in turn should be taken before advanced and capstone classes. Sometimes students decide they want to put off some requirements as long as possible. For example, many psychology students try to postpone taking research and statistics for as long as they possibly can (recall our earlier discussion about math anxiety). Doing so, however, is counterproductive because basic skills in methodology and analysis are important for getting the most out of intermediate and advanced psychology courses. By taking classes in the designed sequence, you maximize the opportunity to learn the most from the course material. The skills acquired in earlier

courses will inform later courses, refining both knowledge and your proficiencies in the major in the process.

2. *Give time and attention now to identifying the pathway that you would most like to follow after graduation.* At this stage, it is very useful to determine in which area your interests are strongest: research/academic; clinical/human services, or practical/workforce related. This strategy will help you decide which electives to take in your advanced coursework. The first two paths move students in the direction of graduate school. Students who want to follow those paths need to pursue research opportunities, lab courses, and other activities that can provide evidence of intellectual rigor and fitness for graduate school. Students who are interested in practical applications of psychology should focus on workplace-simulating experiences through internships, field placements, service learning, or volunteer activities. Every student should build a strong **resume** (a summary of education and experience) that will interest future employers.

3. *Actively consider your personal connections to the coursework you take in this stage to maximize the impact of the material.* Not only do developing learners survey their personal lives for relevant examples that make concepts come to life, they think about the ways in which a given course could connect with their future plans.

4. *Identify research questions that can sustain your interest through the rest of the major.* Students who want to go to graduate school can benefit from identifying some core concepts or theories that might serve as the basis for the demands they will face in undergraduate research. For example, Tina recognized early on that she liked social psychology more than other specialized areas and was especially drawn to the factors that prompt people to help one another. She took a related course in positive psychology and got excited about doing research on empathy for her term paper. In her capstone project, it was easy for Tina to come up with an associated topic—charitable giving patterns—in the area where she had already developed some expertise. Concentrating her undergraduate interests then helped her identify graduate programs in which she could continue doing the research that she found so stimulating.

5. *Nurture helpful relationships.* As you develop expertise in some more specific topics, make a strong connection to the librarian on your campus who specializes in social science research.

6. *Identify professors who will be good references for the steps that follow graduation.* Letters of reference sound more compelling when written by professors who know their students well. If you ask professors whom you admire at an early stage of your schooling whether they would be willing to write strong letters of recommendation when the time comes, they will appreciate how thoughtful you are being about

your future. That favorable reaction can contribute to a praise-filled recommendation. See *A Major Success Story: The Power of Professors Who Know You Well* for an example of how important the right letter of recommendation can be to opening doors.

7. *Join an active research group.* In the developing stage, you should be learning firsthand about the fun and frustration of research projects. Ideally, you should aim to conduct your own research or be a member of a research team by the end of this stage. If you hope to go to graduate school, successfully completing independent research will weigh heavily in your favor. If you plan to join the workforce, conceiving and managing a research project provides evidence of capable project management skills.

8. *Seize opportunities to talk about psychology in academic settings.* If you are like most students, you will have to complete quite a few projects in your advanced courses. Presenting the results of those projects is a great way to practice speaking like a psychologist. You might volunteer to do a presentation in class or present your projects during student research celebrations; making any such presentation will help you overcome the anxiety that accompanies the beginning of being a public speaker.

A **Major** Success Story

The Power of Professors Who Know You Well

Nadine Kaslow knew she wanted to be a clinical psychologist from early on and was prepared to do the hard work required as an undergraduate to get where she wanted to go. She had a stellar grade point average, developed her leadership in appropriate extracurricular activities, and became an active contributor in a faculty member's research group, resulting in having publications even before she graduated. There was just one hitch: Nadine was one of the legions of psychology majors who typically don't test well. If graduate faculty used the usual criteria to determine whether she should be admitted, she may not have been able to get into graduate school.

However, Nadine's development of her resources as an undergraduate included building mentoring relationships with people who wrote effective, attention-getting letters of recommendation that ultimately made a persuasive case regarding her fitness for graduate work. Her mentors were able to write wonderful descriptions of her capacity to do high-level research and her exceptional abilities in solving clinical problems. Nadine's relationships with her mentors reaped huge dividends. She was accepted to multiple graduate programs. She completed her PhD at the University of Houston and launched her career. Her research is impressive for its breadth, depth, and originality.

Her research interests include child and adolescent psychopathology, women's mental health, and family violence. She is a member of multiple academic departments—psychiatry, pediatrics, and emergency medicine—at Emory University School of Medicine. Due to her long-standing service at the American Psychological Association, she was enthusiastically elected as president, serving in 2014. In her limited spare time, she consults for—and works out with—the Atlanta Ballet.

9. *If you plan to go to graduate school, dedicate some activity at the end of the developing stage toward making that happen, including scheduling the GRE, securing reference-letter writers, and identifying possible careers that might be most satisfying.* This stage is also the time to target graduate programs that would be appealing and get the application process underway.

10. *Build a portfolio.* Consider pulling together samples of your best work electronically into a **portfolio** so that you can easily access evidence of the quality of your thinking. A portfolio can come in handy for graduate school interviews and can set you apart in a job search. A portfolio can be online or hardcopy (paper). See **Table 6.1** for an example of what the content of a psychology portfolio may include based on the APA's *Guidelines 2.0.*

11. *Play like a psychologist.* Find out whether your department has social outings or attends conferences together. If possible, try to join in the travel to begin to understand what might be expected in that lifestyle.

12. *Be your own best critic.* The best developing students begin to evaluate the quality of their own work conscientiously and strive not to turn in anything but their best efforts. Before you submit work for evaluation, think about its strengths and weaknesses. When you receive feedback, read it with the idea of improving your learning.

TABLE 6.1

The Psychology Portfolio

Construct your portfolio to correspond with a specific set of performance standards, such as the APA's *Guidelines 2.0 for the Undergraduate Psychology Major*, or use the standards that have been adopted by your own department. Here are some examples that are based on the APA performance categories:

Psychology Content

- A transcript highlighting your undergraduate courses and grade point average
- A copy of a capstone project
- A discussion of your preferred framework or theory
- A brief context paragraph explaining any clusters of courses (e.g., human resources, human development) that reflect your special interests
- A description of how your minor has informed your psychology major

Scientific Inquiry & Critical Thinking

- A list of all projects you completed during your undergraduate career that demonstrate critical thinking
- Abstracts of successful research projects you've completed

Continued

■ Acceptance letters or awards for research projects
■ Grant proposals
■ Theoretical reviews

Ethical & Social Responsibility in a Diverse World

■ A copy of an Institutional Review Board approval
■ Service-learning project descriptions
■ Letters attesting to high-quality volunteer work that you have done

Communication

■ A copy of your best paper
■ A Powerpoint of your best class presentation
■ A videotape of a speech you've given
■ Recommendations that address your interpersonal effectiveness

Professional Development

■ A formal career plan
■ A resume
■ A list of people willing to serve as references
■ An analysis of your strengths and weaknesses in self-regulation
■ Testimonials regarding the effectiveness of your teamwork skills

The Advanced Learner

Toward the end of the major, strong programs offer **capstone courses** that facilitate integrating learning across courses (Dunn & McCarthy, 2010). Capstone courses typically are smaller-sized seminar classes that may be devoted to a specific topic (e.g., history), or capstone work may involve internships, participation in a research team, or any other high-level integrative activity. Our discussion that follows focuses on the nature and quality of student capstone performance.

Characteristics of the advanced learner. Advanced students in psychology should have a comfort level that derives from having chosen the major wisely. In Perry's (1970) framework, advanced learners can be described as **committed learners**—learners who forge decisions despite the presence of ambiguous conditions. As apprentice psychological thinkers, they enjoy complexity and more readily rely on empirical data than on personal experience. They have become "variable minded" because they assume that behaviors stem from a variety of factors and enjoy the work involved in creating tentative speculations about cause and effect. They can pick and choose from an array of strategies, selecting specific approaches that best suit the questions being considered.

As advanced learners, psychology majors are genuinely enthusiastic about the power that comes from working with empirical evidence. They have more ease with using an approach of **amiable skepticism**, which helps them more thoroughly consider matters under discussion. They are vigilant about complying with the ethical requirements of the disciplines.

Particularly in their capstone projects, advanced learners concentrate on developing **coherent** arguments. They read the literature selectively. Advanced learners pay attention to the credibility of the authors and the plausibility of the authors' arguments. Their performances in front of professional audiences are less anxiety inducing. Advanced students also tend to be more comfortable in leadership roles; they are conscientious about involving group participants broadly to help ensure that contributions from all members are of high quality. They are also reflexively self-critical in ways that can help them generate the best possible projects.

Recommendation for the advanced learner. Before their senior year, advanced learners should have developed a plan for the period after graduation. Think about your final courses, especially your capstone, as an opportunity to improve your professionalism. If you plan to go to graduate school, you will already have established a track record, so you can devote your senior year to preparing for graduate school. If you don't plan to go to graduate school, then your primary consideration should be getting ready to enter the workforce.

1. *Capstones should represent your best work.* Strive to make your project a good indication of your work capacity. Pay attention to the quality both of the product and of the process through which you produce the work. Be prepared to articulate what you accomplished, recognizing that your description should vary depending on whether you are trying to impress prospective graduate school representatives or potential employers.

2. *Consolidate your faculty fans.* When approaching faculty for letters of reference, look your prospective letter writer in the eye and inquire about whether they can write you a strong letter. Go with the ones who enthusiastically say "yes." If a faculty member hesitates or cannot reassure you that their recommendation will be helpful, be gracious, thank them, but move on to someone whose enthusiasm will increase the likelihood that they will write a persuasive and positive letter. Waive your right to read what the faculty has to say to ensure candor and demonstrate your confidence.

3. *Show off your public speaking skills.* If you have a chance to participate in a research showcase, participate! It will help you practice explaining psychology to the public and will strengthen your resume. It signals your seriousness as a scholar. Some student research exhibits also have prizes for the best student research projects, which would provide even more evidence of your high caliber for future employers or graduate admissions committees.

You might also be asked to help with prospective student recruitment by describing the quality of your undergraduate experience. By all means, accept this opportunity to help build your resume and demonstrate your responsible performance as a representative of the university.

4. *If you took the GRE and weren't thrilled with your score, work on your plan B.* Consider creating a study group to prepare for retaking the exam, or signing up for a review or prep class. However, if you don't make additional effort, don't expect a better score if you take the test again. Your plan B can also include figuring out a way to find a job that can either help you gather more experience to reapply to graduate school or launch a satisfying career.

5. *If you are hoping to head into the workforce, become familiar with your campus career center.* Connect with the staff member who knows the most about placement of students with psychology or social sciences degrees. Complete the inventory tests that help you identify fields that are most suited to your interests. Write a compelling resume (a brief description summarizing not just what you have done but what your skill sets are) and be prepared to tailor it for specific audiences. (See pages 138–140 for a discussion of resume writing.)

6. *Maximize your experiences in applying psychology in different kinds of contexts.* Service learning, internships, field experiences, volunteer activity, and even psychology-related jobs can add depth to your resume.

7. *Compete for special designations.* Most departments have activities that distinguish high-achieving students from their peers. Don't be shy. Strive to achieve distinction. Volunteer for leadership positions. Submit your papers to competitions. Every award you receive and leadership position you accept provides a new and impressive entry on your resume and demonstrates the seriousness of your intentions about your future.

8. *Solicit feedback on nearly completed works to ensure your best performance.* Even professional psychologists take advantage of peer review to ensure that they communicate their key ideas. Learning how to absorb constructive criticism will be a valuable skill as you enter the workforce or graduate school.

9. *Keep your ethics squeaky clean.* You are not just building content expertise about psychology, you are building your reputation. How your peers and faculty feel about you can be permanently altered with even a single ethical misstep.

10. *Don't complete your graduation requirements by taking throw-away courses.* Eight hours of advanced yoga to fulfill your graduation requirements may help your spirit. However, taking advantage of the opportunity to enroll and succeed in more rigorous courses will help you make a stronger argument for your work ethic and intellectual rigor.

FREQUENTLY ASKED QUESTIONS REGARDING ADVISING

Navigating Registration

What's the best time to declare the major? As a general rule, declare the major as soon as it feels right. Although psychology courses are not always tightly sequenced in the major, some classes are **prerequisites**, courses that have to be taken before other, more challenging classes. Obviously, you will have your best opportunity to accommodate sequenced class requirements if you declare early.

On the other hand, we discourage you from declaring before you genuinely know that you have found an academic home. Ronan (2005) suggested that 50% of students change their majors at least once. Some students change two or three times before settling into an academic home. If you make frequent changes to your major, you will protract your time in college and add significantly to the cost of your schooling. In fact, some states (e.g., Florida) charge higher tuition for students who exceed the target number of undergraduate hours, in order to move students efficiently through a 4-year program.

Am I out of luck if a course I want is closed? Maybe. Find out whether the course has a wait list; if it does, recheck the list regularly. It may help to talk directly with the professor, but she may not be able to exceed the limits established by the registrar (the limits are often related to fire codes). You might also go to the class the first day in case some "no shows" create some room. Be polite and persistent but understand that you may not get into the course.

Must I see an advisor to plan my course list? Many programs require oversight by a professor or advisor on students' schedules. This practice tends to reduce costly errors and curbs students' impulses to register for courses that aren't in their long-term best interest. Other programs allow students to make their own schedules but may not be too accommodating if students make mistakes in their planning. It is always a good idea to find someone in a position of authority whom you trust who can give you objective suggestions about the most effective ways to make your choices. Some programs ease the challenge of getting registration advice by offering peer advising programs in which more seasoned students can help identify potential pitfalls of newer students' plans (Nelson & Fonzi, 1995).

My advisor seems disinterested. Should I ask for another one? Yes. Some departments may not allow for changes, but if the chemistry isn't good between you and your advisor, do all you can to get someone who seems genuinely interested in your future and your well-being. If you can't officially change advisors, then identify a knowledgeable mentor who can fill in that gap and rely on your official advisor to "sign off" on the choices you make based on input from others. Ask for help from the head of advising or the department chair.

Navigating the Faculty

Should I ask a professor if I can get into a class once it has already begun? Most colleges will allow you to join a course in progress if you haven't missed too many classes. However, missing the first hours of class will mean that you miss hearing the context set for the course. A better decision might be to defer registration for the course until you can join the class the first day. If you do get into the class, do not expect the professor to recap the lectures you missed. Develop a relationship with someone in the class from whom you can borrow notes.

If I miss class, should I talk to the professor about what I missed? We don't advise it. Not all professors pay close attention to attendance because they operate on the assumption that they are dealing with adults. The professor might not have noticed you were missing. But professors also can be offended if you obviously prioritize other activities, especially if they are trivial, over attending class (Kuther, 2014). If you miss a class, it is your responsibility to do the make-up work. Anticipate this probability by sharing your contact information with another strong student in the class who can provide you with details of any class you might miss.

Whatever you do, don't ask the professor, "Did I miss anything important?" [One of the best answers we have ever heard was from a quick-thinking professor who responded, "Yes, that day was the day we gave away the Porsche in class and you had to be there to win."] Professors are rankled because your professor may infer you think the class doesn't usually do important things in the class, even if that wasn't what you intended to convey.

What's the best way to ask a professor for help? Professors maintain office hours and respond to email as part of their job responsibility. That doesn't mean that all professors will be thrilled to hear from you or be responsive to your requests, but it helps for you to know that part of their paycheck should cover time spent answering students' questions. Alert the faculty member that you'd like some help and, if possible, estimate how much time you might need. Prepare a set of questions to make the most efficient use of the professor's time. Don't overstay your welcome and be sure to express your appreciation for the time spent.

What's the best way to get invited to join a professor's research team? Excel in the classroom. Visit the professor during her office hours. Read what the professor has written so that you are informed when you talk with her. Ask her directly if there are any roles you can play to assist in the research. If she says no, ask her if she knows of any other possibilities that the professor can recommend.

I want to avoid this professor in the department because his ratings are so low on Rate My Professor. Is that reasonable? Not really. First, recognize that social media evaluations of professors tend to pull opinions either from extremely happy or extremely unhappy students, so the ratings might not be an accurate characterization or correspond well to the standard you have in mind for great teaching (Otto, Sanford, & Ross, 2008). In addition, even unpopular teachers make a connection with some students in the class. Strive to be one of those with whom any teacher can make a more positive connection. We recommend taking time to visit the professor during his office hours to demonstrate your good intentions.

I'm in a course that feels toxic. Should I drop it and take it later? It is rare that a course is hopeless. However, especially if you have in mind braving a high-stakes competition (e.g., admission to graduate school) in the future, you may need to drop the class to protect your grade point average. Before you do, be sure that there will be other faculty who offer the course or you may simply be postponing rather than avoiding the experience. In the worst-case scenario, consider taking the course elsewhere and transferring it in if your perception is that the faculty member's performance is unacceptable or damaging to your academic record.

What if a professor treats me unfairly? We hope you don't have to experience the disconcerting challenge of having a professor treat you unfairly or disrespectfully. Nearly every college graduate has a memory of at least one professor who was not ideal. Most of the time the best course of action is to ride it out, do your best, and move on. However, if the maltreatment reaches levels that cause you serious distress or poses a serious threat to your well-being or future, you may need to take some protective action.

Arrange to visit the professor with another person you trust (a potential witness if things go badly) and lay out your concerns. It helps if you can be specific about the behaviors that have led you to conclude that there is a problem that needs to be addressed. Recognize that professors tend to hold more power than students, so your evidence will need to be compelling if you hope to have a positive outcome. If the problem cannot be fixed informally, you may need to move up the hierarchy in the department and speak with the department head. Some serious problems may even require the intervention of a dean. Your college may also have a specific officer in charge of investigating discrimination complaints, and your exploration may need to start in that office.

I'm uncomfortable because one of my professors seems too friendly. What should I do? Sometimes professors have poor boundaries (Halonen, 2002). They can show preferential treatment toward a student based on interests that are personal and romantic rather than academic. If you think a professor is coming on too strong to you, take some steps to protect yourself. Redirect unwanted attention back to the class. Do not meet alone with the professor behind closed doors or off campus. If the attention is unrelenting (and sadly both of us have seen professors who have created such situations), then consider reporting your concerns to the head of the department.

If you are tempted to develop a relationship with your professor, be aware that most campuses prohibit professor–student romances. To avoid a variety of negative consequences, wait to begin a romance with a professor after that professor no longer has grading power over you.

Navigating the Curriculum

I'm not good at math. Why do I have to take statistics? Psychologists emphasize description and measurement in their work. Statistics is a potent tool that helps us determine whether or not the manipulations we design produce the outcomes we intend. Most curricula require a basic statistics class that helps students learn the most familiar and useful tools in the psychologists' statistical toolbox: correlations and analysis of variance. Becoming comfortable knowing when and why one uses these tools, and being familiar with using **SPSS®** (a powerful statistical program) to manage masses of data should empower you to conduct studies that have some impact. If you believe you will struggle in a statistics class, participate in study or review sessions before your exams and use whatever tutoring services are available.

Can I take courses if I haven't completed the prerequisites? You may be able to persuade a professor into waiving a prerequisite, but it usually isn't a very good idea. Why? Because those who design the program curriculum recognize that students simply need to have prior experience with certain concepts to be successful in the next classes in the sequence (Dunn et al., 2010; Stoloff et al., 2010). Consequently, prerequisites assist students in building their knowledge base through **instructional scaffolding** by providing a sequence of challenges that increase in difficulty over the major. Although it's possible to do well in a course without taking its prerequisite, a course taken without a prerequisite will almost inevitably require more work than it ordinarily would. In addition, those students who abided by the rules will have an advantage in the class—they can focus on the concepts being presented instead of spending time doing background reading to catch up.

Do I need to have a minor? And if so, what should it be? A minor may not be a requirement for your program. But if you do want to have an additional concentration, think about what other areas may be useful for the future you have in mind. Courses in business and management can make you more attractive in the workforce. Graduate schools like to see rigorous minors, such as philosophy, biology, or another science. Plans to enter the helping professions can be improved with additional social sciences. If writing has a place in your future, courses in communications or English literature will be helpful. A foreign language minor can make it easier to get into study-abroad programs as well as broaden your employment options.

Should I double major? Many students can manage a double major in the confines of a 4-year program. However, you must recognize that having a double major means the faculty of both majors will expect you to be hard-working in each of your respective majors. Finishing advanced coursework in two majors at the same time can be especially taxing. For those who are committed to graduate work in psychology, a double major does not confer a particular advantage and potentially can delay your graduation. On the other hand, if you truly love the second major, then pursue it—but do so with your eyes open, knowing that you will need to work hard to stay on track and graduate on time.

Can I put off taking the experimental psychology class as long as possible? (I hear it's hard!) This is one of the worst strategies you can use. Don't do it! Because research constitutes the backbone of psychology, you will have a big advantage if you take the research class as soon as possible. Many schools require that students complete this course before taking any upper-level classes. Understanding what good research involves will make it easier to begin to make connections among your advanced classes.

Should I pursue a certificate if one is available in my program? Some programs offer certificates, which show evidence that a student has taken a concentration of electives in a certain subject. Certificates are given in child development, human development, and industrial organizational psychology, among other psychology subfields. Certificates provide a little something extra to impress potential employers but don't tend to carry much weight for graduate school.

I have to do an independent study. How can I come up with an idea to research? Grab an introductory textbook. Open it up to the table of contents. Pick the chapter that is the most appealing to you and skim it to see which concepts pique your interest. Take a list of two or three concepts and visit your professor during office hours to see if that conversation might inspire an interesting idea and help you develop a manageable design.

Navigating Disappointing Performance

What if I get a D in a core class? First, make absolutely certain that your grade was calculated properly. Mistakes do happen, and when professors are shown that something went awry on their end, they will usually apologize (with some embarrassment) and make the correction. Make every effort to calculate your own grade accurately rather than expecting the professor to perform the math on the spot. Don't be offended if the professor recalculates your estimate; it is just part of the job.

If the grade is accurate, analyze what prompted you to turn in such a lackluster performance. Not enough sleep? Taking too many credits? Long-winded roommates? You will need to fix the conditions that sabotaged your potential if you expect your performance to improve.

If your program has grade forgiveness for poor performance, file the appropriate paperwork as you register to take the class again. However, don't make the mistake of thinking that you already learned a lot the first time so you won't have to work hard when you retake the course. A bad grade means that you didn't learn the concepts the first time. Half-hearted effort on a second try almost always fails to help students do well on the material that originally caused them trouble.

Can I ask to be assigned to a more functional group in my class? You can try, but it probably won't work. Professors who rely on group projects as part of grade assignment are helping you build your teamwork skills. When you graduate, you won't always get to pick and choose the people with whom you will work. Try to adopt the attitude that you are learning not only about the content of the project but refining your project management skills. Actively strategize about how to help the group function better. If those efforts fail, ask the professor to provide some assistance in helping the group figure out better ways to collaborate.

Some of my friends cheat whenever they can. How do I withstand the pressure? It can be hard on a person's morale to observe so much undetected academic misconduct. However, taking the easy way to your degree can taint your school years for you, producing some lifelong regrets, and it adds a level of risk that can cost you your degree. An earned degree is a proud accomplishment; a stolen one is tarnished.

Navigating the Future

How do I secure the best letters of recommendation? When you ask your professor for help, bring with you a one-page summary of your key achievements so the professor has the detail that will help her write an informed letter. Remind the professor of how you did in her course and explain why you have chosen her in particular to write your letter. Ask if there is any other information she would like to have to write you a strong letter. Be sure to follow up with a thank-you note and with news of the outcome. The latter is especially important if you need to ask for additional letters in the future.

If the professor turns you down, don't protract the conversation. You want letter writers who are enthusiastic and positive. Move on until you find someone who is pleased to help you. Obviously, if you have given a lackluster performance, your options may be fairly limited.

How can I find a mentor who can assist me with career planning? If your assigned advisor is reluctant to help you chart your path, ask your advisor or the head of the department for some assistance in identifying a **mentor** who might be able to serve in that role. One of the alumni of your school or a current graduate student might be just the person to help you talk through your options.

How important is extracurricular activity in getting where I want to go? Having a lot of extracurricular activity won't provide the same kind of influence in important future decisions as having strong academic performance. However, the by-product of extracurricular activity—the development of leadership skills—should strengthen your workforce or graduate school applications. Be sure to talk about the impact of what you did in your extracurricular activities. But don't spread yourself too thin with too many outside activities, as they will detract from the more important indicator of your capability as a student—your academic performance.

Is a field placement a good idea? Absolutely. Field placements and internships provide practical experiences in which principles of psychology can be applied. If the field placement comes close to the kind of workplace you envision for yourself, it can help you see whether that type of work will be satisfying. In our experience, some students perform so well in field placement sites that they receive job offers because the host agency is so pleased with their work and wants to continue the relationship. On the other hand, if the field experience is not satisfying, then you may be able to rule out work of this kind as a future option.

When should I take the Graduate Record Exam? Deadlines for taking the **Graduate Record Exam (GRE)** depend on the schools to which you will be applying. It is usually best to take the exam early in the fall of your final year. Receiving your results in early fall can help you then be considered for assistantships or grants in many programs.

Does it help to prepare to take the GRE? Usually. Using a practice exam book allows you to develop the pace necessary to deal with the huge number of multiple-choice questions on the GRE. The practice questions may also cover specific content that is on the exam. Another strategy for preparing is systematically to review a current introductory textbook the summer before you take the exam. Study groups are also useful for building your confidence in the material.

If I do poorly on the GRE, should I retake it? Do an appropriate analysis to determine the cause of your poor score. See if you can identify whether you didn't really know the material well or if anxiety got in your way. If the former, then you need to refer to the strategies we will describe in preparing for the GRE and try harder (see pages 159–160). If anxiety was the problem, consider making use of whatever counseling services might be available on campus to help you figure out how to reduce your anxiety. Happily, if you take the GRE more than once, you can choose the score that you want to be forwarded to your prospective graduate programs.

What if I don't get into graduate school? It happens (Jane didn't get in the first year she applied). It's not the end of the world. Psychology graduate programs are remarkably competitive, especially in the clinical arena. Plan to strengthen your application by doing some work in research or clinical settings. If possible, attempt to stay aligned with an active research team as a volunteer.

LOOKING BACK

At the conclusion of your major, you will want to feel satisfied that you chose your major well and did all you could to make the major work for you. If you practice an intentional and thoughtful approach to your decisions, we can virtually guarantee that you will not just be a happy major but a valuable one.

THOUGHT QUESTIONS

1. Why should you strive to be an intentional student?
2. What are the hallmarks of students' thinking when they are just starting out in the study of psychology?
3. Why are research concerns so prominent among the milestones of the developing student?
4. How do the pathways differ for majors who plan to enter the workforce versus those who want to go to graduate school?
5. Why should you seek help when you are registering for your courses?
6. What should you do if you start having serious difficulties with a professor?

7

Doing Psychology Research from Start to Finish

Smita enrolled in a research methods in psychology class because it was required for all psychology majors. During the first class, the instructor announced that everyone was going to come up with an original research idea. They would all be designing and executing their own **experiments** that semester. Smita started to panic. She had no experience doing research, wasn't sure what the instructor meant by "experiments," and had no idea how to use the library to locate information on psychology. She was thinking about dropping the class until the instructor explained that she didn't expect the students to be familiar with the research process; they would all learn about it together in a gradual, incremental way. Smita breathed a sigh of relief. In a flash of insight, it occurred to her that she might be able to do something in the area of student stress and academic anxiety for her research project. She certainly had a head start in understanding the phenomenon and she thought her research could be personally helpful in the adventure ahead.

□ □ □

Psychologists are critical thinkers and researchers. They know how to pose research questions and create plans for carrying out investigations. They also know how to present their findings in different ways to different audiences. We designed this chapter to help you find good, researchable ideas, develop an appropriate strategy for answering questions, and present your findings in written and oral formats.

Sometimes psychologists' research is **empirical**, which means the investigators might design an experiment where they manipulate some **variables** while measuring other variables. One group of people—the **experimental group**—gets a "treatment," that is, an experimental level of a manipulated or independent variable that represents the researcher's hunch regarding what factors lead to a particular behavioral outcome. Another group serves as the **control** or **comparison group** in that they don't experience the manipulation of the independent variable. A simple example of this design strategy is the clinical trial when researchers test the effectiveness of a new medicine. Volunteers are randomly assigned either to receive the drug of interest (similar to a treatment) or they receive what is called a **placebo**, a sugar pill that should produce no medicinal effect. **Random assignment** refers to a process that ensures that all volunteers in an experiment have an equal chance to be assigned to either the treatment or the control condition. The placebo group constitutes the control condition. If there are differences in the two groups, researchers will know the effects are caused by the drug since everything else has remained the same due to the **controlled conditions** used in the experiment.

How might that strategy apply when studying behavior? Suppose we want to know whether studying is more successful if the person studies against a backdrop of classical music. Researchers might require experimental subjects who have been randomly assigned to the treatment condition to turn on Mozart during every study session. The people in their control group study in quiet conditions. Comparing the groups to look for any differences in the academic performance of the two groups allows the psychologist to discern cause-and-effect relationships based on manipulated variables.

Other research—the **literature review**—is based on available peer-reviewed information about a particular topic. A researcher investigates existing scientific literature, whether in journals and books or online, pertaining to some research topic to make a claim about it or to frame what is already known in a novel way.

Psychology majors are also critical thinkers and budding researchers. As students of the discipline, they learn to identify **independent** (manipulated) **variables** and **dependent** (measured or outcome) **variables** in various research designs found in the published literature. (In the classical music example, the independent variable is presence or absence of music, and the dependent variable could be exam grades.)

Students should be able to interpret literature related to a topic of interest and even to add to that literature by designing and possibly executing their own research projects. Part of the learning curve in becoming a psychology researcher involves getting familiar with relevant peer-reviewed sources either in print or through online searches. Based on the literature (instead of on personal experience), researchers learn to make scientific claims and write stylistically appropriate research papers and lab reports.

This chapter is about learning how to conduct psychological research and to communicate the findings. We explore how to make the best use of available resources in psychology to develop your own ideas about the underpinnings and causes of behavior in humans, animals, or other organisms. To help you develop relevant critical thinking and research skills, we offer guidance on sources that work best, followed by information on how to do library research to explore the available psychological literature. We discuss the importance of navigating cyberspace by using its resources wisely and constructively. We then introduce the writing style psychologists and psychology majors use to communicate their ideas and research findings with each other. We also take a look at other kinds of writing you may be asked to do as a major. We close with tips on how to make presentations to professional audiences.

We begin the chapter by addressing an important question—how do students generate research ideas?

CREATING RESEARCH IDEAS

Where do students of psychology get ideas for research papers and projects? The origins of psychological questions that spur research can appear to be a mystery to some students, especially the first time or two they have to think of a researchable project topic. There are many ways to develop ideas. Here are some popular guidelines that both psychologists and students routinely use (for other ideas, see Dunn, 2013a,b; Martin, 2007).

Look around. Rely on your observation and intuition—what interests you about what you see around you? Why do members of your campus community behave as they do? Are there any common or unusual behaviors displayed by students or other members of the campus community that are worth examining more closely? For example, why do people sit in the same seat every day in class? How do professors differ in their office décor? What attitudes shape whether students cheat or stay honest in taking exams?

Extend already published research. If a psychological topic you learned about in class or in a course reading piqued your interest, consider extending what is known about it. Research psychologists often test the limits of experimental effects by changing conditions, adding new variables, or employing different groups of participants. Locate a published work (you will learn how to do this shortly) and think of ways to alter its current hypothesis by looking at it from a different angle.

Find a paradox. People love information that contradicts expectations. Consider romance: Many people assume that attraction occurs most strongly when a person finds someone whose personality type is completely different from his or her own—in other words, when "opposites attract." Although this sounds reasonable (and may well be in a few cases), generally people actually prefer to become partners with similar rather than dissimilar others—in effect, "birds of a feather flock together" (Luo & Klohnen, 2005). Such everyday paradoxes make excellent starting points for researchable questions, and they always draw people's interest.

Identify a real-life problem. Everyday life is filled with problems that could be constructively addressed by simple psychological interventions. Many college cafeterias have done away with trays, for example, a change that has prompted students to take only the food they really want to eat (Curry, 2008). These "natural experiments" reduce food waste and cost while promoting student health.

Here's a real-life problem to mull over: How can you motivate students to use the stairs in academic buildings (thereby getting valuable cardiovascular exercise) instead of taking the elevator? What sort of message (say, on a sign) will encourage and persuade rather than offend or annoy students? These and other practical ways to change attitudes on campuses are common; it's just a matter of identifying and exploring them. What is happening on your campus right now that could serve as your inspiration?

A research program can flourish and become a way of life. See *A Major Success Story: Sound Decisions* for a great example of one psychology major's journey into a professional life in auditory research.

A **Major** Success Story

Sound Decisions

Jim declared a psychology major at the outset of his college career. He first was drawn to psychology when he worked on his high school senior thesis, in which he began exploring the work of Sigmund Freud. Although he thought Freud's observations were both extraordinary and important, he concluded that Freud's theories were not just arbitrary, but maybe "a little insane." However, working on his thesis inspired Jim to want to be a clinician in part because he thought there must be better ways of explaining and improving human behavior.

During graduate school Jim got sidetracked by experimental psychology, especially by psychophysics, the branch of psychology that deals with how sensation and perception define human experience. In particular, he was fascinated by auditory perception, in part due to his love of music and sound. He liked how work in the physiology of hearing blended with the experimental methods he had learned in psychology. He joined his university's perception lab and happily reports that he never left. He currently serves as the director of the lab, writes grants to secure funding for the lab operations, publishes his findings, and teaches on the side.

His primary work focuses on digital strategies for altering speech signals so that communications can be more intelligible. For example, his lab was able to determine the voice pitch that can be most easily understood in a noisy cockpit. His work has specific implications for helping people with hearing impairments who need modifications in the quality of the signal for sounds to be audible.

Being in a profession that involves asking and answering questions satisfies Jim's curiosity. He especially enjoys designing experiments and analyzing the results. Sometimes he feels challenged by getting the results written up for publication when what he really enjoys is getting to run more experiments. Writing grant proposals is a necessary evil to support the work of the lab, but the economic necessity of this aspect of his role "wonderfully concentrates the mind," he says, adding, "like a hanging."

Jim believes that being a successful researcher depends on how well a person can communicate his or her findings. "As a writer of science, I try to be concise, absolutely clear, and compelling so the reader doesn't wander off until you've made your best case." He suggests that clarity and being compelling are just as important in speaking. "Being compelling shouldn't be that difficult if you keep it personal. We're talking about psychology. What's more personal than that?"

What about you? What psychological issues puzzle you, either about yourself or those close to you? What do you think about when you evaluate the choices and actions of close friends, peers, or perfect strangers? Or consider the social or political issues on campus. Do any bother you or cause you to wonder about them? Is there anything there you can capitalize on in the form of an interesting research question?

Once you have a topic in mind, you need to flesh it out with supporting evidence. What sources should psychology students like you use when conceiving papers or projects?

Sources for Developing Psychological Claims

Marcus took a course in developmental psychology during his freshman year. One of the first assignments was to write a research paper on birth-order effects on child development. For example, do firstborn children differ in some psychologically meaningful and measurable ways from their later-born siblings? Are firstborns more introverted than siblings born later? Do later-borns engage in more risk-taking behavior than do firstborns? Are there any other birth-order effects? Marcus wrote a draft of his paper and sought feedback on it from his instructor a few days before it was due. In the draft, he mined his personal experience, describing the ways his older sister and younger brother's attitudes and actions were distinct from his own.

The instructor explained that research papers need to incorporate *published* research found in the psychological literature, rather than casual observation or personal stories, no matter how compelling and interesting these might be. The instructor cautioned Marcus about making subjective assumptions and conclusions, encouraging him to use library resources to make objective arguments about what developmental psychologists already know and still don't know about birth-order effects. Although he had to rewrite most of the paper, Marcus was glad he shared the draft with his instructor. When he left her office, he went to the main library on campus and worked with a reference librarian who helped him locate four helpful journal articles on birth order. He ended up earning a good grade on the paper and thereafter relied on library sources rather than on his personal and highly subjective experience when writing papers.

When they first arrive at college, many students are like Marcus: prone to using their own experiences when they are unsure about which sources are appropriate for writing and research projects. Some instructors specify the sources that are appropriate for assignments but others do not, so it's always a good idea to ask teachers for clarification about their preferences. Generally, professors in psychology and the other social sciences expect that the data will be scientifically reliable rather than based on personal experience, casual observation, and hearsay. Popular sources, such as newspapers, magazines, social media, television programs, YouTube videos, and the like are not usually considered scientifically reliable. No matter how interesting it might be, information from *Psychology Today*, the *Huffington Post*, or the *Onion* does not meet academic standards. These sources can sometimes be used to introduce or illustrate an idea but are usually not considered to provide sufficient or valid support by themselves.

Like professional psychologists, psychology students should rely on journal articles as their primary sources, followed by chapters and books that summarize empirical evidence. What follows are descriptions and rationales for why this is so.

Journal articles. Journal articles are peer-reviewed scientific or scholarly articles that make claims supported by agreed-upon theories, research methods, and public evidence. The process of "**peer review**" refers to evaluating the ideas and argument in a manuscript or other work by other professionals working in the same field. These peers often remain anonymous and expend efforts to be objective when assessing whether to accept or reject a submission for publication. Peer-reviewed journal articles tend to make one main argument and to provide supporting evidence in the form of a review of the relevant psychological literature and typically an experiment or series of experiments that support the author's claims. Major journals tend to be published monthly or on some regular schedule, which means that articles appearing in them discuss what is currently known about the topics presented therein.

Your institution's library probably has a periodical room or section where many print journals are housed. If it does, you might stop by to browse through a few psychology journals to get an idea of what they are like and to see what has been published recently. **Table 7.1** lists journals published by the American Psychological Association (APA) and the **Association for Psychological Science (APS)**, both excellent sources of top-quality research.

Chapters and books. Book chapters often summarize a psychologist's research on a question or the available research of many investigators dealing with a topic. Peer-reviewers or editors who are experts in the relevant topic usually review chapters before they are published as a book. A book might deal with one topic—there are many books on birth order and psychological development, for example—or the book might contain work on a variety of topics including birth order, such as a handbook on issues in human development. Because chapters and books may take much longer to publish than journals, the information in them is often less timely. Nonetheless, chapters and books on psychology can be a solid source of psychological information.

Start your literature review with recent journal articles dealing with your issue of interest and then supplement those articles with relevant chapters or books, if needed. All else being equal, articles, chapters, or books that have been published recently (within the last 5 or so years) are apt to be preferable over those that are older, unless a resource has been recognized as classic or markedly significant. Naturally, these decisions depend on the topic and its current scientific popularity; sometimes you may rely on older works, but it is always best to look for recently published sources. Where to look for these sources? The best place to begin is in an academic or research library.

TABLE 7.1

Journals Published by the American Psychological Association (APA) and the Association for Psychological Science (APS)

APA Journals

American Journal of Orthopsychiatry

American Psychologist

Archives of Scientific Psychology

Asian American Journal of Psychology

Behavior Analysis: Research and Practice

Behavioral Development Bulletin

Behavioral Neuroscience

Canadian Journal of Behavioural Science

Canadian Journal of Experimental Psychology

Canadian Psychology

Clinical Practice in Pediatric Psychology

Clinician's Research Digest: Adult Populations

Clinician's Research Digest: Child and Adolescent Populations

Consulting Psychology Journal: Practice and Research

Contemporary Psychology: APA Review of Books

Couple and Family Psychology: Research and Practice

Cultural Diversity & Ethnic Minority Psychology

Developmental Psychology

Dreaming

Emotion

Evolutionary Behavioral Sciences

Experimental and Clinical Psychopharmacology

Families, Systems, & Health

Group Dynamics: Theory, Research, and Practice

Health Psychology

History of Psychology

The Humanistic Psychologist

International Journal of Play Therapy

International Journal of Stress Management

International Perspectives in Psychology: Research, Practice, Consultation

Journal of Abnormal Psychology

Journal of Applied Psychology

Journal of Comparative Psychology

Journal of Consulting and Clinical Psychology

Journal of Counseling Psychology

Journal of Diversity in Higher Education

Journal of Educational Psychology

Journal of Experimental Psychology: Animal Learning and Cognition

Journal of Experimental Psychology: Applied

Journal of Experimental Psychology: General

Journal of Experimental Psychology: Human Perception and Performance

Journal of Experimental Psychology: Learning, Memory, and Cognition

Journal of Family Psychology

Journal of Latina/o Psychology

Journal of Neuroscience, Psychology, and Economics

Journal of Occupational Health Psychology

Journal of Personality and Social Psychology

Journal of Psychotherapy Integration

Journal of Rural Mental Health

Journal of Theoretical and Philosophical Psychology

Journal of Threat Assessment and Management

Law and Human Behavior

Military Psychology

Motivation Science

Peace and Conflict: Journal of Peace Psychology

Personality Disorders: Theory, Research, and Treatment

Practice Innovations

Professional Psychology: Research and Practice

Psychiatric Rehabilitation Journal

Psychoanalytic Psychology

Continued

Psychological Assessment

Psychological Bulletin

Psychological Methods

Psychological Review

Psychological Services

Psychological Trauma: Theory, Research, Practice, and Policy

The Psychologist-Manager Journal

Psychology & Neuroscience

Psychology and Aging

Psychology of Addictive Behaviors

Psychology of Aesthetics, Creativity, and the Arts

Psychology of Consciousness: Theory, Research, and Practice

Psychology of Men & Masculinity

Psychology of Popular Media Culture

Psychology of Religion and Spirituality

Psychology of Sexual Orientation and Gender Diversity

Psychology of Violence

Psychology, Public Policy, and Law

Psychomusicology: Music, Mind, and Brain

Psychotherapy

Qualitative Psychology

Rehabilitation Psychology

Review of General Psychology

Scholarship of Teaching and Learning in Psychology

School Psychology Quarterly

Spirituality in Clinical Practice

Sport, Exercise, and Performance Psychology

Stigma and Health

Training and Education in Professional Psychology

Translational Issues in Psychological Science

Traumatology

APS Journals

Clinical Psychological Science

Current Directions in Psychological Science

Perspectives on Psychological Science

Psychological Science

Psychological Science in the Public Interest

Information from: American Psychological Association (2016) and Association for Psychological Science (2016).

DOING EFFICIENT LIBRARY RESEARCH IN PSYCHOLOGY

Academic libraries are social and cultural hubs that connect users to all kinds of information from an incredible variety of disciplines and fields of study. Our focus here is a narrow one—navigating the psychology literature—but when you can, familiarize yourself with your school's library, as its resources will help enrich your learning in all of your undergraduate courses.

Using PsycINFO

Locating the psychological literature requires you to use library resources; whether you do so by physically visiting the library or by going online is up to you. Searching the literature entails the use of databases, many of which are found online through most college and university libraries. The most useful database for students is **PsycINFO**, a reference tool maintained and continuously updated by the APA. This database contains citations and abstracts (brief research summaries) from journals, book chapters, books, book reviews, and other materials published in psychology since 1887. PsycINFO also allows users to search for research sources from sociology, nursing, psychiatry, and education. Another APA database, **PsycARTICLES**, gives users access to the complete text of electronic articles that were originally published in APA journals. Because PsycINFO is more commonly available and used by students, we will center our discussion on how to use this database. (Other helpful databases include PubMed and Bio Abstracts.)

To begin searching a database, you need to rely on **search terms**, the key words that are linked to a given topic in psychology. If you choose a topic from a textbook, for example, then you could rely on some of the terms that are discussed in the chapter or chapter section that interests you. For example, if you are interested in prejudice, then you could focus on a particular type, such as racism or sexism. Alternatively, you can use an encyclopedia of psychology, selecting search terms from entries of interest found in the encyclopedia. **Table 7.2** lists several common encyclopedias. Your library may have others; any one of them will provide you with viable search terms. For college-level assignments, rely on discipline-specific encyclopedias and dictionaries rather than general ones.

After you have a working list of search terms, you can expand it by accessing some of the index terms in PsycINFO. Once you are in the database, you can look for and then click on *PsycINFO's online thesaurus of psychological index terms*. Other search terms can be found in the thesaurus and then added to your existing list.

Once you have your search terms, you can begin to use PsycINFO. The main search screen is very straightforward. You can insert a search term to begin looking

---

TABLE 7.2

Some Common Encyclopedias of Psychology: Good Sources for Search Terms

Baumeister, R. F., & Vohs, K. D. (Eds.). (2007). *Encyclopedia of social psychology* (Vols. 1–2). Los Angeles, CA: Sage.

Corsini, R. J. (Ed.). (2010). *The Corsini encyclopedia of psychology and human behavior* (4th ed., Vols. 1–4). Hoboken, NJ: Wiley.

Eysenck, H. J., Arnold, W., & Meili, R. (Eds.). (1982). *Encyclopedia of psychology.* New York, NY: Continuum Press.

Harré, R., & Lamb, R. (Eds.). (1988). *Encyclopedic dictionary of psychology.* Oxford, England: Basil Blackwell.

Kazdin, A. (Ed.). (2000). *Encyclopedia of psychology* (Vols. 1–8). Washington, DC: American Psychological Association.

Ramachandran, V. S. (Ed.). (2012). *Encyclopedia of human behavior* (2nd ed., Vols. 1–4). San Diego, CA: Academic Press.

for references, for example, or you can refine your search by selecting one of many field options, which narrow the search for a term. You could, for example, look for the titles of works that include the search term "birth order" or you could search for abstracts that include the specific phrase "birth order," and so on. Perhaps you have learned that a particular psychologist publishes about birth order; you can also search by name to find all the articles published by that author.

The point is that PsycINFO is extremely flexible; in fact, the only challenge you are likely to face is that it often provides too many research citations—you may want five but you get 500. If it returns too many results, narrow your search further by looking at only empirical articles, those that were published in the last year, and so on. If you are unsure how to refine your search, ask a reference librarian to help you. These professionals are trained to search for and find material for users—working with one can only help you to develop quicker, more effective search strategies.

Once you find some references about your research topic, capture them to begin to build your research argument. If the reference is available electronically, print or download it. If it isn't available in digital form, go to the periodicals section of the library, locate the bound journals, and make a photocopy of the article. If your school's library does not have a subscription to a particular journal and you cannot obtain a copy through some other online database, you can probably order a copy through what is known as **interlibrary loan** (you can probably do so online; ask a reference librarian for assistance). Once you have copies of the articles, you can read them and take meaningful notes from them at your leisure.

Check the Library's Catalog

Virtually all college and university libraries are searchable online. You can search by author, title, or keywords. You can also use the **Library of Congress Subject Headings** (LCSH; Library of Congress, 2012), a six-volume alphabetized guide often found in a library's reference department. Use the LCSH by looking up one of your search terms to see what other search terms are related, then continue your catalog search using them. If you find promising books listed in the online catalog, look for the subject headings associated with them, which will be hyperlinked. Click on one of the headings to start a search of all the available books in the library linked to that particular subject heading.

If your PsycINFO search suggests chapters or books, you can check the library's catalog to see if the library has a copy of the book (either a physical copy or an online version). If it doesn't, you can likely borrow a copy of the book by ordering it through whatever interlibrary loan service your school uses.

One important suggestion: As you search the catalog, keep a record of the call numbers of the books you intend to consider. Many catalogs are hooked up to printers, making keeping track of titles easy, or you can download your list or simply write down the call numbers in a small notepad or on your phone before you head to the stacks. Don't erase the numbers or throw them away; you may need to refer to them again before the project is over.

Use Known References to Locate Other References

Another good way to obtain sources for your assignments and writing projects is to look through the reference sections of the works you already have in your possession. Reading reference sections will not necessarily inform you about the most recent publications but will usually provide you with the major or "classic" references on a topic. As you examine the reference sections of the articles, chapters, or books you find, you will readily recognize those sources that are cited frequently, an obvious clue to their relevance and importance to the research topic.

Use the reference lists to identify the names of the main authors working within a research area. Once you know their names, you can search by author in PsycINFO to make certain you have found the author's publications that are relevant to your research topic. You can even search for their publications within a particular journal or that appeared during some time frame (a year or range of years).

Always Ask for Assistance

What happens if you are unable to locate useful sources in your initial search? Allow yourself a half an hour or so of searching on your own. If you cannot find published material on a topic, assume that you are probably not using the right approach. Lack of success is perfectly normal. Don't despair—ask a reference librarian for assistance. You won't be imposing; reference librarians treat student requests as mysteries that they not only can solve but love to solve. Reference librarians, in particular, know how to search effectively for information no matter how obscure it might be. Don't be afraid to ask for help—they can be very helpful when it comes to searching multiple databases, narrowing search parameters, and suggesting new search strategies. They also know your school's library intimately, including what is and is not available, so they can locate sources quickly. There is never any shame in consulting an expert, especially one who wants to help! It takes a little time to develop search expertise.

Many academic libraries offer tutorials on using reference, technical, and other resources. If your library does, take the time to sign up for this valuable instruction.

Searching the Internet

The Internet is an amazing tool, one none of us would want to do without. However, it should be used with moderation and care because the way it performs searches is not selective or necessarily intelligently—no guiding filters focused on quality are involved. The nanosecond results of a web search for "birth order" or "prejudice" will not rate the relevance or accuracy found in the listed results. Unless you know with certainty that a website's content is valid or peer-reviewed, using it for college-level work is problematic. Whatever your information source—*especially* when it comes from an Internet source—your wisest course is to evaluate it critically and to seek independent verification of its veracity. It pays to be a skeptical consumer and user of the Internet.

Here are some questions to ask yourself when evaluating evidence from the Internet:

■ Who is the author? What are the author's credentials?

■ Was the Internet document published by an established organization? Was there any peer or professional review involved? Self-published documents are rarely considered to be reliable sources and should be avoided in scholarly work.

■ Is the evidence from the Internet clearly placed within the established research tradition? Is the material informed by existing evidence? If not, then it is highly suspect.

■ Science strives to be a neutral enterprise even if scientists don't always achieve neutrality. In contrast, the Internet doesn't foster neutrality. Does the Internet site have a point of view, particular perspective, or even an agenda? Is the site at all politicized?

■ How up to date is the Internet evidence? Is there a date of publication? When was the website updated last?

Using established websites maintained by professional organizations in mainstream psychology is always a good idea. Consider visiting those sites maintained by the APA, the APS, and Psi Chi (the psychology honorary society). Websites from college and university psychology departments and those maintained by specialty organizations in psychology (see the list of APA divisions in Table 2.1) are apt to be useful sources, as well.

Table 7.3 summarizes the steps in the search process we reviewed in this section. Refer to this table to carry out your search of the psychological literature efficiently when you get a new paper or project assignment.

TABLE 7.3

Recommended Steps for Searching the Psychological Literature

Step 1—Identify your research topic by using one of the topic-generation strategies or choose a topic from a course, psychology book, or a reading.

Step 2—Gather search terms for the research topic (consider using a source from Table 5.2) and search for them in PsycINFO.

Step 3—Collect copies of journal articles from periodicals at the library, and from downloadable sources, books and book chapters, and interlibrary loan.

Step 4—Search the reference lists in the sources you collect; repeat step 3 as needed.

Step 5—Consider consulting a reference librarian who can help you expand or focus your search of the literature.

Step 6—If needed, carefully search the Internet for additional sources, but be appropriately critical and skeptical about what you find.

Once you locate some sources to use for your research, you will need to evaluate whether they are useful to you. The questions provided below can help you assess whether a source is appropriate for your needs. Use the *Reality Check* to assist you in developing the right critical thinking approach to references.

One final piece of advice: You will have to review many more sources than you will actually use in your paper. If your paper requires 10 sources, don't be satisfied with the first 10 articles you read. You will end up struggling to construct an argument that is forced and unsatisfying. A better goal is to locate two to three times more articles than you need so you have a rich landscape from which to build an appropriate and compelling argument.

✔ Reality Check

Evaluating Psychology Sources

When reviewing a source ask yourself the following questions:

Accuracy
Is this an original or primary source?
Are facts provided?
Are they supported with sources?
Was the research peer-reviewed by other experts?

Authority and Credibility
Is the author an expert in the field?
How do you know if the author is an expert?

Objectivity
What are the goals of the research?
What opinions are expressed by the author?
Who is the intended audience?

Currency
When was the research published?
Has it been updated since then?
Are there new studies being conducted by others on the same topic?

Coverage
How narrow and detailed is the research topic?
Does the author give any background about or context for the research?

Overall Evaluation
Is the research helpful to you? Is it believable?
Would the research be useful in helping you form a reasonable opinion or decision?

WRITING ABOUT PSYCHOLOGY

Besides being critical thinkers who rely on the scientific method, psychology majors are also storytellers. They develop narratives exploring the implications of hypotheses (empirically testable questions) and research findings. Before we explore the two types of papers that psychology professors are most likely to assign—lab reports or literature reviews—we first review the writing conventions that psychologists practice using APA style.

APA Style in Brief

APA (American Psychological Association) style is an agreed-upon set of rules for communicating the results of scientific research in psychology. By using these shared rules for writing and presentation, all psychologists and psychology students can understand one another more easily; that is, what appears in APA style is predictable, consistent, and accessible to educated readers. Moreover, the writing is sufficiently clear that anyone could take the directions found in an empirical article and repeat (psychologists and other scientists say "replicate") what was done in a given research project to verify the validity of the original author's arguments.

The tradition of science also involves careful scrutiny by those who read research claims in the disciplinary community. Professionals read and analyze psychological arguments or claims to see if they are plausible. Ultimately, if the report is plausible, they verify the claim and regard the work as valid. Or they instead may challenge the conclusions drawn by the investigators because of flaws in the logic, design, or clarity of expression. This professional give-and-take advances science because it makes theories, methods, and explanations as open and objective as possible (as this book was being written, the discipline of psychology was moving to make all published research data open, available, and accessible to anyone).

The most complete summary of APA style can be found in the *Publication Manual of the American Psychological Association* (APA, 2010). Our review in this chapter is necessarily compact. Still, the information here is sufficient for crafting an APA-style lab report or literature review. If you have more specific questions, you can find the answers or guidelines you need in the *Publication Manual* or in one of the various available books on how to write about psychological research (e.g., Dunn, 2011).

The Research or Lab Report

Sometimes students will conduct an experiment or **correlational study** from start to finish—collecting data, analyzing it, writing it up, and presenting it orally. Other times they will propose a study and describe what findings they anticipate observing if the project were actually conducted.

Research reports usually follow the conventional outline of APA-style papers and published empirical studies, including a format that has four main sections: the introduction and three sections entitled "Method," "Results," and "Discussion," respectively.

Introduction. The **Introduction** of any APA-style paper gives readers a focused and detailed review of the literature related to the question or issue being explored. A thorough introduction provides a concise overview and then addresses the following points:

- What scholarly evidence is already known about this topic?
- Why is the current study being conducted? What question does it address?
- How can any new findings extend what is known about the topic?
- What variables were measured and manipulated in this study?
- What hypothesis was tested? Why?

An introduction begins broadly, identifying the area of interest and then increasingly narrowing the focus by reviewing relevant prior studies and leading up to the rationale for the current work's hypothesis.

Method. The **Method** section provides a specific road map or guide for understanding exactly what was done in the study from start to finish. The level of detail must allow a reader to recreate the study from scratch if desired. When reading a good Method section, a reader should be able to envision herself taking part in the study, answering questions, and engaging in the various behaviors required by the experimenter.

The Method section of a research report usually features three subsections. The **Participants** section describes the people who took part in the research, including whatever demographic information (e.g., sex, age, education) might be relevant to the study. The **Materials** section describes any equipment, surveys, questionnaires, and the like that were employed in the work. A chronology of what took place, who said and did what, and when they did so is in the **Procedure** section, as well as any important details about the experimental design and the ethical debriefing of the participants at the study's conclusion.

Results. APA-style **Results** sections describe the research findings clearly and concisely, indicating how participants behaved, along with supporting statistical analyses. Readers get a clear sense of whether the research supported the hypothesis, but there is no interpretation included in this section. Results are factual and focused; researchers may include tables or figures displaying data or graphing findings for clarity. A full account of the findings, their implications (if any) for understanding the larger research literature pertaining to the topic, waits for the Discussion section.

Discussion. **Discussion** sections put findings into perspective: What do the results mean for understanding behavior? Why do they suggest one interpretation over others? Where should future research turn? This last main section of the research paper or lab report represents an opportunity for the author to consider "the big picture" concerning the research topic, to interpret what was found and to place it in proper perspective. Researchers often use the Discussion section as an arena for explaining which aspects of the methodology worked well and which did not, as well as to qualify any observations, and to highlight the limits of the study and what could be improved upon in any future investigations. All studies have limits—no single research project can address or answer all questions.

Although **Table 7.4** outlines all sections of the APA-style paper, the four main or central sections are indicated in **boldface**. Additional information regarding layout and content is also included in Table 7.4.

TABLE 7.4

Characteristics of Sections, Layout, and Content of the APA-Style Manuscript

Title page—Appears on page 1 of the manuscript

Title explaining the nature of the work (12 words or fewer)

Author name and academic affiliation (name of your college or university)

Running head (an abbreviated title), with page numbers beginning on the title page in the header; see the sample paper in Appendix A for formatting

Author notes can also be added to the bottom of the title page

All information on the page is centered

Abstract—Appears as page 2 of the manuscript

This short summary in one paragraph (not indented) notes the hypothesis, method, results, and implications of the work; 120 words or fewer

Keywords (five or fewer that connect the research to the psychological literature, should be double-spaced and centered under the last line of text)

Introduction—Begins on page 3 of the manuscript

The centered title of the paper appears above the first line of text

Includes an overview of the research question, a review of relevant studies, and the purpose and hypothesis of the present experiment

Method—Immediately follows the end of the manuscript's introduction

Participants (who took part, how many, their sex, and any other pertinent demographic information as needed)

Materials used (surveys, questionnaires, personality measures, equipment, tools)

Procedure (a step-by-step narrative description from the beginning to the end of the study, including what participants were told, what they did behaviorally, and their provided information was gathered and recorded for analysis)

Results—Appears immediately after the Method section.

Concretely presents what happened behaviorally and any statistical outcomes, but *not* interpretation; tables and figures are included as needed to explain what was found

Discussion—Appears immediately after the end of the Results section

Addresses questions such as: Did the results support the hypothesis? Did the investigation broaden what is already known about the research area?

Continued

What do the findings mean? What do they imply about our understanding of the research question? How should future research proceed? Can improvements be made? What's next?

References—Begins on a new page following the last page of the Discussion section

Follows APA citation style: List of authors alphabetized by author's last name (no first names, initials only)

Any citation in the body of the paper must be listed in the references

Table(s)—Begins on a separate page after the last page of the references

Figure(s)—Follows any table(s) on a separate page

Information from: APA (2010).

Papers in correct **APA format** must be typed, that is, word processed. Here are the basic formatting requirements (others are noted in Table 7.4):

- Double-spacing is used throughout the paper—there are no exceptions to this guideline.
- Each page has a 1-inch margin on all four sides.
- The right margin should *not* be justified, that is, it should be "jagged" in appearance.
- Only a 12-point font should be used, one that is clear and easy to read (Times New Roman is the default font).
- Every page is numbered in the top right-hand corner and inside the 1-inch margin (only the Figures pages lack a page number).
- With the exception of the Abstract paragraph (which appears on page 2 of the APA-style paper), the first line of every paragraph is indented (use the tab key, which usually indents five spaces).

The best way to understand the layout, structure, and function of an APA-style paper is to look at some examples. Appendix A in this book contains an annotated APA-style student paper that will serve you as a helpful template when you are drafting and writing your own paper. You might also go to the periodicals section of your library and look up one of the APA journals from the list in Table 7.1. Open the journal (or bound set of journals, usually a year's worth) and pick a published article to review. Pick a second article at random in the same journal and compare it to the one you already reviewed. Although they are structured the same, the subheadings that create meaning and order in the introduction, Results, and Discussion will differ in each article. However, the overall outline—title, Abstract, introduction, Method, Results, Discussion, and References—will be the same.

References. The theme of standardization is continued with the style and presentation of citations appearing in the **References** section of the APA-style paper. Although all citations are similar, the most recent edition of the *Publication Manual* (2010) lists 77 categories of references—from the basic journal article to video blog posts (or vlogs). **Table 7.5** provides common reference formats that students are likely to use when writing lab reports or literature review papers. These samples will probably serve you well (note that the entries in Table 7.5 are not double-spaced—they would be in a student paper or a research manuscript). You can also consult the References section of this book for other examples. If you have a more exotic reference to cite (say, a photograph or a film), look up the formatting information in the *Publication Manual.*

One important note: References appear in what is called a hanging-indent format (see the entries in Table 7.5). That is, the first line of each reference aligns with the left margin; however, any text on the second and subsequent lines is indented five spaces.

TABLE 7.5

Basic Examples of APA-Formatted References

Journal Articles

Bem, D. J. (2011). Feeling the future: Experimental evidence for anomalous retroactive influences on cognition and affect. *Journal of Personality and Social Psychology, 100,* 407–425. doi: 10.1037/a0021524

Mehl, M. R., Vazire, S., Holleran, S. E., & Clark, C. S. (2010). Eavesdropping on happiness: Well-being is related to having less small talk and more substantive conversations. *Psychological Science, 21,* 539–541.

Books

Bruyère, S. M., & O'Keefe, J. (1994). *Implications of the Americans With Disabilities Act for psychology.* Washington, DC: American Psychological Association.

Pennebaker, J. W. (2011). *The secret life of pronouns: What our words say about us.* New York, NY: Bloomsbury Press.

Edited books

Fiske, S. T., Gilbert, D. T., & Lindzey, G. (Eds.). (2010). *Handbook of social psychology* (2 vols.). Hoboken, NJ: Wiley.

Nelson, T. D. (Ed.). (2009). *Handbook of prejudice, stereotyping, and discrimination.* New York, NY: Psychology Press.

Book Chapters

Chan, F., Livneh, H., Pruett, S., Wang, C.-C., & Zheng, L. X. (2009). Societal attitudes toward disability: Concepts, measurements, and interventions. In F. Chan, E. da Silva Cordoso, & J. A. Chronister (Eds.), *Understanding psychosocial adjustment to chronic illness and disability: A handbook for evidence-based practitioners in rehabilitation* (pp. 333–367). New York, NY: Springer.

Funder, D. C., & Fast, L. A. (2010). Personality in social psychology. In S. T. Fiske, D. T. Gilbert, & G. Lindzey (Eds.), *Handbook of social psychology* (5th ed., Vol. 1, pp. 668–697). Hoboken, NJ: Wiley.

Materials from the Internet

American Psychological Association. (2016). *The road to resilience.* Retrieved from http://www.apa.org/helpcenter/road-resilience.aspx

World Health Organization. (2011). *World report on disability: Summary.* Retrieved from http://www.who.int/disabilities/world_report/2011/report/en/

Literature Reviews

Literature reviews are psychology term papers that summarize what is known about some psychological topic. The best review papers propose some point of view for examining the studies available on a topic. For example, it's likely that a paper comparing the incidence of depression in firstborn versus only children would be more focused and insightful than one comparing firstborn with only children in general. Specificity is a good rule to follow: More specific reviews say quite a bit about one topic, in contrast to broad reviews, which say little about many aspects of whatever is being considered.

Literature reviews typically also follow the basic outline of APA-style papers. However, because they do not usually contain original experiments by the author, they do not have methodology and results sections. A quality student literature review has three main parts (Thaiss & Sanford, 2000, p. 88):

1. *A topic overview*—A clear explanation of the paper's theme and the purpose of the review.

2. *Main section of the paper*—Contains a review of specific topics and issues drawn from a close reading of relevant studies. The main section can include subheadings to highlight key ideas.

3. *A closing section*—Identifies main conclusions to be drawn from the reviewed studies and suggests directions for future research.

Other Writing Formats

Although professors tend to have students write lab reports and literature reviews as a means of teaching the students how to write in psychology, they also assign other kinds of writing. What follows is a list of some of these types of writing assignments, with some pointers for writing effectively in those formats.

Posters. Your professor may ask you to convert a research project into a poster either in place of or in addition to a traditional research report. The poster should include the same kinds of headings that would appear in a paper, but the limitations of the format require you to summarize the key ideas and write with precision. Be sure that you use a font that is readable and use graphics to add some visual interest to your work. Include at least a partial list of the most important references (in APA format) for your work.

Grant proposals. Especially for those students who may be headed into the nonprofit sector of the workforce after graduation, learning how to write **grants** can be a useful talent. A **grant proposal** is a detailed request for funding to carry out a specific research project to solve a particular problem. At minimum, grant proposals include a list of the authors ("principal investigators" or "PIs"), a statement of the problem that needs funding, a brief literature review (with an APA reference list), a specification of how success will be measured, a timeline, and a clear and adequate budget to accomplish the aims of the grant proposal.

Your campus may have an office that specializes in writing grant applications, with experts who may be able to provide additional assistance.

Technical reports. Your professors may assign you to complete a project or technical report as part of their goal of preparing you for life after graduation. A **technical report** outlines the process, progress, or results of a technical or scientific research problem. For example, a class assignment might require you to serve as a consultant to a campus-based day-care center by helping them work with toddlers. You might write a report recommending use of particular play activities that promote active learning for toddlers. This assignment simulates the experience of providing consultation. The report written about the experience should summarize the impact of your work. The writing in a technical report needs to be precise and objective. Your instructor will specify whether you need to include APA-style references.

Case notes. Some students may get internship placements that allow them to work directly with clients. In such cases, the agencies may require students to document their interactions in **case notes**, or client files. Although case notes do not require APA format or literature citations, case note writers do have to abide by some specific conventions. Clients technically may have access to their records so the notes need to be objective and free of bias or judgmental description. Unlike other, more public, forms of writing, case notes must be treated confidentially. Interns need to follow the policies of the organization in which they are working. Be sure to seek some feedback to ensure you are meeting the agency's expectations.

Journal entries. Certain classes may require you to create a record in which you reflect on your learning experiences in **journal entries**. Beyond observing rules of grammar and spelling, journal entries tend to have fewer constraints and no reference citations. Exercise discretion about disclosing too much personal information in this context. Faculty members do have professional obligations to report certain criminal acts, such as child abuse.

Memoranda. Email has become a dominant medium for getting things done. However, casting the message in a formal business **memorandum** format, even if the memo is forwarded via email in an attachment, increases the importance of the communication. Using a conventional memo approach sets the communication apart from the deluge of messages most professionals must wade through each day. Put the following information at the top of a formal memo:

> To: Bruce Wayne, President, Batman Foundation
> From: Dick Grayson, Lab Assistant
> RE: Request for Batmobile Renovation
> Date: March 15, 2016

If you use memos to conduct business about your coursework, be sure to provide enough context information to clarify your problem, including which class you are taking. Be clear about specifying if you need some action taken by a specific deadline. You do not need to have a separate sign-off from the heading.

If you send a request via email, the normal format of email will do some of the context-setting work for you, such as the date and some identifying information from the sender. But remember, your email name might not clearly communicate who you are to people who don't know you well (e.g., jwt29@ just won't help the reader know who is writing). Be sure to add your full name in the body or closing of the email, along with a good subject heading that orients the reader to what you need or want.

STAND AND DELIVER

Your work may not be over when you submit your paper. Many faculty include a speaking component as part of the research and writing experience. Here are some tips to make the most of that opportunity:

1. *All good speakers started out NERVOUS.* With practice, you will be able to overcome your jitters.

2. *Even if people know who you are, introduce yourself and state your purpose in the presentation.* Good introductions give the audience an idea of the main points you plan to cover.

3. *Rehearse, rehearse, rehearse.* Don't wing it. Research studies especially have details that should be presented precisely. Rehearse so that you don't read from your index cards or PowerPoint but create a more conversational approach.

4. *Practice with technology.* You will lose precious minutes of your allotted time if you have to fuss with the volume controls or a recalcitrant video.

5. *Stay on topic.* Don't allow tangents to divert you from your main message.

6. *Look professional and act professionally.* Dress for the occasion in comfortable clothes that you won't be adjusting through the presentation. Don't fuss with your hair or pull your earlobe. Avoid using placeholders such as "um," "like," "you know," "literally," and "stuff like that...".

7. *Engage your audience through creative language, examples, or involvement.* Maintain eye contact by sweeping your eyes across the room. Humor also helps presentations to be more memorable.

8. *Don't end abruptly.* Summarize the key ideas that you want your audience to remember long after you have stopped talking.

9. *Be thoughtful in response to questions.* If you are stumped, ask the questioner what his answer might have been. That response will give you more time to think through a better response. An honest "I don't know" is a better strategy than bluffing.

10. *Target your presentation to match the allotted time.* Talking too long indicates you aren't in control. Talking too little suggests you might not have done sufficient work.

We offer one final note, this one about your role as an audience member during your peers' presentations. Listen carefully to the presentations and try to formulate questions that will help elevate the experience for everyone. You will stand out as a critical thinker and get practice at being a good colleague.

THOUGHT QUESTIONS

1. Do you have any other suggestions for ways to generate research or paper topic ideas?

2. Why are journal articles the preferred resources in psychology?

3. What are some challenges associated with obtaining research from Internet sites?

4. If you had to write a research paper in psychology right now, what would your topic be? Why?

5. Why is it important to meet appropriate time or page limits in your communications assignments?

6. What situations would require you to write a memorandum? What problems might be more appropriate for a memo rather than an email?

7. Which presentation tip addresses a public speaking weakness you might have experienced? How will you address that problem?

Using Psychology to Become an Effective Leader

As Sam hoisted a big bag of mulch into the back of Jane's SUV, he described himself as being in a "holding pattern." Just graduated with an undergraduate degree in psychology, he was continuing to work as a stockperson at a local lawn and garden business, a job he had begun while he was working on his degree. When Jane asked what he hoped to do with his degree now, Sam confessed that he had blown it. "I screwed up. I didn't take that **internship** course and now I won't be able to get a job in psychology. So I guess I'm just stuck."

□ □ □

Conversations like these are challenging for students and professors alike. Sam's lack of vision and his limited hopes for the future were certainly disheartening, but buried in his confession were both a flawed conclusion and a painful reality. Sam was wrong about the damaging effects of missing out on an internship. Internships do provide a great opportunity to apply what you have been learning in professional contexts, making you more valuable to a potential employer, but the obverse isn't accurate. The lack of an internship doesn't prevent you from getting a job; it simply makes proving that you "have the chops" harder. Unfortunately, Sam was right in that his holding pattern was a morass of his own making.

The painful reality inherent in Sam's current dilemma is that he recognized he didn't fully invest in the opportunities he had that would have made him a better job candidate after graduation. Sam is not alone. According to the National Center for Education Statistics (http://nces.ed.gov/pubs98/98137.pdf), nearly half of traditional-aged full-time students work while pursuing a degree. One out of every 10 full-time students works a minimum of 35 hours a week. Unfortunately, between overbooked social lives, substantial work commitments, and a full-time academic load, students have little discretionary time available to pursue activities that will make them more valuable to the workplace following graduation.

According to Pascarelli and Terenzini (2005), the most successful undergraduates are good at blending academic, personal, and extracurricular pursuits. This involvement tends to translate to higher grades and to a higher likelihood of remaining in college. Kuh et al. (2010) suggested that students fare best in college when they have one **high-impact practice (HIP)** in their first year and another HIP in their senior year. High-impact practices are special opportunities that allow students to make a deeper connection to their chosen discipline, their faculty, and even their institutions or communities, such as participating on a professor's research team or in a food drive for the homeless. Some HIPs are embedded within courses; others involve extracurricular activities. Happily, psychology abounds with many HIP opportunities that enhance basic academic life.

The goal of this chapter is to explore the value added by participating in ways that create high-impact experiences for the undergraduate psychology major. We systematically review the more popular HIPs in psychology to make the case that investing your time will produce multiple positive opportunities in your life, potentially including:

- applying concepts and principles of psychology in assorted work projects;
- exercising leadership skills when completing projects;
- developing more personal relationships with people who might write letters of recommendation for you;
- expanding your portfolio with evidence of abilities and traits that will impress a future employer; and
- demonstrating your commitment to improving the lives of others

But first, we explore the importance of making strategic decisions about how to allocate your limited discretionary time.

MAKING STRATEGIC DECISIONS

You will have a variety of opportunities to develop leadership skills as a psychology student. Some will be easy to participate in because of their close connection to your major. For example, organizing and participating in study groups or working as an assistant in the department will give you a chance to develop leadership in ways that directly support your academic work. Taking a term abroad can also provide an excellent opportunity to refine your leadership as you master a new environment. Other activities may require significant commitment of your free time; being an officer in a psychology club or campus fraternity or sorority, serving in student government, or taking on significant projects in the community are all worthwhile but have a serious impact on how much time you can devote to your studies.

Choose your leadership opportunities carefully. Consider this: Your number one priority in completing your major is creating an academic track record that will give you maximum opportunities after graduation. Don't allow yourself to be swept away by activities that you really don't have time to complete, no matter how exciting or ego-boosting they might be.

Josh's story provides a good example. He enjoyed his psychology major but really loved being involved with student government. Eventually he had an opportunity to run for president but was concerned that the time demands of being president would be problematic. He chose the presidency and eventually fell behind in his studies. Although he did get leadership experience, it cost him. His grade point average fell and he had to stay in school an extra year to complete his requirements. In retrospect, his choice was not a good one. He gained leadership experience at the expense of a clean academic record that would have given him a wider range of options after graduation.

If you do decide to pursue a leadership position, recognize that a lot of effort goes into being a successful leader. See *Reality Check: Do You Have What It Takes to Be a Leader?* to assess what strengths you already show as a leader and to identify some areas where you could use some more experience.

We turn our attention now to some of the places in which you might develop your leadership skills. We will start with a HIP that has a direct, positive impact on your academic success—establishing and leading study groups in psychology classes.

Organizing Study Groups

You don't have to move too far from the classroom to develop important leadership skills. Consider organizing a study group for a class, particularly if the course is challenging. Campuses may provide some infrastructure for launching a study group; however, if you let your instructor know that you're interested in starting one, she or he can probably solicit interest from your classmates.

Discussing the course materials will reinforce your comfort with and recall of the content. The normal challenges (e.g., using time efficiently and effectively) that result when students work together will provide a great opportunity to develop team skills and leadership. Improving your own performance and helping your peers with theirs through a study group may make it easier to figure out whether you would like to work as a teaching assistant in graduate school.

✔ Reality Check

Do You Have What It Takes to Lead?

College offers an array of leadership opportunities that can help you develop your skills and character. Whether you are organizing a study group, serving in student government, or presiding over Psi Chi, check off from the list below the items that you think characterize your style. When you have finished, go back over the list and mark with an "X" the top three features you could work on that would make you a better leader.

Personal Attributes

☐ Are you more extroverted than introverted?
☐ Are you energetic?
☐ Do you have self-discipline?
☐ Do you keep your promises?
☐ Are you punctual?
☐ Are you known for having high standards of integrity?
☐ Do you speak with authority?
☐ Can you rebound from setbacks?
☐ Are you visionary?
☐ Do you maintain a positive outlook?

Problem-Solving Skills

☐ Do you notice problems that need to be fixed before others do?
☐ Do you make sure you understand situations thoroughly before taking action?
☐ Are you willing to do extra work in background research and planning?
☐ Can you take immediate action once you have formulated a plan?
☐ Do you strive to identify the consequences of the plans you implement?
☐ Do you develop a "plan B" just in case your original plans don't work out?
☐ Do you enjoy change?
☐ Can you take calculated risks?
☐ Do you show courage under pressure?
☐ Can you take responsibility when you make errors and then correct those mistakes?

Team Skills

☐ Are you oriented toward serving the needs of others?
☐ Can you relate to and appreciate a wide variety of people?
☐ Do you make a point to include others' ideas in your plans?
☐ Can you persuade others to take action?
☐ Do you build and maintain effective collaboration?
☐ Do you encourage team members to work from their strengths?
☐ Can you manage conflict?
☐ Do you have strategies for working with difficult people?
☐ Do you recognize and celebrate achievements?
☐ Can you share the glory that follows an achievement?

What's the best way to ensure your success? Weimer (2013) suggests that study groups can meander if they don't have a specific focus. She recommends several ideas to make the group experience a good one:

1. Each member predicts five things that are test-worthy, then the group constructs a master list of the concepts that were most frequently identified.

2. Each member writes a potential test question for a concept that is "fuzzy" or hard to understand. The group spends time answering each fuzzy concept question.

3. The group devotes a small amount of time to constructing one master summary sheet and uses the sheet to foster discussion.

Undergraduate Teaching Assistants

Some psychology faculty show special interest in students who express a desire to become teachers or especially college professors. In fact, some programs allow undergraduates to serve as teaching assistant (TAs) so that they can become familiar with aspects of being a teacher. Some undergraduate TA positions are paid; others are structured as a directed (or an **independent study**). If the latter, the supervising faculty member will likely assign the TA readings and perhaps some reflective writing to help the TA get the most from the experience.

Undergraduate teaching assistants can have a variety of responsibilities, including grading low-level assignments, processing Scantron tests, coordinating and conducting study groups, meeting with students during office hours, and coming up with suggestions for active-learning activities. In some cases, undergraduate TAs might give a mini-lecture and get feedback on the strengths and weaknesses of their lecture.

Even if there is no formal undergraduate TA program in your department, you can approach a professor about volunteering as a teaching assistant. If you perform well, your professor will be in a splendid position to write a strong letter of recommendation for graduate school, where you can pursue your dream of being a teacher.

Honors Program

Many campuses allow students who have proven their talent to enroll in an enriched program. Students can enroll in **honors programs** from the outset if their high school records qualify them as high performing; other students can earn their way into honors programs through a strong first-year performance. Typical honors programs provide some serious advantages for students, including smaller class sizes and being able to register for classes in advance. Honors programs tend to draw the most vibrant faculty, who thrive in working with small, highly motivated classes. Many honors programs also provide a social program in which students might find a comfortable place to develop what may become their most enduring friendships.

For all their advantages, honors programs also require a great deal from their participants. Small classes means that there is little chance a student can get away with not doing the work. Honors faculty design examinations and assessments to evaluate student knowledge at the highest levels of complexity. Honors programs require students to do a lot of writing, often including a thesis. This usually guarantees that honors students get to work one-on-one with a professor whose research interests them.

According to Astin (1999), honors programs produce multiple positive outcomes. Students who successfully complete honors programs in college report high interpersonal and intellectual self-esteem and have more well-developed enthusiasm for the arts. Honors students describe greater satisfaction with the quality of instruction they receive and with their relationships with faculty. They also demonstrate more persistence and are more inclined to pursue additional education in graduate or professional schools than students who are not enrolled in honors programs. Students who graduate from honors programs can proudly add to their graduation regalia items such as honor cords to publicly display their achievements in their undergraduate major.

Psychology Learning Communities

Learning communities within majors are a relatively new HIP. Typically, these communities are designed to establish a strong *esprit de corps* among a limited number of first-year students who are all taking a common curriculum. The students are often housed together. The communities tend to attract exemplary faculty members who enrich their courses by inviting faculty guests and by incorporating field trips that illustrate psychological principles. Zhao and Kuh (2004) praised the potent positive outcomes of being involved in these communities, including stronger retention patterns through graduation, higher GPAs, marked improvements in skills and competencies, significantly enhanced student involvement that is sustained through later years, and higher student satisfaction. Learning communities tend to be somewhat selective. Students routinely report that the intensity and scope of activities in the discipline-based learning community gives them a head start on knowing what they want to do professionally.

At James Madison University, students who participate in the Psychology Learning community can register earlier than other students for experimental methods classes (see http://www.jmu.edu/stories/orl/2014/05-08-rlc-caroline .shtml). At Rutgers, students in the Psychology House are ensured of being able to taking blocked courses with their peers. **Blocked classes** means a cohort of students take a specified number of classes together. They can also participate in related social activities, a quiz competition, and a resource fair for summer funding (see https://rulc.rutgers.edu/content/psychology-discovery-house).

Psychology Study Abroad

If you have the financial wherewithal, consider studying abroad. Study-abroad programs can provide a particularly eye-opening experience in which to strengthen your background in psychology while you enjoy adapting to a new culture. Most people who have been in a study-abroad program say that it was transformative in part because their comfort zones were stripped away. Students must rely on what they have learned to help navigate the various daily challenges—language, social customs, novel foods—they hadn't even conceptualized before the trip.

Unless they are part of a language-immersion curriculum, most study-abroad programs are conducted in English. Students can secure an independent study arrangement through the variety of options hosted by specific psychology programs (Google "psychology study abroad" to see a dazzling array of options). However, it may be smartest to work with the international studies office on your own campus. That office may have preexisting agreements that will not only narrow down the wide range of choices available to you but also can help you solve the problems entailed in international travel.

Studying abroad can have a significant effect on personality development and leadership (Zimmerman & Neyer, 2013). Travelers must face and conquer ambiguous conditions, from those involved in making travel arrangements through the various adjustments to living in a new culture. Coupling travel vagaries with academic demands produces near-perfect conditions for developing confidence, problem-solving skills, and more tolerance for and appreciation of people from different backgrounds.

Many students report that studying abroad is life changing, that it has an impact on how they think about politics, additional education, and career directions. Not surprisingly, studying abroad can increase openness and agreeableness (two dimensions of the Big 5 personality framework) as well as decrease neuroticism (McCrae & Costa, 2003).

Undergraduate Research

Dana got engaged with undergraduate research in his freshman year. He served as an undergraduate research assistant to a graduate student who was finishing a dissertation. Although his responsibilities were limited to data entry, it was a pretty heady experience to be mentioned in the footnote of a *Journal of Personality and Social Psychology* article. He was then able to secure a second research assistant position for a high-profile social psychologist. His responsibilities included recruiting students from the department's human subject pool, scheduling data collection times, and collecting data. Not only did he learn a great deal about the rigor involved in social psychology experiments, he learned about the importance of having a strong work ethic. That experience served him well when it was time for him to design and execute his honors thesis, which he completed on short-term memory effects on voter decision-making.

Dana's experience is typical of students who understand the value of building a strong portfolio of experience in research. Lopatto (2010) praised involvement in undergraduate research for the improvements it brings about in the skill sets of scientists, including critical thinking; the ability to work with primary literature; communication; and teamwork. He also emphasized that overcoming the inevitable obstacles in undergraduate research builds self-confidence and improves independence. He recognized that successful experience seems to inspire students to want to pursue more complex research designs. Lopatto concluded that these benefits give people an advantage in any career path they choose.

Experiential Learning

Students who give back to the community through volunteer work in psychology-related settings, in more organized efforts through service learning or in career-focused internships and field studies, can demonstrate civic engagement. The caliber of volunteer experience depends on the quality of supervision and the scope of the volunteer's responsibilities. In psychology, especially for students with a clinical bent, volunteering in clinical settings may provide some advantages in developing employment planning. For example, students who volunteer at a local state-sponsored institution often begin to see that working with people with serious mental disorders requires enormous effort and patience. Seeing the nature of the work from such a close perspective can help students make better career choices, even if it means learning that kind of occupation is not for them. Volunteer work may be personally meaningful but supervised learning experiences will provide more tailored feedback that reflects the use of psychology in the setting.

Service learning promotes content and skill learning linked to specific classes (Bringle & Hatcher, 1995). Typically, service learning is project-based so that it can be adapted to the constraints of the academic term. Students take on a project, such as building a house for an organization like Habitat for Humanity, but ground their experience in the relevant research literature. For example, they might look at the effects of income inequality or what constitutes quality of life. "Service learning" can be the title of the course or it can be a special assignment embedded within a course. For example, Jane's introductory psychology class consulted with a child abuse agency to make some recommendations for changes to the agency's parent-training curricula after they learned some basics about child development in their course.

Internships typically deliver the most intense experiential learning. Students move outside the traditional classroom structure and try out professional roles in settings that deal with psychological concerns. In the best internships, students receive feedback from both an on-site mentor and a faculty member with pedagogical expertise about activities at the site. Students might work in a politician's office, for example, solving problems for constituents. They can run leadership training sessions for the Girl Scouts. They may go to work as an extra pair of hands in a research laboratory. Internships can be valuable for helping students decide what directions not to pursue before they get too far down the professional path.

Student Interest Groups

Psychology students are often passionate about their major. It is not unusual to find psychology interest groups or clubs established on campus to help students spend more time in the discipline they are learning to love and to connect with other students and faculty who share their passion. Psychology clubs usually have a faculty sponsor who can provide light guidance about the kinds of activities that the club should undertake, including field trips, alumni visits, careers days, and service learning. See *A Major Success Story: Parlaying Student Leadership Into Professional Success* for an example of positive outcomes that can result from wise extracurricular choices.

Many students find that becoming a member of an organization that honors strong academic work is helpful to their development. Begun in 1927, Psi Chi confers membership on students who have a particular GPA overall (top 35% of the class) and in the major (a minimum of 3.0 on a 4-point scale). There are well over 1,000 chapters of Psi Chi around the world and the organization reports that it has 600,000 lifetime members. Members can apply for awards and grants, as Psi Chi gives away $350,000 annually to its membership. Psi Chi

A **Major** Success Story

Parlaying Student Leadership Into Professional Success

Annie had a good track as a student throughout her major, but it wasn't until she became involved in her department's psychology club that she began to get an inkling of what her future might be. Her first official responsibility to the membership involved volunteering to coordinate special events for the group. That task involved working directly with professors on scheduling sessions in which they could informally talk about their research. She also persuaded several alums to speak at a career night. Annie did such a fine job that she quickly rose to the presidency of the club where she had an opportunity to roll out her vision for what the club could become. Her leadership was inspiring and resulted in favorable commentary in her letters of reference when she joined the workforce.

Her skill at coordinating diverse projects while maintaining laudable academic achievement appealed to a local collective of mental health practitioners who hired her to become an office manager for their private practice. Her academic background in psychology, especially her classes in personality and abnormal psychology, helped her understand the challenges of working with the agency's clientele. Her social psychology and organizational behavior classes helped her cope with the diverse personalities and styles of the private practitioners. Her marketing minor contributed to effective strategies in publicizing the fine quality clinical care of her employers.

After 6 years in her management position, Annie decided to use her leadership skills and accumulated experience to launch her own mental health care business. Within 10 years of her graduation, Annie was managing a mental health enterprise with three locations and 20 practitioners. She was grateful for her early extracurricular experiences that helped her develop her multi-tasking strategies in the service to the discipline she loved.

publishes *Eye on Psi Chi*, a magazine for members that features articles of interest to the psychology community. Psi Chi also sponsors special sessions at regional and national conferences. A career-enhancing advantage of being selected to Psi Chi is that members automatically meet a requirement for joining the civil service at the GS7 level. Visit the Psi Chi website at http://www.psichi.org.

An honorary organization operating at the community college level, Psi Beta selects its members based on meeting similar high standards of scholarship. Many of the advantages that attach to Psi Chi membership are also available through Psi Beta. See the Psi Beta website at http://psibeta.org.

On-Campus Employment

Recall that our chapter opening story about Sam's poor engagement choices suggested that he was working too much and exploring enrichment activities too little. Not all employment is a bad thing. In fact, faculty members expect that most (but not all) students can reasonably manage between 10 and 15 hours per week and still do well in their studies (Pena, 2010). If you need to work to cover your expenses and can handle the strain without compromising your academic success, we strongly recommend finding employment on campus and encourage you to work with the campus offices that streamline screening and selection.

There are multiple advantages to on-campus employment (Mayfield & Mayfield, 2012). Employers tend to be especially sensitive to the rhythm of the academic term and may allow you to work fewer hours during periods when academic demands (e.g., project completion, finals) increase. If a job has downtime, the employer may let you do your homework during the slow period.

On-campus jobs might also be part of a work-study program, which can have a positive impact on your financial aid. If you have been deemed eligible for work-study—which is based on financial need—you can apply for an on-campus job that is jointly subsidized by the school and the federal government. There are limits to the number of hours you can work and how much you can earn. Work-study money can help you pay for tuition and other college expenses and, most importantly, the money you earn does not count against the amount of financial aid you receive for future semesters. The jobs available are often in the library, campus bookstore, cafeteria, the admissions office, or even in campus residence halls.

Psychology majors who end up working in psychology departments—a great way to learn more about the faculty and the discipline—are required to abide by confidentiality rules, particularly where handling course materials (including quizzes and exams) and student records are concerned. Students can use the experience of being a part-time student-employee to explore how a psychology department functions. This experience can make it easier to figure out whether to apply to graduate school, as it provides a close-up look at what life in an academic department entails.

CONFERENCE AND CONVENTION PARTICIPATION

Professional Conventions

One of the powerhouse high-impact experiences Jane remembers was participating in the Midwestern Psychological Association (MPA) convention as an undergraduate. Everything about the trip was exciting. She got to see some famous psychologists and attend some stimulating presentations that whetted her appetite for graduate school. She was also impressed with the side features of conference life (e.g., great restaurants, access to museums, networking) that made the prospect of regular attendance very appealing.

Academic psychology sponsors a wide array of conventions and conferences, giving students ample opportunity to try out this aspect of professional life. Many faculty are active in the professional organizations that sponsor conferences. Consequently, those faculty may foster student travel groups to the conferences they would normally attend. They might also build in expectations for advanced or top-performing students to participate in student poster sessions.

Conferences that are friendly to student participation, either undergraduate or graduate, happen at three levels: state, regional, and national. State psychology organizations tend to be more focused on concerns of clinical practice, but still may have presentation or poster sections to showcase high-quality student work.

Many regional and national conferences hold special sessions to promote the submission of excellent student work. Regional psychology conferences (e.g., the Southeastern, Eastern, Midwestern, Western conferences) tend to be scheduled near the end of the spring semester. In some cases, the conference traditionally takes place at one particular hotel, such as MPA's Palmer House in Chicago. Most other regional conferences rotate among larger cities within the region.

National conferences also tend to dedicate specific parts of the program to students, but most tend to be geared to graduate students rather than undergraduates. The convention of the American Psychological Association (APA) draws thousands of psychologists and is typically scheduled in late summer, tending to rotate among the largest cities in North America (e.g., Toronto, Chicago, Los Angeles, Washington, DC). The convention for the American Psychological Society (APS), a newer national organization that focuses on research, takes place in late spring, over the Memorial Day weekend. With a slightly smaller number of participants, it moves among a variety of U.S. cities. See **Table 8.1** for a listing of regional and national conferences.

Well-organized programs tend to offer orientation information for students so they know what to expect when they are away from campus. Preparation for

TABLE 8.1

Regional and National Psychology Convention Venues

National Conventions

American Psychological Association (APA)

http://apa.org
August 4–7, 2016, Denver, CO
August 3–6, 2017, Washington, DC
August 9–12, 2018, San Francisco, CA
August 8–11, 2019, Chicago, IL
August 6–9, 2020, Washington, DC
August 12–15, 2021, San Diego, CA

American Psychological Society (APS)

http://www.psychologicalscience.org/
May 25–28, 2017, Boston, MA
May 24–27, 2018, San Francisco, CA

Regional Conventions

New England Psychological Association
http://www.newenglandpsychological.org/
October 15, 2016, Worcester, MA

Eastern Psychological Association
http://www.easternpsychological.org/
March 16–20, 2017, Boston, MA
March 1–4, 2018, Philadelphia, PA

March 1–4, 2019, New York, NY
March 12–15, 2020, Boston, MA

Southeastern Psychological Association
http://www.sepaonline.com/
March 30–April 2, 2016, New Orleans, LA
March 8–12, 2017, Atlanta, GA

Rocky Mountain Psychological Association
http://www.rockymountainpsych.org/
April 6–8, 2017, Salt Lake City, UT

Western Psychological Association
http://westernpsych.org/
April 27–30, 2017, Sacramento, CA
April 26–29, 2018, Portland, OR

Midwestern Psychological Association
http://www.midwesternpsych.org/
May 5–7, 2016, Chicago, IL

Southwestern Psychological Association
http://www.swpsych.org
April 8–10, 2016, Dallas, TX
2017, San Antonio, TX

going to a conference often involves holding fundraising events—such as bake sales or carwashes—to supplement departmental funds and make it financially easier for students to attend. Student fees for participation in these conferences tend to be fairly modest. If faculty from a particular school are involved in the leadership of the conference, their students may be able to work at the registration table and thus reduce their cost of attending the conference.

Conferences will offer keynote speeches by some of the most prominent psychologists in the country. Research papers are often presented in shared sessions. If students have been part of a research team that produced the paper, faculty may ask them to participate in the paper presentation. An increasingly popular format for student work is poster sessions. In some cases, faculty may assign projects with the intention of presenting them at conferences receptive to student work. **Table 8.2** shows a feedback sheet for poster sessions that may be used to judge program quality, particularly when the posters are in a competition.

TABLE 8.2

Sample Rubric for Undergraduate Posters

IUP Undergraduate Scholars Forum
Poster Session Evaluation Rubric

Poster Number: _____   Judge: _____

The following judging rubric lists and explains the 7 elements used to evaluate the poster. The total number of points possible is 35 (7 elements × 5 pts).

	1-2 Points	3-4 Points	5 Points	Total
Organization of Content (5 pts)	Poster **lacks a clear organization.** Components and content are difficult to identify and find.	Most components and content can be found, but they are not clearly identified and/or **not logically organized.**	Components and content are easy to identify/find and follow. Appropriate, **logical organization.**	
Scholarly Presentation (5 pts)	Presentation may be informational or educational, and may be creative or appealing, but it **does not reflect a scholarly presentation.**	Poster contains some elements of a scholarly presentation, but **does not consistently reflect a scholarly approach** to presenting content throughout.	**Reflects a scholarly presentation,** includes components common to scholarly presentations in the discipline (i.e., abstract, research question, review of the literature, methods, results, etc.).	
Scholarly Knowledge (5 pts)	Content may report information but includes **little or no scholarly knowledge** (theory and/or research); includes **no original research** by the students.	Content **reflects scholarly knowledge** (theory and/or research), but **no original research** conducted by the student(s).	Content **includes scholarly Knowledge** (theory and/or research), **and reports on original research** conducted by the student(s).	
Clarity of Information Presented (5 pts)	**Fails to convey key ideas and/or information;** or information does not clearly convey the pragmatics of the topic/project.	**Some lack of clarity.** Some connections may be unclear. Some **information not presented concisely** (e.g., presents raw data or output rather than summarizing results succinctly).	**Information is presented clearly** and concisely (e.g., effectively synthesizes scholarly knowledge and **summarizes results** of the research project). Provides a clear picture of the pragmatics of the topic/project.	
Accuracy of Information (5 pts)	Poster contains **substantial inaccuracies.** Three or more **errors in grammar and/or spelling.**	Poster reflects **minor inaccuracies.** One or two **minor grammatical or spelling errors.**	Poster contains **no discernable inaccuracies.** No grammatical or spelling errors.	

Continued

References (5 pts)	No citations in text and/or no list of references, or cited references missing from reference list.	Only one or two errors in citing references (failures to cite sources or include a reference in list of references).	All references are cited in the text and included in a list of references.	
Aesthetics (5 pts)	Presentation is neither neat nor professional looking. Colors may not coordinate or may distract from content. Title and/or font in text are too small. Font types and/or margins are not uniform.	Presentation is neat in appearance but lacks professional polish. Colors may coordinate, but still distract. Fonts may not all match. Title not quite large enough and/or text slightly too large or too small.	Presentation is neat and professional in appearance. Colors coordinate. Fonts are uniform. Title is large and easy to read; font of text is easy to read.	
Total Points Possible: 35			**Total Points:**	

Comments:

Student Conventions

Regional conferences dedicated to showcasing student work provide another opportunity for students to sample conference life. These conferences accept presentations by students at all levels whose papers meet the published criteria. In addition, conferences routinely feature stimulating keynote speakers who can keep undergraduates engaged. The conferences can also include career advising sessions to help students prepare for the steps after graduation. **Table 8.3** summarizes some undergraduate research conferences that were held in 2014.

MENTOR RELATIONSHIPS

Consider finding a mentor from among students who have experience in the path you plan to follow. Seeking advice from seasoned students can help you avoid classes that are deadly. Such connections may also lead to your being able to join a research team as early as possible in your college career. When you consider adopting a mentor from among seasoned students, make sure you recruit someone who has been successful and is recognized within the psychology program.

Faculty can also serve as mentors. Undergraduates may be particularly drawn to the nature of the work being done by a specific faculty member in the department. Especially in this digital age, when so much communication takes place over the Internet, faculty welcome in-person visits from students, particularly those who show enthusiasm for their work. If the connection is a strong one, the relationship can become one of the most important that collegiate life has to offer, as

TABLE 8.3

A Sample of Student Research Conferences

General Conference

National Council on Undergraduate Research (NCUR)
http://www.cur.org/conferences_and_events/student_events/ncur/

Psychology Conferences

Great Plains Students' Psychology Convention
http://www.greatplainsconvention.com/

Mid-America Undergraduate Psychology Research Conference
http://www.eiu.edu/psych/mauprc/

L. Starling Reid Undergraduate Psychology Conference
http://cacsprd.web.virginia.edu/Psych/Conference

Georgia Undergraduate Research in Psychology Conference
http://academics.georgiasouthern.edu/ce/conferences/gurc2015/

Hudson Valley Undergraduate Psychology Conference
http://www.dc.edu/events/hudson-valley-undergraduate-psychology-conference/

Minnesota Undergraduate Psychology Conference
http://www.macalester.edu/mupc/

Stanford Undergraduate Psychology Conference
www.stanfordconference.org

your mentor will tailor advice to you about your plans for after graduation and will be receptive to your requests to write strong letters of reference on your behalf.

SUMMER OPPORTUNITIES

Especially if you are not taking summer classes, use your summertime wisely to gain more psychology-related experience and potentially enhance your leadership skills. Your campus may provide a service to help you locate work that will allow you to apply psychology principles, exercise your leadership skills, and earn money to support you in your next academic year.

CONCLUSION

The variety of ways that psychology majors can become more engaged is impressive. Students who are headed to graduate or professional school may see the greatest gains through increasing their research involvement, but virtually any outside activity can have a huge effect on developing leadership and building a strong portfolio. However, students should be mindful about the choices they make, as these activities should enhance and support rather than interfere with academic work.

THOUGHT QUESTIONS

1. What kinds of high-impact practices hold the greatest appeal for you?
2. What are the advantages and disadvantages of studying abroad?
3. How motivated might you be to participate in a study-abroad experience while you are an undergraduate?
4. Where and when have you been able to exercise leadership?
5. What would you need to do in general to make a study group effective?
6. What would be your ideal on-campus job?
7. What kind of research team would be most attractive to you? What kind of research team would you want to avoid?
8. How would you manage the cost of attending a student research conference?
9. What style of mentor would best suit your needs for planning for your future?

9

What Career Options Are There for Students with a BA or BS in Psychology?

Austin is a senior psychology major. He enjoys his course work but has decided that graduate school in psychology is not in his future. He wants to apply what he has learned about behavior into some business setting, perhaps doing marketing or sales. When he graduates in 6 months, he will have a BA in psychology. Austin knows he should start looking for a job sooner rather than later, so he makes an appointment at his university's career center to learn about job opportunities, job search strategies, and resume writing. He is pleased to find out that there are a lot of jobs out there that appeal to his interests and abilities. Austin plans to spend the months before graduation trying to narrow down his interests and to apply to as many entry-level positions as he can.

□ □ □

Austin's plans may be similar to yours. Like Austin, you probably need to know how to find meaningful work that fits your skills and interests. This chapter is about career options and job searches for psychology majors. We discuss what employers tend to look for in new hires, how work life differs from life during college, and the many types of jobs available to psychology graduates. We offer suggestions for doing a job search, writing a resume and cover letter, requesting letters of recommendation, and asking someone to be a reference, and we review behaviors that help interviewees do well in face-to-face interviews. We close the chapter by considering what to do if you don't get a job after an interview. We begin by describing the three basic types of undergraduate degrees.

DEFINING DEGREES: THE BA, BS, AND AA/AS (ASSOCIATE) DEGREES

There are essentially four degrees that undergraduate students—including psychology majors—can earn: a Bachelor of Arts degree, a Bachelor of Science degree, and an Associate of Arts or Associate of Science degree.

Bachelor of Arts. A **Bachelor of Arts (BA) degree** is usually awarded to students who complete 4 years of undergraduate study in the humanities or the social sciences. On many campuses, psychology departments are part of the social sciences. In addition to completing the psychology requirements, BA psychology majors also complete a series of courses in the liberal arts—classes from the humanities (English, history, philosophy) and the social sciences (political science, sociology)—as well as in mathematics and statistics, and one or more in the natural sciences (biology, chemistry, physics). Most BA degrees also provide students with a number of electives; that is, classes the student freely chooses out of interest or to pursue a minor or a second major, or even to do a combination of these.

Bachelor of Science. The **Bachelor of Science (BS) degree** is awarded to students who finish 4 years of undergraduate student in the sciences. On some campuses, psychology is housed with the natural science departments and seen as being part of the STEM (science, technology, engineering, and mathematics) disciplines. In some schools students can also opt to receive a BS in lieu of a BA degree in psychology by completing a more extensive set of math and lab-oriented science classes beyond the math and science requirements typically outlined in general education. Students who choose the BS can also take electives; however, the additional math and science requirements often reduce the number of slots available for optional courses. With some planning, most BS degree candidates can still complete a minor or even a second major.

Associate degree. An associate degree is an undergraduate degree earned at a community college, a junior college, a technical school, or a 4-year college or university. There are **Associate of Arts (AA) degrees** and **Associate of Science (AS) degrees**. Generally, AA/AS degrees are equivalent to the first 2 years of coursework in a bachelor's degree. For some jobs, a person only needs an AA/AS degree and not a bachelor's degree. Many lab technicians, paralegals, drafters, teachers in early childhood centers, people who work in some computer and data processing positions, and machinists, for example, often have only an AA or an AS degree. People with an AA/AS often work in human or social services agencies, in mental health agencies (e.g., clinics, crisis intervention centers), and in drug and alcohol rehabilitation counseling centers (not necessarily as counselors but as aides to the counseling staff or case managers).

Should you pursue a BA, a BS, or an AA/AS? That depends on your career goals, your time, and your resources. For many students, a bachelor's degree in psychology can be either a terminal liberal arts degree or preprofessional preparation. In other words, the liberal arts degree provides students with a wide array of skills enabling them to pursue a variety of careers. As a preprofessional degree, the BA or BS is solid preparation for a graduate degree in psychology (see chapters 10 and 11) or some other field. Compared to an AA/AS degree, a bachelor's degree provides more career flexibility, the potential for mobility, and greater career earnings. On the other hand, an AA/AS degree is a solid choice for someone who is looking for marketable employment in a particular skill area.

CAREER MATTERS FOR BACHELOR'S DEGREES IN PSYCHOLOGY

Psychology majors can pursue an impressive array of employment opportunities. A study published in 2016 found that 27% of recent graduates with a bachelor's degree in psychology work in jobs that can be described as closely related to their major (American Psychological Association, 2016). Another 35% said that their work was "somewhat related" to their psychology major, and 38% indicated their job was "not related" to psychology. So, close to 62% of former psychology majors have careers that deal directly with or are somehow related to psychology.

Figure 9.1 illustrates the results of a second survey, one published in a 2015 issue of the APA *Monitor on Psychology* on the range of directions a psychology major can pursue and the relative popularity of those jobs. Graduates work in STEM (science, technology, engineering, and math) fields such as computer and social sciences; in the STEM-related health-care fields; and in a variety of non-STEM occupations, such as social services, management, business, and education. Although the range of options underscores psychology's flexibility, job hunters may feel frustration because the pathways into specific options are sometimes not very clear. In this section, we discuss employer expectations and places where those with psychology degrees work.

FIGURE 9–1 In What Contexts Do BA/BS Graduates Work?

Originally published in Christidis, P., Stamm, K., & Lin, L. (2015, May). How many psychology bachelor's-degree holders work in STEM occupations? *Monitor on Phychology, 46*(5). Retrieved from http://www.apa.org/monitor/2015/05/datapoint.aspx. Copyright ©2015 American Psychological Association. Reproduced with permission.

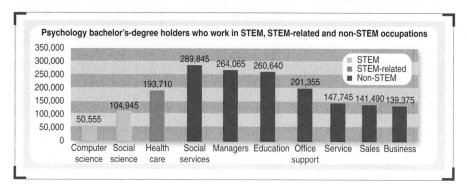

Note: STEM = science, technology, engineering, and math. Occupations with less than 5 percent of psychology bachelor's degree holders were not included in the figure. These occupations include engineers, mathematicians, and statisticians, life scientists, architects, legal, arts and entertainment, construction, production, and agriculture. Data source: U.S. Census Bureau, American Community Survey. (2012). Retrieved from http://www.census.gov/dataviz/visualizations/stem/stem-html.

What Do Employers Want From New Hires?

One of the most reasonable questions psychology majors ask is, what do potential employers look for in new hires? Generally, employers who hire bachelor's-level students want to employ those who earned good grades in college and who, while there, learned how to learn. They want to hire people

✔ Reality Check

Developing Valuable Workplace Skills

What are the skills and qualities employers seek in people with a bachelor's degree in psychology? Review this list of attributes that make for workplace success and generate some specific examples from your college experience that would illustrate your accomplishments in these areas. Remember to return to this list before you interview for a job.

Workplace Skill	Example from College Experience
Solid work ethic	
Computer/digital technology skills	
Honesty/integrity	
Ability to function well on a team	
Oral and written communication skills	
Analytical/research skills	
Self-direction/initiative	
Interpersonal/social skills	
Adaptability/flexibility	
Self-confidence	
Professionalism	
Listening ability	
Problem-solving skills	
Willingness to learn new things	
Client/customer focus	
Quantitative skills	
Multicultural awareness and sensitivity	
Planning/organizing skills	
Leadership skills	

Information from: Landrum & Harrold (2003); Appleby (2000); Hansen & Hansen (2014).

who are enthusiastic and committed to doing high-quality work. Most employers are willing to teach or train their employees to perform the kinds of work necessary to their success, but they want the people they hire to arrive possessing some skills already. We already reviewed the APA (2013) *Guidelines for the Undergraduate Psychology Major 2.0*, which highlight skills linked to psychology's knowledge base, scientific inquiry and critical thinking, ethical and social responsibility, communication, and professional development.

Beyond good grades and psychology-related skills, what are employers looking for? *Reality Check: Developing Valuable Workplace Skills* lists a variety of skills and character qualities that many employers say they want from those they hire. The entries here are all positive qualities that are self-explanatory and can be developed and refined during college. Most are qualities that students demonstrate in class, on writing assignments, when engaged in group projects, and by taking part in extracurricular clubs and organizations. To complete this exercise, think about what evidence you could provide to an employer to indicate you have these sorts of skills and character traits. Whenever possible, point to specific behaviors or incidents that support your claims. Consider using your list to create a personal portfolio of your skills and experiences during your college years that would be useful in the workplace.

Work life is distinct in many ways from college life. You may be surprised to learn that responsibilities in most workplaces are actually less structured than those in school. Having a career means that you must be a consistent self-starter who is punctual, prepared, and able to accomplish job-related tasks in a timely manner. The transition from the campus to the office or other work setting will likely not be a struggle if you know what to expect. **Table 9.1** lists some of the

TABLE 9.1

Some Perceived Distinctions Between the College Campus and Workplace Cultures

College campus	Workplace
Professors	Managers or supervisors
Individual effort and performance	Team effort and performance
Frequent and concrete feedback on performance	Infrequent feedback on performance, often not specific
More freedom and control to set schedule	Less freedom or even control over schedule
Frequent breaks, time off, vacations	Limited time off. Vacation days are often limited until after you have been there a while.
Structured courses and curricula	Less structure, fewer directions
Few changes in routine	Constant and unexpected changes
Academic or intellectual challenges	Organizational, coworker, and client challenges
Environment of personal support	Usually less personal support
Correct answers are usually available	Few "right" answers

Information from: The Senior Year Experience (p. 102), by J. N. Gardner, G. Van der Veer, & Associates, 1997, John Wiley & Sons; permission conveyed through the Copyright Clearance Center, Inc.

perceived distinctions that former students identify as making their work life different from the life they enjoyed on campus. Review Table 9.1 to develop a sense of what to expect in the future, and plan to use your energy and efforts accordingly. As Hettich (2004) noted, starting a new job out of college is like being a freshman again—you have to learn the written and unwritten folkways of a new culture.

What Jobs Attract Psychology Graduates?

People with a bachelor's degree in psychology get hired in a wide range of jobs, including as sales agents, educators, health-care providers, and consultants. Quite a few former psychology majors find careers as human resource managers and personnel specialists, as probation officers, employment counselors, and even as writers. **Table 9.2** includes a list of job titles that have attracted former students with a bachelor's degree in psychology. The entries have been grouped by category: some are linked to psychology, some to business, and some are part of the wide variety of other opportunities that are available. This list is representative but not exhaustive—there are many jobs that at first glance may not seem in the realm of possibility for psychology majors but turn out to be a good fit. Use this list as a starting point to help you identify some possibilities that may not have occurred to you before.

TABLE 9.2

Selected Job Titles for People With a Bachelor's Degree in Psychology

Jobs linked to psychology	
Academic advisor	Intellectual disability unit manager
Alcohol/drug abuse counselor	Life skill counselor
Behavior analyst	Mental health technician
Career counselor	Parole officer
Career planning and placement advisor	Political campaign worker
Case-management aide	Probation officer
Caseworker	Program manager
Child-care worker	Public affairs coordinator
Child protection worker	Public relations specialist
Community outreach worker	Publications researcher
Community support worker	Radio/TV research assistant
Corrections officer	Rehabilitation advisor
Counselor aide	Residential counselor
Day-care center supervisor	Residential youth counselor
Director of volunteer services	Secondary school teacher
Family services worker	Social services assistant
Gerontology aide	Social work assistant
Group home coordinator	Urban planning research assistant
Housing/student life coordinator	Veterans' advisor

Continued

Jobs linked to business	*Miscellaneous jobs*
Administrative assistant	Activity director
Advertising agent	Assistant youth coordinator
Advertising trainee	Camp staff director
Affirmative action representative	College admissions officer
Airline reservations clerk	Community organizer
Bank manager	Community recreation worker
Claims specialist	Community relations officer
Customer relations agent	Congressional aide
Customer service representative	Crime-prevention coordinator
Employee counselor	Director of alumni relations
Employee relations assistant	Director of fundraising
Energy researcher	Driving instructor
Events coordinator	Educational coordinator
Financial researcher	Fast-food restaurant manager
Hotel management	Foster home parent
Human resources director	Film researcher/copywriter
Human resources recruiter	Historical research assistant
Insurance agent	Hospital patient service representative
Insurance claims/underwriter	Juvenile probation officer
Intelligence officer	Laboratory assistant
Job analyst	Law enforcement officer
Loan officer	Neighborhood outreach worker
Lobbying organizer	Newspaper reporter
Management trainee	Nursing home administrator
Marketing representative	Parks and recreation director
Marketing researcher	Private tutor
Media buyer	Research assistant
Occupational analyst	Security officer
Office manager	Statistical assistant
Personnel worker/administrator	Statistical reports compiler
Property management	Store manager
Public information officer	Task force coordinator
Sales representative	Teacher
Small business owner	Technical writer
Staff trainer and developer	Vocational rehabilitation counselor
Store manager	Volunteer coordinator
Technical writer	Warehouse manager
Warehouse manager	Work activity program director
	Youth minister

Courtesy R. Eric Landrum (2001).

A **Major** Success Story

Human Resourcefulness

One occupational direction that many psychology majors pursue is human resources (HR). An HR specialist serves both the employer and the employees by offering guidance regarding benefits, feedback on the rules of the job, and interventions to keep employers on track. Effective HR people foster positive employee feelings toward their employers and generally earn among the highest salaries of those with a bachelor's degrees right out of college. (Those with a master's degree earn even more.)

David serves as a good example. He decided to major in psychology because he found the content fascinating. He was initially drawn to forensics but after he took additional psychology classes, he thought more about the idea of working in business settings, so he decided to minor in business. He went into a masters' program in industrial/organizational (I/O) psychology, and found himself more drawn to the "O" side (consulting with people) than the "I" side (working with statistics). He captured a plum internship at QVC as part of his program and within 3 years was a human resources (HR) director for QVC. He developed his niche in change management consultation.

After 8 years, David decided that he wanted a job that was closer to his home state of Florida. He is now in the process of building an HR department in the commercial division of a prominent cruise line. In his new role he works with marketing, guest services, and fleet deployment, including figuring out new ports of call.

Describing his undergraduate degree as "very purposeful," David claims that he uses his undergraduate degree every day. Although the idea of getting a PhD was tempting for him, David counsels students to simply think about the "sweet spot" where experience and level of education will support the kind of work they might find most interesting. For him, the masters' degree was a great passport into a satisfying professional choice and lifestyle.

Bear in mind that there are many other jobs that do not appear on this list. You may discover still other career options as you begin your job search. Our profile in *A Major Success Story: Human Resourcefulness* highlights a successful psychology major who has some good advice for job seekers.

SEARCHING FOR JOBS: WHERE TO BEGIN

Effective job searches rely on using a wide variety of resources. Most of these resources will be convenient and accessible to you.

Campus career center. If your college or university is like most, it has an on-campus office dedicated to helping students explore their career interests and options. This career services center or office can often help students identify possible careers through vocational tests and inventories. Many career offices bring recruiters to campus and arrange for senior students to sign up for information sessions, mock (practice) interviews, and actual job interviews. They typically offer help with resume writing (an important matter discussed in detail below) as well. Make a visit to the career services office on your campus to learn what resources are available and to talk with the director about your interests.

Alumni networks. Your school may maintain a very valuable resource—an alumni network that allows current students to seek job advice and career guidance from graduates. Alumni who sign up to help in this way are delighted to share their experiences, insights, expertise, and even potential job leads with students who are graduating from their alma mater.

Internships. Doing an internship in a community or a business setting can provide you with invaluable insights into whether a line of work or a workplace setting fits your skills and interests. Your college may run an internship office that keeps a list of local sites. Some students do internships for course credit during the regular academic year, while others do them during the summer months. While many internships are volunteer experiences, others include some remuneration. Having an internship on your resume can be an asset as you enter the job market—and many times a successful internship leads the site to extend the student intern an offer for a permanent job after graduation.

Job shadowing. Some career services offices offer students the opportunity to **job shadow**—to spend a few hours or even a day following a professional as he or she "lives" a typical workday. This "shadowing" affords students a chance to discover whether a given career and its routine responsibilities appeal to them. Check with your campus career center to find out whether any job-shadowing program is available. Alternatively, if you know someone whose career is of interest to you, ask if you can be his or her shadow for a day—what have you got to lose?

The Occupational Information Network. The **Occupational Information Network** (O*NET, at http://www.onetonline.org/) is an online center dedicated to providing information about a wide variety of occupations. For each job, the site lists details about the knowledge, skills, and abilities required, as well as a description of the work context, salary information, and other important details. The website is very user friendly and provides specific information on more than 1,000 occupations.

Informal networks. Do not overlook your personal connections for job and career opportunities. Ask your family, friends, and coworkers about the work they do, why they do it, and whether they know of any job leads. The people in your informal networks will often want to help and may be able to provide helpful suggestions on the job search.

Other resources. **Table 9.3** lists some other resources you should use to locate information on jobs for psychology majors. The top of the table lists three specific books that discuss careers in psychology—including the profiles of many professionals—in depth. The bottom of the table lists some helpful websites on general job searches, jobs in the government, and a website that offers salary data on various positions.

Writing a Resume

A good **resume** is your entry to an interview and a possible career. Your resume is a brief written account of your personal, educational, and professional qualifications. As such, it must be thoughtfully conceived, well-written, polished, and focused. You should have both a hard copy and an electronic version available, as many websites want applicants to upload a copy. You should edit or modify the contents of your resume as necessary to fit the requirements of particular job descriptions or ads. Here are the basic requirements for a good resume:

- Set the text on high-quality, standard 8.5 × 11 inch white, ivory, or light beige paper (the electronic version should be on a white page). Print on only one side of a page.

- Do not write in complete sentences and avoid using the word *I*. Instead, begin each entry with an action-oriented word that highlights an achievement or a goal you met ("Reduced staff attrition" or "Supervised peer tutors").

TABLE 9.3

Other Resources for the Job Search

Books	*Websites*
Kuther, T. L., & Morgan, R. D. (2013). *Careers in psychology: Opportunities in a changing world* (4th ed.). Belmont, CA: Cengage.	**General job searches** www.CareerRookie.com www.collegegrad.com www.monster.com www.rileyguide.com
Landrum, R. E. (2009). *Finding jobs with a psychology bachelor's degree: Expert advice for launching your career.* Washington, DC: American Psychological Association.	**Government employment** www.governmentjobs.com www.usa.gov/job-search www.usajobs.gov
Sternberg, R. J. (2007). *Career paths in psychology.* Washington, DC: American Psychological Association.	**Median salaries for various occupations** www.salary.com

- Personal information that is unrelated to the job you are seeking, such as hobbies, should not appear in your resume. At best, it looks like filler; a worst, it creates a negative impression of you in the mind of the reader.

- The resume should be brief—one page is the rule for college students and recent graduates. Never go beyond two pages. If an employer specifies a required length, do not exceed it.

- There should be no spelling or grammatical errors. Have someone from career services, your academic advisor, and someone you know to be an excellent writer proofread a draft of the document. Having multiple reviewers increases the likelihood of catching errors, correcting phrasing and spelling, and of having a clearer resume.

- Do not use elaborate or outsized fonts—stick with a basic font; for instance, Times New Roman in a 12-point size.

- Never fold or staple your resume, even for mailing purposes (send it in a large, flat mailing envelope).

The basic parts of a resume include:

Heading. Center your name at the top of the page. Put your address and contact information below your name using a format that makes the heading easy to read. Don't use a wildly oversized font, as it distracts readers' attention from the resume's content.

Objective. The objective is a concise and precise statement regarding the sort of position you desire for employment. The objective should be revised or edited for different positions, which means you will be creating different versions of your resume.

Education. List the degree or degrees you have earned, the school from which you received your degree, and your college major. Academic honors and awards can also be noted here (briefly). Once you have a college degree, you no longer need to note that you have a high school diploma.

Experience. This section usually has a chronological list of your previous work experiences (from most to least recent). Each entry should include the dates of employment as well as your work responsibilities and any noteworthy accomplishments—bulleted lists of these are fine. Avoid listing mundane duties.

Activities. List any key extracurricular activities, including internships and volunteer or community work, in this section. Avoid listing too many things or you will give the impression that you are padding your resume.

Awards. If you have been honored for an important contribution or achievement, by all means mention it briefly.

References. Indicate at the end of the resume that the contact information for your references is available upon request. If you are asked for specific contact information for your references, then list each person's name, title, academic or work affiliation, mailing address, phone number, and email address.

A sample resume appears in **Table 9.4**. As you can see, the formatting is simple and straightforward and the information is easy to follow. Clarity is important, as an evaluator will only spend between a few seconds and a couple of minutes reviewing a given resume—that's it. If your resume is odd or too "busy," chances are it will be passed over in favor of one that is easier to read.

TABLE 9.4

A Sample Resume for a Student with a Bachelor's Degree in Psychology

Susan L. Whitman

Current and Permanent Address:

27 Beverly Avenue

Foxbridge, MA 02175

(555) 875-9901

slwhit@gomail.com

OBJECTIVE

Seeking employment in marketing and sales where I can use my knowledge of human behavior.

EDUCATION

Bachelor of Arts in Psychology, cum laude, May 2016
Moravian College, Bethlehem, PA
GPA 3.5/3.75 in major

EMPLOYMENT

Intern. Creative Marketing Solutions, Allentown, PA (1/5/15–5/1/15). Designed marketing campaign for orthodontic group; researched local competition; worked with firm's principal to prepare for client meetings.

Sales Associate. Your Line Apparel, Norton, MA (5/8/14–8/25/14; 5/10/13–8/20/13). Greeted customers, shared new stock, and managed register; restocked shelves; arranged clothing displays; managed web closeout sales.

Waitress. Hometown Diner, Wexley, MA (5/15/12–8/20/12; 5/17/11–8/22/11). Took and delivered customer orders, bused tables, and prepped for food service.

ACTIVITIES

Campus Marketing Club. President, 9/1/14–4/20/15; member of executive board, 9/1/13–4/20/14; member since 9/5/12. Updated bylaws; invited local CEOs and advertising executives to speak at bimonthly speakers series; recruited new members.

Sigma Iota Tau Sorority. Chaired membership and recruitment drive; doubled sorority membership in one year; member since 11/5/12.

AWARDS

Dean's List
"Best Student Poster" in Campus Research Symposium, 2016

REFERENCES

Available upon request

Writing a Cover Letter

A **cover letter** must accompany your resume. Like the resume, it is tailored and brief, usually one page or less in length. Most cover letters will have three parts that translate into three paragraphs. The first paragraph explains the reason for your letter, identifies the position you are applying for, and indicates how you heard about the opening. The second paragraph describes your background and why you believe you would be a good fit for the position. You might, for example, briefly explain how your skills match the needs of the organization or how your experiences match the needs of the position. The third and final paragraph highlights your interest in the job opening and invites the reader to contact you.

Table 9.5 shows a typical cover letter, which, like the resume, should be on white, ivory, or light beige paper. The letter should look formal, not friendly.

TABLE 9.5

A Sample Cover Letter

June 25, 2016

Mr. John Harcourt
Human Resources Department
Alliance Pharmaceuticals
427 Ridge Avenue
Pleasant Vale, NJ 07022

Dear Mr. Harcourt:

Please allow this letter and my attached resume to serve as my application for the assistant marketing manager opening in the sales division of Alliance Pharmaceuticals. I learned of this position when I visited the job openings listing on the company's website.

My education and work background fit the job description for the assistant marketing position, as I have a liberal arts degree and have completed several courses in accounting, marketing, finance, and economics. My internship with Creative Marketing Solutions in spring 2014 allowed me to work on a marketing and sales campaign for an orthodontics group. Working with the firm's principal partner, I met weekly with the clients, drafted agendas, researched competitors, and outlined a radio commercial script that was eventually produced as part of the campaign. I believe my experience in marketing dental health care can serve as a solid bridge to marketing pharmaceutical products.

I enjoy working with others on teams and I am quite willing to relocate to New Jersey. I would be delighted to speak with you further regarding the job opening. I may be reached at (555) 875-9901 or via email at slwhit@gomail.com. My mailing address may be found on my resume. I look forward to hearing from you.

Sincerely,
Susan L. Whitman
Enclosure

Keep an electronic copy, which you can edit or update for other positions, as well as upload with a copy of your resume.

INTERVIEWING SKILLS

If your resume, cover letter, and references pass muster, then you will be invited for a face-to-face interview, a formal part of the personnel-selection process. Organizations often interview several people for one opening, so understand that you are likely to be competing with others for the job. Additionally, it is not at all unusual to be interviewed more than once for the same position (one of our friends was eventually hired after four separate and lengthy interviews spread across several weeks).

Before you go to the interview, make certain that you have learned all you can about the company or organization by reviewing any materials available on the web. You want to appear both knowledgeable and very interested in the position—this is not the time to play hard to get. Indeed, your goal is to convince the interviewer(s) that you are the right person for the job, someone who will fit in and contribute to the organization's enterprise. While you do that, the interviewer(s) are looking for any weaknesses, aspects of your behavior or character, that make you a risky choice.

Interviewers will ask you a variety of questions about your educational and work background. They want to get to know you and to learn what skills you could bring to the work setting. **Table 9.6** shows examples of two types of interview questions. Trained interviewers—often those employees whose sole role is hiring—often rely on **structured interview questions**, which are a company's standard questions that all prospective employees are asked. Untrained

TABLE 9.6
Examples of Structured and Unstructured Interview Questions

Structured questions

Describe a work incident in which you had to develop a creative solution in order to solve a problem.

Tell me how you handled working with a difficult person. Be specific.

Provide a specific example of an instance in which you demonstrated leadership in your last job.

Give me some specific examples showing how you worked effectively with coworkers on a team.

Unstructured questions

Why do you want this job?

What are your strengths? What are your weaknesses?

Tell me something about yourself that I cannot learn from your resume.

What would your former supervisor say are your greatest accomplishments in the workplace?

interviewers tend to use **unstructured interview questions**, which have an informal and unplanned quality to them. You should be prepared for both types of questions because you likely will not know much about the person who will be interviewing you.

Presenting Yourself Well

Your ability to answer questions, to provide concrete examples of your work skills, and to discuss your career goals is only half of the interview strategy. The other half entails how you present yourself to others. You want to make a very favorable and lasting positive impression. Here are some suggestions for doing so:

Appearance. How you look matters, as first impressions are often lasting impressions. One way to make a good first impression is to learn how current employees at your prospective employer dress and come to the interview appearing just a little more formal than that. For many positions, you should be dressed in conservative business attire. Your appearance, from your hair to your shoes, should be neat, not flashy. Give yourself a once-over to make sure you are stain-free. [Jane recalls with some mortification that she gave a job talk during an interview, looked down, and realized she was wearing one blue and one black shoe. She got the job despite her uncoordinated attire].

Poise and eye contact. Although you may be nervous, you should look relaxed and attentive. However, you should not look too comfortable—don't sit back and lounge in a chair, for example. But don't be rigid, either. Sit up straight with a slight lean toward the interviewer. Smile. Make and maintain comfortable and friendly eye contact. Avoid displaying nervous tics, such as playing with your hair or biting your nails. When the interviewer speaks, watch closely and listen carefully—don't look around the room. Also, silence your cell phone; if it rings, quickly turn it off, apologize, and turn your attention back to the interviewer. Under no circumstances should you check your phone during the interview as it signals that you may inappropriately do so on the job as well.

Questions to ask—and not ask. At some point, you will be given the chance to ask questions. Be certain you have at least three or four in case one or more of your questions are answered in the course of the interview. "I don't have any questions" does not convey interest in the job. Asking if there is a timeline for making a hire is a reasonable question as long as you don't press the matter. Asking about the salary or the salary range is *not* a good idea—it's presumptuous. Wait until (and if) the employer extends a job offer to you; at that time, he or she will also present you with a salary figure. Asking how many vacation days you would have in the first year is also not a good idea. That, too, will be explained later, if there is a later. Focus on questions about the job and what it's like to work there—people usually enjoy talking about where they work and the interviewer is unlikely to be an exception. You will be able to tell a lot about the workplace's culture from the interviewer's response.

Initiate, don't just answer! Besides the questions you prepared prior to the interview, it is absolutely reasonable—and it conveys your genuine interest—to ask questions that naturally emerge from the flow of the interview. Once you have answered a question, for example, it's fine to say, "May I ask you a question? As I was talking about the leadership I showed in my last job, I remembered I was curious if each work team here has a designated leader?" You don't want to fire back a question after each interview question, but a few in the course of an interview makes the setting more like a friendly conversation, allows the interviewer to get to know how you think, and lets you present yourself a bit more.

Send a thank-you note. Once the interview is over, you should follow up with a thank-you note to the person who met with you. In the note, acknowledge that you enjoyed the interview, that you remain very interested in the position, and that you would be pleased to answer any additional questions. Mailing a thank-you note is fine as long as it gets there within 3 or so days. Emailing a note is fine, too. Just do so the next day, indicating you took some time to reflect on the interview. Emailing a note immediately after the interview looks a little needy. Whether written or digital, keep the note professional and brief.

Be prepared to wait a bit. You may not hear for a while whether you received the job. Be patient and understand that there may be other interviewees, for example, and that the task of hiring someone involves steps internal to the organization. In the meantime, be hopeful but continue looking for other jobs.

If you don't hear back, should you follow up with the interviewer? Unless the interviewer told you a probable date when you could expect to hear back about the position, you can send a friendly follow-up inquiry a week or so after the interview. Doing so can illustrate your interest in the job. Don't inquire more than once, however.

AFTER THE INTERVIEW: WHAT'S NEXT?

You Don't Get the Job

What happens if you follow the advice in this chapter but don't get the job? Unfortunately, this may happen—you may not get the first job you interview for, or even the second one. Try not to be too discouraged if a job you want does not pan out. There are many different reasons why a person may not get a particular job offer, even when all the signals seemed to be positive ones. There are often multiple variables in play, many of them beyond your control. These include:

- the economy;
- the qualifications of the other applicants;
- the possibility that an internal candidate has the inside track for the job;
- the number of applicants in the hiring pool;
- the impact of factors that actually influence hiring decisions in the organization (such as budget constraints or sudden hiring freezes— factors that you would not be privy to).

Instead of second-guessing the hiring process and ruminating about the variables involved, focus on what you can control. Reflect on the interview and ask yourself if there were things you might have done differently. If there were, then make those changes for your next interview. If there weren't, then assume you did what you were supposed to do and that you did it well. Continue your job search and look ahead to the next interview. Be persistent. Ideally, you are looking for an employer who will be as enthused about hiring you as you are in working for them.

Here's another suggestion to consider: Are there any skills you might hone or any additional training you might get while you are in the interview stage of looking for a position? Acquiring more skills while you are searching can make you a better candidate for future interviews.

You Get the Job

Congratulations! Let's assume you decide to accept the position. What's next? Your work is just beginning because now you need to focus on doing well in the job. In a way, getting an offer is actually the easy part; now you need to succeed and keep the job. You will not be surprised to learn that many new employees end up losing their jobs for rather predictable reasons (Gardner, 2007), including:

- not meeting required deadlines;
- being late for work;
- acting in unethical ways;
- showing little or poor motivation;
- failing to follow directives.

Note that these same behaviors should be avoided during your undergraduate years; indeed, these are precisely the sorts of actions that lead to bad grades and negative impressions. Thus, while an instructor's deadline for a paper or project, for example, can seem arbitrary, keep in mind that meeting deadlines is a requirement out in the "real world". It is never too soon to develop professional habits.

Avoid making these sorts of mistakes on the job by having a positive attitude, taking initiative, setting priorities, seeking regular feedback on your performance, and being committed to the job and the people in your workplace. Being a well-regarded employee is similar to being a good student—you must work consistently and concentrate your efforts effectively.

THOUGHT QUESTIONS

1. What degree are you seeking? Why?
2. Do you have any idea what sort of work appeals to you? What would your ideal workplace be like?
3. Have you considered doing an internship? If you have, what sort would you want to pursue?
4. What would you say are your current skills? What other skills would you like to develop before you seek employment?
5. What experiences have you already had that you can put on a resume?

10

How Do You Apply To and Get Into Graduate Programs in Psychology?

Cavan had known she wanted to become a psychologist since she was in high school. She loved what she learned in her high school psychology class and, once she began college, she looked for opportunities to volunteer in her college's psychology department. During her 4 years there, she worked with a professor on his research, served as a teaching assistant and tutor, and during her senior year, did a year-long honors project. All throughout college, Cavan studied hard to get the best grades she could, as she heard that graduate admissions to top programs were very competitive. Once her senior year began, Cavan felt confident that she had prepared as best she could for the application process—all she had to do was to submit her applications and then wait.

□ □ □

Cavan is probably a bit unusual as a student: she knew after one class in psychology that she wanted to be a psychologist and that she was willing to make the sacrifices her goals would entail. At this point in your academic career, you may be wondering whether graduate school is right for you. This decision is not a simple one.

SHOULD YOU GO TO GRADUATE SCHOOL IN PSYCHOLOGY?

Graduate school in psychology requires energy, enthusiasm, and a major time commitment, minimally 4, very often more, years. But the most important issue to address is why you want to go. See *Reality Check: Do You Have the Fire?* to sort out your motives for applying to graduate school.

You must be realistic about your genuine motivation to attend graduate school. If your reasons are sound, then you should begin to prepare sooner rather than later.

✔ Reality Check

Do You Have the Fire?

Undergraduates have a mix of motives for going into a graduate program in psychology. Decide whether each rationale below is part of your reason for wanting to be admitted. Which of the following are true of your quest?

- ☐ 1. I would like to become a scientific researcher or a professional in the discipline.
- ☐ 2. I earned good grades in psychology during college so I probably should become a psychologist.
- ☐ 3. I hope to contribute to the discipline through research, practice, or a combination of both.
- ☐ 4. I don't really want a "real" job.
- ☐ 5. I want to educate people about basic and applied psychological science.
- ☐ 6. I want to be addressed as "Dr." or "Professor."
- ☐ 7. I want to dedicate myself to promoting psychological well-being and to ameliorating distress.
- ☐ 8. I don't know what else to do now that I have my undergraduate degree.
- ☐ 9. I enjoy research, writing, publishing, and giving professional talks.
- ☐ 10. I don't want a 12-month job—I want to be a college professor and have my summers off.
- ☐ 11. I am deeply curious about the human condition.
- ☐ 12. I've always been a student and I'm pretty good at it—why stop now?

Interpretation

If you checked off any of the odd-numbered rationales, your motives are consistent with those who are likely to be in graduate school for the right reasons. Adopting one or more of these reasons entails a serious commitment to your education, very hard and often solitary work (studying, critical thinking, writing, research), and entering what is a very competitive job market. On the other hand, if you checked off even-numbered items, then you may want to reconsider. Those rationales tend to be more shallow and your commitment will be hard to sustain during the rigor of graduate school.

PREPARING FOR GRADUATE SCHOOL DURING COLLEGE

Preparing to apply for graduate school is not something that can be done quickly. The decision to apply is a mature response, one that should motivate you to assess your strengths and weaknesses as a student (and we all have both), to engage in a series of systematic steps during college that can help to ensure your success, and to formulate a plan for submitting applications. You should begin to develop a comprehensive application strategy as soon as you begin to believe that graduate school in psychology might be in your future. Ideally, as a rising junior-level college student you should begin to think about and carry out some of the steps suggested in this chapter. Once you enter your senior year, you will not have a lot of time to pull together materials. Many applications are due in late fall—by November or early December, possibly sooner in some cases.

Of course, preparing for graduate school is in large part about your course work and what you do with it. Not surprisingly, grades matter for admission; the higher your **grade point average (GPA)** the better your chances of getting in to graduate school. Keep in mind that you will be competing with students who have worked hard during college to develop academic records that reflect sincere interest in graduate study in psychology—getting into many graduate programs is much more difficult than getting into undergraduate programs, for example.

As a result, when you are looking for the graduate programs that fit your needs, you will need to evaluate the level of selectivity that is right for you. Rigorous programs admit only a handful of students each year. Other programs recruit larger numbers of students. There is a variety of published lists of nationally ranked graduate programs in psychology, including lists that focus on particular subfields (e.g., clinical psychology, social psychology). Naturally, programs at the top of such lists tend to be the most selective, inspiring the most intense competition. Don't limit your search just to these lists, however. Speak to your instructors about which graduate programs they know, their perception of the quality of those programs, and whether one of them might be a place for you to consider applying.

In addition to examining the likelihood of your being admitted to the program of your choice, consider some other factors about graduate school, such as:

- *Cost.* Some graduate programs support their students with fellowships, teaching assistantships, or sources of funding; others don't. You may have to decide if you want to take out loans to cover tuition and living expenses, for example.

- *Location.* Are you willing to move to another state or even across the country to attend graduate school? Would a university in the Midwest or South work for you? Or must you be in the Northeast or California?

Would you prefer to live in the city or attend a university in a more rural setting? Are there reasons you must stay close to home?

■ *Placement.* How well do the graduates of the programs you are considering do in the job market? Do they tend to pursue teaching, research, or other sorts of careers? How well do their choices match with your plans for the future?

To apply to graduate school, you should have taken an array of courses in psychology. A well-designed undergraduate psychology major requires you to complete introductory psychology, at least one research methods course and one statistics course, as well as one course in each of the four core areas of the field: neuroscience, developmental, cognition, and sociocultural (comprised of courses such as social psychology, personality, and clinical psychology) (Dunn et al., 2010). Taking at least one applied course like health psychology, industrial/organizational psychology, or environmental psychology is also recommended. Finally, some capstone course—an advanced seminar, for example—that ties together the skills you learned across the psychology major is an ideal way to wrap up your undergraduate schooling.

Some psychology curricula have nine or so course requirements—this is likely the minimum number of courses for a psychology major. Other curricula include many more psychology classes. Take advantage of every opportunity you have to demonstrate your rigor as a student. Avoid taking "filler" classes and opt for classes that will help you build the best foundation for graduate study.

It is not the number of courses per se but the skills that you acquire along the way that will have the greatest impact on your candidacy. Can you design (and ideally execute) experiments, to collect and analyze resulting data? Can you navigate the psychological literature to find studies pertaining to issues of interest? Can you write a standard lab report using appropriate conventions? These and other acquired skills, as well as the varied content of the courses, give evidence of breadth in your disciplinary learning. But what about depth?

Depth: Choosing an Area of Interest

An important part of applying to graduate school in psychology is identifying and pursuing a specific area of interest. Generally, student interest is linked with course work. Perhaps you took a course in cognition and found the abundant research on memory to be fascinating. Or you became interested in how people differ from one another, so you were drawn to the study of personality. A lab-based experience in neuroscience might have wakened your interest in the biology and chemistry of the brain—and so on. Although you should take the recommended set of core courses, you certainly can take one or more courses in the subfield of psychology that interest you most (recall the list of APA divisions that correspond to interest areas—see Table 2.1 on pages 13 and 14).

As you learn more about developmental psychology, for example, you may decide to become a developmental psychologist. Thus, when considering where to apply for graduate school, you will want to identify those universities with good developmental psychology programs. By channeling your professional interests in a particular direction, you may target research areas or topics within the field that speak to you. You can then focus on graduate programs that specialize in those research areas—someone interested in adult development, for example, would look for developmental programs emphasizing that focus instead of those programs that focus on child development, and so on.

How do you find out this sort of information? Naturally, the Internet makes gathering information about graduate programs in psychology easy to do: just type in "graduate programs in adult development" and you will get a number of websites. This approach to searching is not very selective, however. A second strategy is to speak to your academic advisor about graduate programs they know by reputation or rank. Speaking to a faculty member who specializes in or teaches developmental psychology (or whatever area you are interested in) is also a good place to begin.

We also recommend that you take a look at the most recent edition of the APA's ***Graduate Study in Psychology (GSIP)***, which is published yearly (e.g., American Psychological Association, 2016). In brief, the *GSIP* provides detailed information on the approximately 600 or so graduate programs in the United States and Canada. Each entry contains contact and department information (mailing address, phone, fax, email addresses, program website), a listing of the programs and degrees offered, APA accreditation status (for programs in clinical, counseling, and school psychology, and for joint professional-scientific degrees), number of students' applications and admissions statistics (including information on required scores on the Graduate Record Exam [GRE], GPAs, and other admissions criteria, as well as how many people applied and were admitted and eventually enrolled in the previous year, and the anticipated number of openings for the next year), financial aid/assistance policies, and employment outcomes among recent graduates. The book has two useful indexes. The first lists programs by the area of study (e.g., biological psychology, clinical psychology, community psychology, personality psychology) and degree(s) offered (e.g., MA, MS, PsyD, PhD), allowing users to quickly locate the schools that offer study in their area of interest. The second index is an alphabetical list of all the programs.

What information does the *GSIP* identify as generally mattering the most for gaining admission to graduate school in psychology? Most graduate programs report that letters of recommendation, college GPA, and applicants' statement of goals are among the most important criteria for admission. Research experience and GRE scores follow close behind. Extracurricular activities are the least important criterion for admission to graduate programs. As should be clear, the *GSIP* is a very helpful and portable publication. Your department might have a copy; if it doesn't, check the reference section of your school's library or career center or consider investing in a copy for yourself. You can also visit APA's Graduate Study Online database, which can be found at http://www.apa.org/pubs/databases/gradstudy/?tab=2.

Research Experience

Traditional graduate programs in psychology are dedicated to producing scientific research in psychology. As an applicant, you will need to demonstrate to the admissions committee that you are capable of doing research. More important for yourself, you need to want to do research—really, you need to enjoy doing it. If you don't, graduate school will not be a pleasant experience and you will be guiding yourself toward a career that you will probably not like very much. We believe it is a very good idea for students to obtain research experience before applying to graduate school in psychology. Not only does this strategy tend to make an application more competitive (recall that the *GSIP* indicates having research experience is almost as important as having good grades), but it also helps you figure out whether research life appeals to you. If it doesn't, better to know sooner than later so that you can choose a different type of graduate education in psychology, rather than the traditional PhD.

There are distinct advantages to doing research as an undergraduate (e.g., Landrum, 2002), including:

■ learning about different approaches to doing research, including diverse methodologies;

■ gaining "hands on" experience doing psychology outside the classroom;

■ improving teamwork skills by working with faculty members and other students on interesting questions;

■ developing writing and speaking skills by learning to summarize research results;

■ potentially contributing to the psychological literature through being a team member or a coauthor on a conference presentation, journal publication, or the like.

How can you gain research experience? The best way is to become involved in research being conducted by faculty members in your undergraduate psychology department by being a **research assistant**. Do so as early in your schooling as a psychology major as you can—that way you are likely to see the results of your labor in the form of some professional product, such as conference presentations or a journal publication. Many faculty members will actively seek out good students to help them with their research projects. Some will advertise openings in their labs, for example. It may be easiest to approach individual faculty to find out if they are conducting research and if they welcome undergraduate assistance with it. Obviously, if you know you are interested in cognition, then you should try to work with a faculty member who conducts research in cognitive psychology. Even if no one is currently doing research in your area of interest, research experience in any area is important, so try to get a placement in a lab—remember, although research topics may differ greatly from one another, the research process is similar across subfields of psychology.

What do research assistants do? Here is a short list:

■ perform library and database searches to locate existing research on given topics;

■ participate in lab meetings to review current research and to plan future investigations;

■ work as part of a research team;

■ run data-collection sessions with research participants;

■ enter data into spreadsheets and perform statistical analyses using software (e.g., SPSS); and

■ write research summaries for conference proposals.

A second way for you to conduct research is to do a *senior thesis*. On many campuses, students with sufficiently high GPAs have the option to do a research-intensive project during their senior year. For psychology majors, this often entails writing an in-depth literature review article; proposing an experiment; or, ideally, carrying out an experiment or other research from start (hypothesis) to finish (results). By the end of the academic year, you would produce a **thesis**, which is usually a written work that is much more advanced than the sort of paper that would come out of a normal course. Thesis work requires high levels of initiative, organization, independence, effort, and tenacity, which makes the experience good preparation for graduate school as graduate faculty assume that you will already have these qualities.

In addition to writing the thesis, you might also have to give an **oral presentation** (sometimes called a *defense*) to psychology faculty, fellow thesis students, and interested members of your college's community.

If the option to do a senior thesis is not available, you may be able to do an independent or directed study on a topic of your choosing. An independent study is a solo project—usually one semester in length and thus much smaller than a thesis—that is supervised by a faculty member. You might want to read in depth about a topic that interests you (e.g., animal personality) but which your school doesn't offer a course about. An independent study enables you to become reasonably expert on that topic. You would likely write some sort of term paper and might meet weekly with a faculty member to report on your progress. It is certainly possible to do an experiment or other research investigation as part of an independent study, so it can serve as a reasonable substitute for the senior thesis.

Collaborating on faculty research and doing a senior thesis (or an independent study) are both great ways to learn about research, to develop relevant skills, and to add weight to your graduate applications. Consider being a teaching assistant (TA) in addition to these other activities. When Dana was an undergraduate, for example, he was a TA in a course on cognitive psychology. He ran a weekly recitation section where a small group of students (12 or so) came to discuss the week's lecture material, do brief in-class exercises, and to ask for help with any concepts they did not understand from the three lecture sessions.

This sort of opportunity can prepare you for more formal teaching during graduate school, where working as a TA or eventually as a course instructor is a source of income.

A final way to gain research experience is through summer programs that offer concentrated undergraduate research. Some universities provide financial support to their most promising students who become part of an existing research team, and there are some competitive national summer research opportunities that provide both funds and experience. Check with your advisor about what options might make the most sense for your application strategy.

Presenting Research at a Conference

Let's imagine you work with a faculty member on his or her research or do some research on you own. What's next? An important part of the research process—some would say its *essential* aspect—is to share what you learned with other people. Admittedly, writing a senior thesis or other paper achieves this goal, but it is also true that few people beyond your research advisor will read it. A very good alternative that will enhance your potential as a graduate student is to present research at a psychology conference. Some conferences are explicitly for undergraduates to share their work with other students (recall Table 8.3), while many regional, national, and even international conferences for professionals have sessions in which undergraduates can present (recall Table 8.1).

One thing: Most conferences are sponsored by an organization (APA, for example), thus, if you want to submit a conference proposal (which must be reviewed and then accepted), you will be required to join as a student affiliate before you can present. Membership costs for students tend to be reasonable. Your research supervisor will probably need to be a full member of the organization in order for you to present. Specific information regarding these and related issues can be found at the organization and conference websites.

There are also many local psychology conferences specifically designed for undergraduate presentations. These tend to be offered by an individual college or university or sometimes a consortia (in which more than one institution sponsors an annual undergraduate conference that moves from school to school). Your own school may host an annual "Scholars' Day" or "Student Research Symposium" where you can present (these events are held annually on both Jane and Dana's home campuses).

Generally, there are two modes of conference presentations: poster sessions and oral presentations. A *poster* is a highly visual summary of a research project that more or less follows APA style (i.e., introduction, Method, Results, Discussion) but does so with little text and an emphasis on tables and graphs. The poster is hung in a conference room or large hall with other posters. Interested attendees (including peers) stop by, read the poster, and then ask the researcher questions about the work. The situation is generally a low-stress one that involves having a quick 2-minute summary to share with the people who drop by (for information about creating a poster, recall the poster rubric shown in Table 8.2; see also Dunn, 2013; Wilson & Schwartz, 2015).

In contrast, an *oral presentation* is a talk where the speaker stands in front of an audience to present his or her research, usually for 15 or 20 minutes. Most oral presentations rely on PowerPoint slides or some other digital graphics package like Keynote or Prezi. Like posters, oral presentations are also brief. If you are giving the presentation, you won't have a lot of time so you will need to focus on the hypothesis, the methods used to test it, what was found, and what it means. In addition, you will need to reserve some time, usually 5 minutes, to allow audience members to ask you questions about what you did or found, why, and so on. Oral presentations are a little more stressful than posters but learning to do them is a valuable skill, one that will pay dividends in graduate school (where you give lots of talks in and outside of classes or lab meetings) and in the workplace (where you will lead discussions in meetings, present reports, and the like). For suggestions on giving talks, see Dunn (2013) or Wilson and Schwartz (2015), as well as the points on good public speaking practices provided at the end of Chapter 7.

APPLYING TO GRADUATE SCHOOLS: PLANNING AND PROCESS

Self-Assessment: Know Yourself and Apply Strategically

When you are deciding where to apply to graduate school, perform an honest and realistic appraisal of your chances of being admitted. Carefully review the admissions information about the programs that interest you in the *GSIP* and on each program's website; again, fit matters. Take the admissions data seriously, no matter how sobering it may be. If your GPA or GRE scores are below the average for a particular program, it's probably not wise to apply there. This is different than the process of applying to undergraduate schools, where students are often told to apply to at least one "reach" school. Unlike undergraduate schools, graduate programs are looking for specific skills and abilities that students must possess before they begin graduate-level training. However, if your application is somewhat balanced by excellence in other areas—sustained research with a faculty member, conference presentations, a senior thesis, excellent letters of recommendation, and so on—then taking one or two application "risks" might be worthwhile. But do not raise your hopes unrealistically. It is best to apply to those programs where you have a reasonable chance of being accepted.

Because most graduate programs rely on an apprenticeship model, in addition to searching for programs that match your interests, you might also look for a specific faculty member in each program whose research appeals to you and with whom you would like to work. You could contact this person directly to express your interest in his or her research. Sending a polite and professionally worded email is fine. In it, you should describe your background and explain why you would like to work with him or her. You may learn that the faculty member is not currently taking on any new graduate students; in contrast, you may be able to stimulate the person's interest in you. Only make such contacts, however, if you are genuinely interested in the person, the research, and that particular program.

Do be prepared for rejection: Even with a strong undergraduate performance record, when Jane applied for clinical programs the first time she only made it onto the wait lists of the schools she applied for. She invested the following year in working at a research-oriented job and applied again to a new set of schools; that second year, she was accepted. Many professionals we know and work with applied to graduate school several years running before they were admitted. There is no shame in this—admissions to competitive programs are just that—competitive. You should only apply to those graduate programs where you have a good chance of being accepted. There is no guarantee that when you "fit" a program's profile you will be admitted, as there is no way to assess that year's applicant pool more accurately.

Applying to Doctoral or Master's Programs—or Both

Should you seek a doctorate or a master's degree—or get a master's first and then go for the doctorate? Generally, pursuing the doctorate from the start is the wiser course, particularly because so many professional opportunities in the discipline, such as full-time tenure-track teaching in a 4-year college or university or being a practicing psychologist, require a doctorate (recall Chapter 8). On the other hand, many people only want to pursue master's-level training, which can be a fine option if it matches their particular career goals. Our point is that you should make a decision about what you want to do well in advance of when application deadlines roll around. When you read entries in the *GSIP* or look at program websites, be sure to find out what type of degree candidates (master's or doctoral) a given program is seeking. In some programs, students can earn a master's degree as they work toward their doctorate; however, these programs only admit those seeking a doctorate—they do not offer terminal master's degrees.

One strategy that some students take is to apply simultaneously to doctoral and master's programs. Their logic is simple: If they are not admitted to any doctoral program on their first (or even second) try, they may be able to attend a master's program. Once they have an MA or an MS, they can reapply to doctoral programs with their master's degree in hand. Presumably, if they work hard in the master's program, their application will be stronger, as they will have completed a number of graduate courses, conducted research, written a thesis or the equivalent, and will have strong letters of recommendation from faculty in the master's program, and so on. We both have friends and colleagues who followed this route; it worked for them, but we do want to point out that it can potentially involve an extended time commitment.

As we end this section, we are mindful of the commitment graduate education requires and how long it can take to complete a degree. One study of graduate education found that the 10-year doctoral completion rate in psychology was only 65% (Council of Graduate Schools Ph.D. Completion Project, 2008). In other words, 35% of the original doctoral students did not complete a degree after being in graduate school for 10 years (and this *after* 4 or so years of undergraduate school). No doubt many of these students left their graduate program to do something else, but some were still hanging on and pursuing their degree after a decade. Some training programs have imposed limits so that if students aren't finished within a certain amount of time (say, 10 years), they are bounced from the program, probably with a pile of debt and no degree to show for their investment. Remember that going to graduate school is a serious decision. Make it with your eyes—and mind—wide open.

In closing, stay mindful of these important factors:

■ Only apply to programs you would honestly consider attending.

■ You will be in graduate school for several years so the location might matter in your application and decision processes.

■ You will likely need to take out loans and find other forms of financial aid for graduate school—how much debt can you reasonably carry?

A Few Words on Applying to Doctoral-Level Clinical Psychology Programs

Admissions for PhD programs in clinical psychology can be extremely competitive. One reason for the competition is that many students associate psychology more or less exclusively with clinical or counseling psychology (recall Chapter 2), so they apply to such programs because they know less about other options. Because of the sheer number of applicants, graduate programs in these areas typically demand that applicants have higher GPAs and GRE scores and rely on other application criteria such as volunteer work in mental health contexts than do programs in most other psychology subfields, thereby making the competition fierce. We offer this information not to dissuade you from applying to clinical programs. Rather, we encourage you to develop a backup plan to strengthen your application if you intend to pursue a clinical PhD and are not admitted the first time you apply.

An alternative to a traditional PhD program in clinical psychology is the PsyD degree (Murray, 2000). **PhD** programs in clinical psychology concentrate on conducting clinical research according to what is referred to in the discipline as the *Boulder scientist–practitioner model*, which came out of a series of conferences in Boulder, Colorado, in the 1940s and was adapted as the APA's model in 1949. **PsyD** programs, which are based on a model developed in Vail, Colorado, in 1973, emphasize clinical practice over the production of clinical research. This alternate degree provided new options for those wishing to complete doctoral-level clinical training. See *A Major Success Story: From BA to PsyD to Rehab Psychologist* for a description of how a PsyD-prepared psychologist found just the right occupation.

Many PsyD programs operate in university settings. Applicants are likely to find such programs to be highly competitive. However, over the last few decades, for-profit PsyD programs, which accept larger classes, have been established. These programs tend not to be as selective and can also generate substantial debt load for students by the time they graduate.

Two additional points to consider in choosing which schools to apply to are the school's accreditation status and its internship placement records, both of which are indices of program quality. Rigorous programs maintain their accreditation through the APA, which evaluates program quality, faculty qualifications, and curriculum structure before accrediting the clinical program. Occasionally programs lose their status if accreditors determine that they have significant deficiencies.

An emerging problem over the last few years, which is being compounded by recent higher numbers of PsyD-trained internship candidates from for-profit programs, has been ensuring that students in clinical PhD and PsyD programs have access to appropriate internships (Clay, 2012). The APA has been dedicating additional resources to increasing the number of quality internships for students. However, clinical programs should be able to describe how successful their students are in getting placements in appropriate internships at the end of the formal internship-selection process at the conclusion of their academic training. You should think twice about applying to programs that have poor internship match percentages. Doing an internship at an unaccredited placement will limit your professional credibility and job options in the future.

A **Major** Success Story

From BA to PsyD to Rehab Psychologist

Joann knew before the end of her undergraduate education that a traditional clinical pathway in which she would complete a PhD was just not for her. She knew her clinical instincts were solid, based on her volunteer experiences in mental health settings. However, she found the research required by PhD programs simply didn't fit with her strengths. She considers herself extremely lucky that the practice-focused PsyD degree emerged at just the right time for her to enroll in a new and rigorous PsyD program, in which she ended up thriving.

During her clinical training, she gained a lot of experience with populations of all kinds. She found herself especially drawn to people whose life circumstances produced massive physical challenges. She became a rehabilitation psychologist, working in an inpatient clinic affiliated with a major urban hospital. She collaborates with a multidisciplinary team in helping people recover from trauma, including accidents and strokes. She admires the resilience she routinely encounters as she works with her patients. Although her work is physically and emotionally challenging, she can't imagine feeling more satisfied with another professional direction.

How Many Applications?

How many graduate school applications should you submit? There is no magic number, really. You need to consider the cost involved in applying, as virtually all graduate schools charge an application fee (however, most will waive that fee if you provide evidence that you are living on a limited income). We advise you to apply to more than one program, but beyond that the number is up to you. Some students become fixated on being admitted to their dream graduate program or to work with a particular researcher in his or her lab or research group. Such desires are understandable but must be tempered by a realistic appraisal of the chances of being admitted into that particular program.

Grades Matter—and So Do Test Scores

The grades you earn in your undergraduate courses matter for admission to selective graduate programs. You should strive do as well as you can in all of your college courses from your freshman year forward. This is critical because graduate schools do not just look at grades in psychology courses, they also examine students' GPAs in classes outside their major. What GPAs do programs look for? The minimum starting cutoff is probably 3.0—and we intentionally use the word *minimum* here. Competitive programs can and do require higher GPAs, if only in the major courses. The best guideline is to consult the GPA requirements listed on program websites and in the *GSIP*.

What about standardized test scores? Most graduate programs in psychology require students to submit their scores on the Graduate Record Exam (GRE), which contains questions that help assess verbal reasoning, quantitative reasoning, and analytical writing, and on the GRE Psychology Subject Test. The latter is comprised of 205 multiple-choice questions covering the experimental and natural science sides of psychology (e.g., learning, cognition, memory, perception), the social science side (e.g., clinical, abnormal, social, and personality psychology), and general questions covering the history of psychology, statistics, research methods, and applied psychology, among other issues.

Official testing centers sponsored by the **Educational Testing Service (ETS)** administer the tests by computer throughout the year around the country. Once you finish the test, you are instantly given your unofficial scores, so you leave the testing session knowing how you fared.

Like the grades on your college transcript, scores on the GRE and the GRE Psychology Subject Test matter—the higher the scores you earn on both tests, the greater your chance of being admitted to competitive graduate programs. If your score falls below the GRE cutoff score selected by a graduate program, you will likely be wasting your time applying to that program. However, admissions officials may make some exceptions to the cutoff scores if there are substantial extenuating circumstances that justify admission. For example, students who have been particularly successful in undergraduate research demonstrate that they can perform at the level that will be expected in graduate school. In such cases, the publication record and exceptionally strong letters of reference may offset a disappointing GRE score.

We strongly encourage you to prepare for both the general (verbal and quantitative) and disciplinary (psychology) tests. Helpful information about the nature and type of questions, scoring and score ranges, as well as tips on test taking can be found on the ETS websites for each test. A variety of books with practice questions are available and, of course, there are also formal preparatory courses that you can take weeks or months before you take the test. These books and courses can be very helpful, especially if you do not feel confident about your performance on standardized tests. On the other hand, each requires money and time. Only you can decide whether such additional investment is a good idea.

If you get disappointing scores, you should consider retaking the exam. However, without additional preparation and practice, chances are very good your scores will fall in the same range as they did the first time. You can decide which scores to forward to your target schools, so there is little risk in retaking the tests.

Requesting Letters of Recommendations

Chances are good that at some point you will want to request letters of recommendation from your instructors—perhaps your academic advisor and professors who know you well—and possibly your former supervisors or employers. Such letters are routinely used in applications for graduate school, but you may also be asked to supply a recommendation letter or two for a job opening. The appropriate etiquette for asking for letters of recommendation is discussed in Chapter 6.

Whether you ask people for letters of recommendation or to serve as references, be sure to provide them with the following:

- ■ a list of addresses and due dates for letters of recommendations, or for references, a list of the employers who may be calling;
- ■ a copy of your curriculum vitae (CV—see page 163); for job applications, a copy of your resume (see Chapter 8, page 77);
- ■ a copy of your personal statement if you are applying to graduate school; or for jobs, a few paragraphs that describe your career interests and objectives;
- ■ a list of courses, dates, grades earned, and meaningful or significant interactions you had with the faculty member you are asking to write your letter;
- ■ an unofficial copy of your undergraduate transcript;
- ■ a copy of your GRE and Psychology Subject Test scores (and the results of any other standardized tests) if you are applying to graduate school;
- ■ any required recommendation forms; and
- ■ a pre-addressed envelope for each recommendation form or letter, with a stamp if your letter writer is mailing the materials directly.

Many letters of recommendation are now uploaded to university websites by the recommenders themselves. You must provide their contact information to the graduate schools you are applying to—remember, you must ask your potential recommenders in advance if they would be willing to write a letter on your behalf. Once they agree and you submit their contact information, they will receive an email from each graduate program containing instructions about how to submit your recommendation information.

The one issue remaining is unique to the graduate school application process—whether to waive your right to see a confidential letter of recommendation. Most recommendation forms contain a statement in which you indicate whether you waive or do not waive your right to see what a recommender wrote about you. If you waive this right, you can never ask the graduate school (whether you are admitted or not) to see what your recommenders said in their letters. If you don't sign the waiver, in theory, you could ask to see the letters once an admissions decision is made.

Which choice should you make? We believe that it is in your best interest to waive your right. Many faculty will give you a copy of the letter they write on your behalf even if you waive your right. However, if a recommender doesn't offer you a copy and you don't waive your right, you run the risk that your recommender may be less likely to write an honest recommendation on your behalf. Instead, he or she may craft a neutral letter that will not say much that would make a persuasive case for your admission. Some recommenders may refuse to write a letter for you unless you waive your right to see it. This is one of the reasons why we stated clearly that it is in your interest to ask potential recommenders if they can write strong letters on your behalf—if they demur or say they cannot do so, then you should find someone else to serve as a reference. When a recommender indicates he or she can write a strong letter for you, then you should not need to worry about the content—nor do you need to see the letter. In summary, we encourage you to waive this right so that graduate programs will receive candid assessments of your abilities and character.

One final strategy is worth mentioning. Follow up with the programs you are applying to in advance of your deadlines to make sure all of your recommenders have sent in their letters. If any are missing at that point, you still have time to gently remind the person who promised the letter but may have not yet written it to send it in. You don't want your application thrown out because a letter is missing.

Writing a Personal Statement

Most of the materials in graduate applications are a matter of record (grades, test scores) or the opinion of others (letters of recommendation). In contrast, the personal statement is your opportunity to present yourself and to describe your interests, skills, experiences, and career goals. Some programs refer to these as applicant or candidate statements, autobiographical statements, or letters of intent. Whatever they are called, short of a face-to-face interview, they are the one personal aspect of the application. Your statement allows you to do a few things:

- introduce yourself;
- explain your particular interest in psychology;
- share valuable background information about yourself; and
- provide a sample of your writing skills.

Issues and areas you should try to cover in your personal statement include (Keith-Spiegel & Wiederman, 2000):

- your academic interest areas in psychology;
- your academic background and achievements;
- why you are applying to this program and what attracted you to it;
- specific research experiences in psychology or related disciplines;
- teaching experiences relevant to psychology;
- relevant internship or volunteer experiences (e.g., youth counseling, work in clinical settings);
- objectives for graduate school and career plans (What do you hope to accomplish? Where do you see yourself in the future?);
- one or two faculty in the graduate program with whom you might want to work because of similar research interests;
- particular skills you possess (e.g., math, statistics, programming, foreign languages); and
- any personal material you think the admissions committee should know (but be judicious in what you share).

Depending on what you are asked to write about as well as any length constraints on the essay, it's unlikely that you can comment on each item on this list. Whatever you do, be sure to provide answers to the questions on the application and stay within the allotted length. Be concise. One effective strategy for writing a personal statement is to avoid discussing information (GPA, GRE scores) specified elsewhere in the application—you don't want to waste space or be redundant. Still, some topics—your research experiences—can be described in greater detail here than in other places in the application.

Once you have a draft of your personal statement, share it with several allies who can help you produce the most polished and persuasive outcome. For example, get feedback from your academic advisor, the faculty member with whom you have done research, and someone you know to be excellent with grammar. Consider asking for help from someone who knows little about psychology; this last reader can identify any part of the statement that is hard to follow for a general reader—you are trying to make your personal statement be clear, not to demonstrate that you know psychology jargon. Listen to the comments from these readers and revise, revise, revise until you are certain the statement reads well and conveys what you wanted to share about your enthusiasm for psychology and your future in the discipline.

After you have written your general personal statement, be prepared to modify it for each individual application. Some programs provide very detailed directions about what they expect applicants to discuss in this personal essay, along with length requirements (often in terms of some number of words, say, 500). Other programs use a more open-ended format. Be certain to read each program's essay requirements and tailor each statement accordingly. You want to make a persuasive case that there is a strong match between you and the program. You can be equally enthused about all your potential options but each argument you make about a high-quality match is necessarily going to be slightly different from the others.

We have one final suggestion regarding the personal statement for students who are applying to clinical programs. Avoid using the personal statement as an opportunity for an extended discussion about your own mental health struggles. Protracted disclosure of such details tends to send up red flags about your motives and may weaken your attractiveness as a candidate. If your own mental health history plays an essential role in your decision to apply, your discussion of these matters should be brief and to the point and should emphasize positive outcomes of the struggle.

Creating Your First Curriculum Vitae (CV)

In Chapter 8 we provided suggestions for crafting a resume to send to potential employers. In this chapter, we discuss the academic version known as the **curriculum vitae**, or **CV**. A CV summarizes your academic life, particularly any scholarly accomplishments or experiences you have had. We introduce the CV here because if you go to graduate school, you will certainly write one, particularly as you get closer to the end of graduate school. So why not start one now, as you apply to graduate school?

Although CVs are somewhat like resumes, they are also different from them. CVs provide personal information (address, contact information), educational background (institutions, degrees), and any honors or awards, but they specifically focus on materials and experiences related to the person's academic discipline—in this case, psychology. CVs often contain:

- ■ professional experiences, including jobs, that are related to psychology;
- ■ research interests, including current projects;
- ■ teaching interests;
- ■ any professional publications (usually listed chronologically and in APA style);
- ■ conference presentations and other talks (usually listed chronologically and in APA style); and
- ■ references (names, addresses, email addresses for three or four professionals who know you and your work, or an indication that you will provide such information upon request).

As a college student or a recent graduate, your CV will probably be brief, but it will grow as you move through graduate school. **Table 10.1** illustrates a CV for a graduate school–bound student. The formatting guidelines are similar to those for a resume (e.g., white or off-white paper, 12-point font; see Chapter 8). Use Table 10.1 as a guide for developing your own CV, which you might want to include in your graduate school application packets.

TABLE 10.1

A Sample Undergraduate Curriculum Vitae

Cavan A. Jeffries
Curriculum Vitae

1742 Roycroft Way
Gotha, FL 34734
555-777-8951
cavjef@gomail.org

EDUCATION

East Florida State University
BS in Psychology (expected May 2016)
GPA in major 3.85/overall 3.90

HONORS AND AWARDS

Dean's List, fall 2012–fall 2015
Wilson Humboldt Scholarship

RESEARCH AND TEACHING EXPERIENCE

September 2015–present	Research Assistant, Perception Lab, Department of Psychology, East Florida State University
Spring 2014	Teaching Assistant, Dr. Susan Willamette, Introduction to Psychology (PS 101), East Florida State University
January 2013–May 2014	Tutor, Statistics and Methods I and II (PSY 221 & 222), East Florida State University

PUBLICATION

Jeffries, C. A. (2016). *A new view of the Müller–Lyer illusion.* Unpublished honors thesis, Department of Psychology, East Florida State University, Statesburg, FL. (Expected May 2016)

PRESENTATION

Jeffries, C. A. (2015, April). *New visual illusions and why they matter.* Presentation at East Florida State University's Annual Student Research Forum, Statesburg, FL.

PROFESSIONAL MEMBERSHIPS

Phi Beta Kappa
Psi Chi

REFERENCES

Available upon request

Putting It Together

As the application deadline draws near, if you have done your best and been organized, you will have a solid application package that you can submit to the graduate schools of your choice. Our advice is to allow yourself some cushion time of a week or so prior to any due date. That way, if need be, you will still have time to complete any last-minute requirements for a given application—things almost always take longer than we expect. Falling victim to the *planning fallacy*, the failure to estimate the time needed to complete a task, will create very stressful conditions in which it becomes easy to make errors (e.g., leaving a critical piece out of the packet). **Table 10.2** lists the components that likely need to be included in a graduate admissions packet or, in the case of undergraduate transcripts and standardized test scores, need to be paid for in advance and sent independently. Keep in mind that some graduate programs require other materials (e.g., an additional standardized test, such as the Miller Analogies Test (MAT), an essay to go with your personal statement) that do not appear in this list. Always review each program's requirements one last time before submitting your application. Good luck!

If a Graduate School Interview Is in Your Future...

Some graduate programs, particularly those in clinical or counseling psychology, invite finalists to campus to meet and interview with the faculty. Following these campus visits, the faculty will convene and use observations from the interview to decide whom to admit to the program. If you are invited for an interview, always go if you can. If you can't attend an interview in person, inquire about the possibility of connecting with the interviewers online (for example, via Skype or Facetime), but recognize that this is not equivalent to an on-the-ground experience with the program faculty and your potential peers.

TABLE 10.2

Typical Materials Required for Graduate School Applications

Undergraduate transcript: Official copies must be sent to graduate programs from your undergraduate institution's registrar.

GRE and GRE Psychology Subject Test scores: Official copies must be sent to graduate programs from ETS; any other required test scores must also be submitted.

Completed application form: Includes a list of major courses completed, in process, or to be completed in the future.

Your personal statement: The content may vary depending upon what a program asks you to discuss in the essay.

Letters of recommendation: Usually three; some letters must be sent directly by your recommender and you send others to the program in sealed envelopes signed by each recommender.

Optional: A copy of your curriculum vitae or resume.

Besides being an opportunity for the program to get to know you, your visit represents a chance for you to get to know the faculty and the location, and to figure out whether you might want to attend that particular program. Keep in mind that being invited to an interview does not mean you have been admitted (unless you have been told that explicitly), thus how you present yourself in person matters a great deal. We suggest you review the section on interview skills in Chapter 9 and follow the recommendations outlined there (see pages 142–144). Instead of interviewing for a job, you are interviewing for graduate school, but the importance of being friendly, interested, open, attentive, curious (having good questions to ask), and so on, is the same in both cases.

IF AT FIRST YOU DON'T SUCCEED

What if you apply to several programs and you aren't admitted to any of them? What then? As we've tried to convey, getting in to graduate school in psychology is often not easy. It can be easy to get discouraged if things don't work out as planned.

Still, we believe there are things you can do to strengthen your chances next time. First, take a hard look at your credentials. Did you apply to programs where the standards were too high? Second, review your standardized test scores. Would taking a prep class help you to increase your GRE scores? Third, should you try to get more research experience? If you still live near a university, can you apply for any research openings or even volunteer to help a faculty member with research? Fourth, did you apply to both doctoral and master's programs? If only the former, then you may want to try the strategy of applying to both types of programs the next year. Fifth, ask your faculty advisor to review your credentials with a critical eye—is there anything missing? What can be improved upon for next time?

Remember, the path to graduate school is a long one, and it requires tenacity. If you sincerely want to become a professional in psychology, then we encourage you to keep trying. Persistence can pay off in the end.

THOUGHT QUESTIONS

1. What specific reasons do you have for attending graduate school in psychology?

2. Will you pursue doctoral- or master's-level training? Why?

3. Is there a specific area of psychology that interests you? Within that area, are there particular topics you might like to study as a graduate student?

4. Have you had any research experience? If you have, what did you like and not like about doing research? If you haven't, do you plan to obtain some research experience? How?

5. If you were to write a personal statement right now to explain your motivation to study psychology at the graduate level, what would you say? Why?

11

What Can You Do With an Advanced Degree in Psychology?

One out of every four undergraduate majors bolsters their courage, orchestrates the funding, and makes the time necessary to pursue an advanced psychology degree. (Interestingly, 45.3% of psychology majors obtain some sort of graduate degree while, overall, only 35.1% of all college graduates earn a graduate degree; APA *Monitor on Psychology*, 2016). However, it is not just a simple matter of deciding to go. As you will learn in the next chapter, applying to graduate school can be extremely time consuming; getting into a graduate program is intensely competitive. Many prospective psychologists don't get accepted to graduate school the first time they apply.

□ □ □

Making the commitment to graduate school is a huge step. Graduate education is costly and will probably end up adding to your student debt. It requires diversion of your attention from family and friends. It may require you to relocate. And you probably need to develop a taste for macaroni and cheese or ramen noodles for the duration of your graduate study. However, completion of a graduate degree opens an amazing number of professional pathways. The vast majority of people who hold advanced degrees in psychology work in one of three areas: research/ academic, clinical/service, or applications/business.

In this chapter, we develop a good approximation of what it means to be employed with an advanced degree in psychology. First, we look at the kinds of degrees that qualify graduates for psychology-related employment, starting with specific opportunities at the master's level. Next, we turn our attention to doctoral-level training, examining the settings in which psychologists are employed. We describe the occupations that psychologists can pursue and explore the job outlook for psychologists over the next decade. We conclude with some advice about mounting a successful job search.

MASTER'S-LEVEL TRAINING

Students may choose to pursue a master's degree for several reasons. First, they know they want to work in a psychology-related context but may not have settled on a specific career goal. If they stop when they complete their master's degree, the degree is described as "**terminal**." On the other hand, the master's degree may be a stepping-stone to additional training at the doctoral level. Students who enter a PhD program directly after they finish their master's degree may execute a master's project as a proof of fitness to enter the PhD program.

Master's degrees also come in two flavors (comparable to bachelor's degrees). The Master of Arts (MA) reflects that the degree has a strong liberal arts orientation. The Master of Science (MS) conveys more of an emphasis on science and research. The majority of psychology master's programs also tend to have identified concentrations in these areas: experimental, clinical/counseling, or industrial/organizational.

Master's training provides a solid means of developing expertise in psychology without the long-term obligations that go with doctoral training. In fact, for many occupations, a master's degree is just the right level of education, whereas a doctorate may be overkill.

Master's-level psychologists do get to work in the discipline they love but their autonomy depends on the context in which they work as well as the type of psychology they practice. In business contexts, the master's degree supports independent function. In clinical contexts, a graduate with a master's degree may need to work under the supervision of those with doctoral-level training. Despite that constraint, people with master's degrees can work in fulfilling jobs in a number of settings. See **Table 11.1** for some suggestions for master's employment.

TABLE 11.1

What Can You Be With a Master's Degree?

In higher education	*In government-sponsored human services*
Community college teacher	Vocational rehabilitation specialist
Four-year college adjunct teacher	Substance abuse counselor
Academic adviser or academic recruiter	Human resource manager
	Parole officer
Career counselor	Rehabilitation counselor

Continued

In clinical contexts	In business contexts
Behavioral counselor	Human resource manager
Health-care coordinator	Employee developer
Mental health technician (someone who implements elements of a treatment plan)	Advertising and marketing specialist
	Public relations specialist
Mental health therapist	Project manager
Rehabilitation specialist	Sales representative
Group home supervisor	Store manager
Child-protection specialist	
Child-care program manager	

FIGURE 11–1 Where Do Psychologists Work?

Data from: D. Michaels, J. Kohout, M. Wicherski, & B. Hart (2011), *2009 Doctorate Employment Survey.*

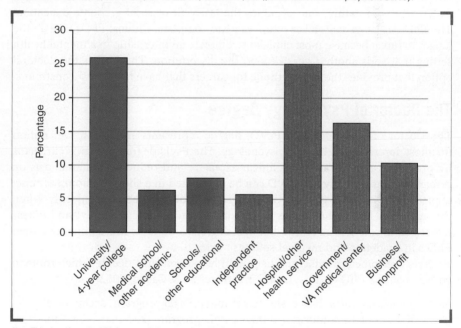

Note: This chart, from the APA Career website, represents employment settings for those with recent doctorates in psychology. Totals amount to 97.7% due to rounding and exclusion of 17 "not specified" responses.

DOCTORAL DEGREE OPTIONS

The term "**psychologist**" is usually reserved for people who have doctoral training in psychology. Let's explore all the ways a person can earn the title of "doctor" in psychology. But first, let's look at where psychologists, prepared at the doctoral level, do their work. As shown in **Figure 11.1**, the vast majority of psychologists are employed in university (25.9%) and health-care settings

(25%) (APA, 2014). Both clinical and research-oriented psychologists tend to predominate in these hires. Government and Veterans Administration (VA) medical centers constitute the third-largest employer at 16.3%. At 10.4%, business and nonprofit settings represent the fourth-largest employer and tend to hire psychologists with an applied orientation rather than those with a research or clinical background. Educational settings (8.1%), medical settings (6.3%), and private practice (5.7%) each employ fewer than 10% of psychologists.

The Doctor of Philosophy Degree

Most people think, with good reason, of psychologists as holding a doctorate degree. It is recognized as the most prestigious degree that can be conferred. A Doctor of Philosophy (**PhD**) degree provides optimal independence for those with psychology backgrounds and prepares students for careers in academia, clinical contexts, and business settings through an emphasis on research. The PhD typically concludes with a research dissertation—an original research effort, often experimental in nature, that occupies the last year or so of graduate education. The PhD degree usually takes 5 to 7 years to complete. Clinical PhDs take a little longer to finish because most clinicians complete an internship in a mental health setting that adds another year beyond the dissertation. The PhD is the doctoral option that provides the most latitude for careers that have the fewest constraints.

The Doctor of Psychology Degree

The Doctor of Psychology, or **PsyD**, degree represents another, newer option for those interested in clinical psychology. The PsyD degree prepares clinicians by providing a wide range of clinical exposure and reducing the emphasis on research. Consequently, the PsyD can be completed in a shorter amount of time, approximately 4 to 6 years. PsyD programs should be considered only when the applicant knows he or she plans to work in a clinical context and is less interested in conducting research. PsyD degrees tend to be less competitive than PhD's in academic and medical settings.

What are some other factors that might help applicants decide which route to go between the PhD and PsyD options (Norcross & Castle, 2002)?

- *Acceptance rates.* It is easier to get into a PsyD program (acceptance of 4 out of 10 applications) than a PhD program (acceptance of 1 to 1.5 out of 10 applications).
- *Program size.* PsyD programs admit 16 students on average, whereas PhD programs average nine admissions.
- *Financial support.* PhD programs have a better track record of providing support through grants and assistantships. Consequently, recent estimates suggest that PsyD graduates tend to bear significantly more student debt (a median of $120,000) in contrast to PhD-level debts (a median of $40,000) (http://psychologygradschool.weebly.com/debt-and-income.html).

■ *Theoretical orientation.* PsyD faculty tend to be drawn from more diverse orientations, including psychodynamic, cognitive-behavioral, and family systems. The dominant orientation of PhD clinical faculty is cognitive-behavioral.

Figure 11.2 shows acceptance rates by subfield of psychology and degree level (master's or doctorate) for the 2013–2014 academic year (Stamm, Michalski, Cope, Fowler, Christidis, & Lin, 2016). More than 110,000 applications were submitted to graduate psychology programs in the United States and Canada, and about 26,000 applicants were admitted (an acceptance rate of 24%). As shown in Figure 11.2, however, acceptance rates vary substantially depending on the subfield and degree level in question. A low acceptance rate should not keep you from applying to a particular field, of course, but it is important to be aware of the competitive nature of applying to graduate school.

The Doctor of Education Degree

The **EdD**, or Doctor of Education, is an option for those interested in more clinically oriented activity but are more likely to focus on more mild rather than severe forms of dysfunction. Typically, EdD programs tend to accept people who already

FIGURE 11–2 Acceptance Rates for Graduate Psychology Programs by Subfield and Degree Level, 2013–2014

Originally published in Stamm, K., Michalski, D., Cope, C., Fowler, G., Christidis, P., & Lin, L. (2016, February). What are the acceptance rates for graduate psychology programs? *Monitor on Psychology, 47*(2). Retrieved from http://www.apa.org/monitor/2016/02/datapoint.aspx. Copyright © 2016 American Psychological Association. Reproduced with permission.

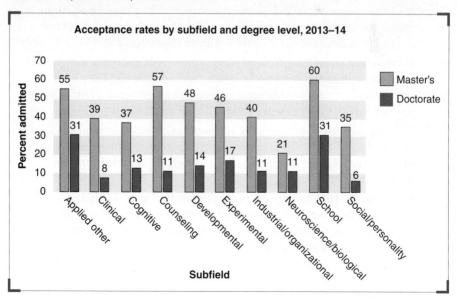

Note: Applied other includes applied behavior analysis, educational, community, forensic, sport, quantitative, and behavioral psychology programs. Data source: American Psychological Association. (2016). *Graduate Study in Psychology.* Washington, DC: Author.

have a master's degree, so it takes from 3 to 5 years to complete the EdD. The area concentration of the EdD tends to be counseling, developmental psychology, or school psychology, and includes an emphasis on research but typically is not perceived as requiring as much rigor in terms of research as the PhD. EdDs are offered in departments of education rather than psychology. Those who earn the EdD tend to work in educational settings, such as secondary schools and colleges and universities. As therapists, they may face some discrepancies in reimbursement rates from insurance companies who are reluctant to place the same value on therapy from EdD's that they do on that from other doctoral-level clinicians.

JOB POSSIBILITIES ACROSS DIFFERENT SUBFIELDS

What follows is just a sampling from the American Psychological Association (APA) of the vocations most commonly held by psychologists (APA, 2014).

- **Clinical psychologists** work in mental health-care settings to alleviate the challenges of emotional or behavioral disorders. They conduct psychological tests and design therapy programs for individuals, groups, and families.

- **Cognitive psychologists** focus on how people think, remember, reason, and make decisions. They work in research contexts and also assist in treatment planning for people with cognitive impairment.

- **Community psychologists** work in larger social systems to improve the lives of those who live in the community. They may be active in delivering assistance after trauma or may concentrate on prevention programs to improve the mental health of the community.

- **Counseling psychologists** focus on problems of everyday adjustment and can be found in schools, hospitals, and businesses. They tend to work with clients whose problems aren't as severe or disruptive as the problems of the clients with whom clinical psychologists work.

- **Developmental psychologists** concentrate on behavior across the life span. Originally focused on childhood and adolescence, developmental psychologists are increasingly electing to work with aging populations.

- **Educational psychologists** explore issues that help or hinder learning. They can design effectiveness studies in classrooms or consult with individual teachers on ways to improve interventions improve learning performance.

- **Engineering (human factors) psychologists** work in the area where machines and humans intersect. They assist in the design of efficient and adaptive devices.

■ **Environmental psychologists** examine the impact of environments on behavior and can serve as consultants. For example, environmental psychologists may advise architects on the potential effectiveness of producing specific effects on behavior from their designs. They can also assist in developing ideas for improving adherence to practices that reduce pollution and waste.

■ **Experimental psychologists** apply their knowledge of good experimental design to advance science in academic settings as well as in manufacturing and engineering contexts. Many academic psychologists publish their work in competitive journals in experimental psychology.

■ **Forensic psychologists** support the judicial system by, among other things, providing expert testimony, conducting research on jury selection, or providing evaluations regarding child custody.

■ **Health psychologists** consult in health-care systems to provide interventions to address psychological reasons why patients may not comply with doctor's orders. They also conduct research on the large-scale health challenges in the culture (e.g., obesity, smoking, high-risk behaviors).

■ **Industrial/organizational psychologists** attempt to make the workplace better through improving systems of production, providing human resource training, and consulting about personnel processes such as hiring and firing. They can serve as agents for change within organizations.

■ **Military psychologists** focus on the unique psychological needs of those who are or have been in the armed services and their families. They work on deployment concerns as well as reentry problems, including the high rates of suicide and substance abuse among military personnel.

■ **Neuropsychologists** examine brain function and may be critical team members working with people who have had traumatic brain injury. They study both normal and abnormal (disease, injury) brain processes.

■ **Personality psychologists** examine individual differences in the patterns of people's thoughts, feelings, and behaviors. Personality psychologists often develop assessment tools that identify people's characteristic and stable responses to stimuli, including situations and other people.

■ **Quantitative psychologists** combine expertise in psychology research design with mathematics to assist in high-quality data analysis. They may propose mathematical modeling for complex behaviors and can quantitatively determine the quality of test instruments.

- **Rehabilitation psychologists** provide direct service to patients with stroke, disability, or developmental delays. They help clients adapt to situations and overcome problems, often working in teams with other health-care professionals. They can also be called on for expert testimony in legal cases related to rehabilitation and disability.

- **School psychologists** provide a wide range of services to children and families in education settings, including counseling, testing, and designing intervention strategies to improve school performance.

- **Social psychologists** are in great demand for their expertise on how people form and change their attitudes. They can consult with businesses to shape advertising and marketing strategies. They also can provide coaching on strategies for enhancing group performance.

- **Sports psychologists** assist athletes to achieve their goals by reducing their fears and improving their motivation to prevail in competition.

ADDITIONAL FACTS ABOUT PROFESSIONAL HELPERS

Psychologists who do therapy for a living must complete some addition steps to establish appropriate credentials to practice. To become licensed to practice, the prospective clinician must pass a comprehensive content and ethics examination and work for 2 years under clinical supervision. The laws that govern professional psychology vary by state. Each state is responsible for addressing public concerns and complaints and has the power to take away a psychologist's license in response to such concerns. The Association of State and Provincial Psychology Boards oversees this process (see http://www.asppb.net/).

There are similar constraints for those who want to practice at the master's level. For example, in Florida, master's program graduates can sit for a state licensing examination. They are then qualified to serve in an internship to earn practice hours. After 1500 hours of supervised practice, they earn the appropriate license. Be advised that states differ in the specific requirements needed to establish credentials. If you intend to reside in a particular state following graduate school, you should consider this as you begin your application process.

However, we would be remiss if we didn't point out another popular option to become professional helpers that doesn't involve the intense focus on science and math required in psychology. Many psychology majors opt to go to graduate school in social work, particularly if statistics and psychological research do not appeal to them. Those with a master's in social work (MSW) degree and appropriate supervision can work in private practice and in mental health agencies. A psychology major provides a great foundation for pursuing an MSW.

JOB OUTLOOK FOR PSYCHOLOGISTS

The news on this front is promising! According to the *Occupational Outlook Handbook* (Bureau of Labor Statistics, 2014), for psychologists, the growth rate in employment from 2012 to 2022 is expected to be 12%, which is slightly better than the expected average growth of all other occupations, at 11%. At the master's level, the rate matches that for all other occupations.

Psychology Salary Projections

Although BA/BS psychology salaries are among the lowest of the liberal arts, salaries improve dramatically with each level of degree. Probably the highest-paid job in a field related to psychology belongs to Phil McGraw ("Dr. Phil"), a media psychologist whose annual income has been estimated to be about $77 million (http://celebnetwealth.com/dr-phil-mcgraw-net-worth-and-annual-salary), but unfortunately, that job is taken. Salaries tend to be the highest for psychologists who combine their disciplinary expertise with management responsibilities (e.g., CEOs, university presidents) or with other enterprises that are more scientific and technological (engineering psychology, neuropsychology, or forensic psychology). Salaries tend to be lower for psychologists working in the community or nonprofit sector. See **Table 11.2** for estimates of current salaries by category.

TABLE 11.2

Estimated Salaries in Psychology by Category*

Doctoral-level training	
Engineering psychologist	$108,348
Industrial/organizational psychologist	$102,570
University administrator	$100,600
Neuropsychologist	$86,000
Forensic psychologist	$85,000
College faculty	$76,060
Clinical psychologist	$69,280
Master's-level training	
Sales manager	$123,150
Advertising manager	$112,870
Public relations	$111,260
Human resource manager	$111,180
Training and development manager	$107,770
Personal financial advisor	$99,920
Educational administrator	$90,670
Management analyst	$89,990

Continued

Social worker	$74,700
Social service manager	$65,750
Claims adjuster	$62,370
Vocational counselor	$56,160
Sports psychologist	$55,000
Health educator	$53,800
School counselor	$53,610
Child-care manager	$52,010
Marriage therapist	$51,690
Mental health counselor	$43,700
Substance abuse counselor	$41,090

Data from: Bureau of Labor Statistics (2013).

*Careful scrutiny of this chart reveals that some occupations at the master's level of training have higher salaries than do those at the doctoral level. The salary discrepancy usually is accounted for by larger salaries generally being connected to business contexts or administrative responsibilities.

FIGURE 11–3 **Average Salaries of Psychologists by State**
Data from: Bureau of Labor Statistics (2014).

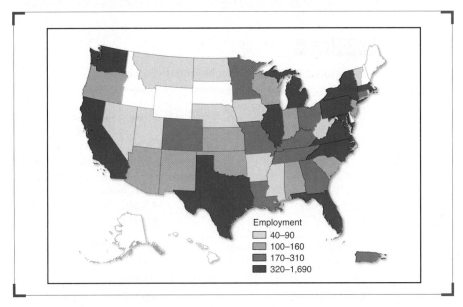

Salaries also vary by region, affected by cost of living and availability of people to do the work. The *Occupational Outlook Handbook* provides a mean of psychologists' salaries by state in 2014. The *Handbook* provides separate distributions for clinical, industrial, and other kinds of psychology. The distribution of the "other" category is shown in **Figure 11.3**. The most lucrative jobs for these kinds of psychologists appear to be in Florida, California, New York, Texas, and Massachusetts.

Calculating Debt Load

Whether you choose to pursue a master's- or a doctoral-level degree, you need to have your eyes open about the financial costs. You will be foregoing a potentially substantial amount of income while you are in graduate school. As well, you may need financial aid to get you through school—in some cases, a great deal of financial aid. You need to do some careful math to determine whether you can afford to start your professional life in such a big hole. See *Reality Check: Can I Truly Afford a Graduate Degree?* to make some realistic calculations about your **debt load**.

✔ **Reality Check**

Can I Truly Afford a Graduate Degree?

Before you sign on the dotted line for graduate school, carefully consider whether you can afford to pursue the degree you want. Calculate the following to determine whether it is in your best interest to go.

1. **Estimate the total cost of the degree.** Each program may feature a net cost calculator on the university admission's website to help you figure out how much money you will need to complete your degree.

2. **Project the total income you can count on during your graduate study.** For example, many programs may provide assistantships (teaching or research-based), grants, or even help you find part-time work within the field that will help with your expenses. This income should offset some of the cost of your degree.

3. **Estimate your first year's salary post-degree.** Using websites that have salary estimates, such as Glassdoor.com or Salary.com, look up the job you are interested in and pick a conservative figure (below the average salary) to project how much you might earn. Also look at the *Occupational Outlook Handbook* (Bureau of Labor Statistics, 2014) to estimate whether the level of training you are aiming toward will be in demand. This action will give you some confidence that you might find a job after you finish your degree.

4. **If the combination of your undergraduate and graduate debt will exceed the estimate of your first-year salary, don't go.** The sacrifice will simply be too great. Currently the average debt load for just an undergraduate degree is a little over $35,000 (Sparshott, 2015). Taking on additional debt may create an insurmountable obstacle for your future financial stability. Determine whether or not you will have enough money after your living expenses to pay back your student loans within 10 years. If you won't, your quality of life, even if you do land your dream job, may suffer.

5. **Calculate the lifetime impact of the potential income generated by the degree.** Determine how many income-generating years you can expect to have between the time you complete your degree and your retirement. Although your salary is likely to increase over time, be conservative in your estimates. Don't forget that every year you spend in graduate school deprives you of income you could have earned with your degree in hand.

6. **Recognize that your estimate doesn't come with guarantees.** You may struggle to land that first job. On the other hand, you might find a job with a high salary. You could also lose the high-flying job should we have another serious economic downturn. Consider the knowns carefully, but prepare for the unknowns.

Information from: Shin (2014).

GETTING READY FOR THE JOB MARKET

Just as you would before receiving a bachelor's degree, prepare for employment with a graduate degree long before the university president hands you your diploma and places your hood over your head. Chief among your considerations should be the following:

What income will support the lifestyle you have in mind? As the Bureau of Labor Statistics have shown, salaries for occupations requiring advanced degrees can be remarkably lucrative, particularly for people whose talents run to management or whose interests include science and technology. On the other hand, people with a bachelor's degree in business can easily out-earn those with a graduate degree who are in social services. Consequently, it's important to understand your values, including your work ethic, as you begin planning for your ideal job. Confucius has been quoted as saying, "Choose a job you love and you will never have to work a day in your life." His wisdom points to the importance of having passion for what you do that can sustain you, regardless of the size of your paycheck.

Psychologists can subsidize their full-time salaries with various types of part-time work. This includes consulting, adjunct teaching, and writing. For example, both Dana and Jane have served as consultants to the College Board as Advanced Placement (AP) readers. In that part-time gig, they commit to a stretch of 10 days in which they read and score AP Psychology exams taken by high school students. Although this particular job is reserved for educators in psychology, it demonstrates that psychological expertise can be used to increase one's income.

What kind of work–life balance will be most satisfying? Quality of life issues have long been a research focus for organizational psychologists; recent data suggest that employees are less willing to work long hours to get ahead than to have a better balance between work and other aspects of life (Korkki, 2010). Professionals can usually expect to surrender more than 40 hours a week in making a living. However, some positions in psychology require more sacrifice of private time than others. For example, launching a private practice in clinical psychology is very time consuming. Factors that can contribute to work–life balance satisfaction include having flexible work hours, being able to work from multiple sites (including home), spending less time in traffic, and having access to compatible colleagues. Carefully consider positions that might rob you of time with your family and friends.

How much independence will you require to be fulfilled? Generally speaking, the more education you attain, the more power and autonomy you have in your professional life. In the case of advanced degrees in psychology, that power differential is quite explicit. Only those at the doctoral level can technically be called "psychologists." In addition, some master's-prepared psychologists, especially those in clinical contexts, may work under the direct supervision of others with more experience and education. The drive for personal and professional autonomy can motivate those with a master's degree to return to school in part to be able to feel in greater control of their professional decisions.

Will jobs exist in the part of the country where you want to live? You may envision an idyllic pastoral lifestyle in the country or the dynamism of living in an urban center; however, psychology jobs may not be plentiful in the area where you wish to reside. You will increase your employability by being flexible about where you are willing to live. That adventurousness means you can apply to any position that gives you the salary that facilitates the kind of lifestyle to which you aspire. It may be possible to use your degree in work outside the country as well.

Can you develop a network that will help you land the job you want? By joining professional organizations (e.g., APA, APS), attending psychology conferences, and making connections at gatherings of local psychologists, you can build a collective of people whom you can ask to help you identify any emerging opportunities that suit your skills and interests. Most psychologists are talented as mentors; they see helping new psychologists get properly launched as a great way to give back.

Can you monitor job availability comprehensively? Think broadly about where to look for employment. Listings for psychology positions don't necessarily lead with "Psychologist wanted." But consider looking at overall categories (human services, research, health care) to see if any descriptions match your desires and skill sets. Job and career fairs sponsored by universities can be a source of inspiration. Job listings in professional organizations (e.g., APA, APS, *Chronicle of Higher Education*) can also be useful. The Internet hosts multiple sites that list job openings. Being familiar with these will help when the time comes to launch your search.

Can you be flexible about moving on? Life throws some curves. That ideal job that seemed to meet all your needs may come with a soul-sucking boss or a toxic work environment. The commute you thought you could tolerate may test your good will toward humanity. Fortunately, having a background in psychology gives you the flexibility and portability that make it easier to find a new job that may provide you with a more satisfying life. In addition, psychologists are well prepared for new and emerging types of jobs that require strong problem-solving and people skills—skills for which psychologists are known.

IS IT WORTH IT?

As psychology professors, we believe we have the best jobs in the world and would follow the same path if we had to do it over again. Recently, the value of the job was confirmed by *Money* magazine's annual publication of the top 50 best jobs in America, in which both "college professor" (ranked #2) and "psychologist" (ranked #10) fared very well (Kalwarski, Mosher, Paskin, & Rosato, 2014). Psychology scores well in terms of flexibility, creativity, and career advancement. Unfortunately, the job market right now is intensely competitive, but, according to

A **Major** Success Story ⬅

Choosing Academic Life

Born in Jamaica, Darren aspired to be an archaeologist until about age 12, when his curiosity about dreaming made him rethink his goal. He began to read psychology texts (Freud, Jung, and others) to understand dreaming better and ended up falling in love with psychology. He became convinced that the mind is the next great unexplored frontier and could picture himself becoming a psychology researcher to indulge his curiosity. Opportunities were better in the States for completing advanced degrees. Darren's interests went beyond pathology to include health, well-being, and social functioning. He completed a PhD in counseling psychology and embarked on an academic career stateside, where he has shown great promise of becoming an outstanding educator.

Darren describes college teaching as an ideal career because it provides a direct impact on many more people than he would have through individual counseling. He also is able to explore new ideas every day and to excite passion in others. He especially enjoys working with students for whom academic success doesn't come easily. He likes to think that his passion for learning will inspire and nurture new generations of psychologists, therapists, and social workers. Because the work is so satisfying, he concludes that none of what he does on a daily basis seems like work.

Darren's advice for those trying to figure out their direction is simple: "Follow your passion. When you pursue a promising direction, all kinds of avenues open up to promote personal growth. Going on that passion-driven journey is a great way to find not just a home for your interests but to discover yourself in the process. Trust that good things will happen when your passion provides the energy."

Psychology Career Center (2014), the job market is likely to grow more than 30% in the next decade as baby-boomer professors retire. If you genuinely liked your experience as a student, consider using your advanced degree to support the development of future psychologists. See *A Major Success Story: Choosing Academic Life*, especially if you are considering an academic career.

THOUGHT QUESTIONS

1. Why would average starting salaries for psychologists differ so widely among different states?

2. What subspecialties for doctoral-level training hold the most appeal for you?

3. Which occupations tend to provide the highest and lowest salaries?

4. What does the master's degree in psychology qualify you to do?

5. What are some strategies you should use during graduate school to prepare yourself for a future job search?

6. How much economic risk are you willing to take to secure an advanced degree in psychology?

7. What do you think the best part of being a college teacher would be?

12

Keeping Connected to Psychology

Jane relishes running into her former students because she loves to hear how their lives have been unfolding. Unfortunately, some of those encounters take a disappointing turn. After the initial greeting, Jane will ask, "So what are you up to?" Students who have gone on to graduate school tend to be ebullient. They detail how much they love what they are doing and how enthusiastic they are about the future. They often express appreciation for the rigor of their undergraduate training that turned out to be so helpful in their pursuit of success.

□ □ □

On the other hand, students who have stopped their education at the bachlor's level often behave very differently. They tend to look away with a sheepish expression. Almost as though they are embarrassed, they confess, "Well, I'm not really doing anything with my psychology degree. I'm doing _____." You can fill in the blank with any number of professions (e.g., running a company, serving as a sales rep, working with children). The point of describing this uncomfortable situation is that there seems to be a serious disconnect between the foundation students build in their undergraduate major and what students do after graduation. For most faculty members, an encounter like this is a real head-scratcher. How could students invest 4 years in learning to think like a psychologist and then see no real connection between that and their current life?

Regardless of the path you choose after graduation, by the time you complete an undergraduate degree in psychology, the imprint of psychology on you should be indelible. Chances are good you will have adopted a psychological worldview that will have an enduring impact on how you relate to the world and its many inhabitants even if you don't pursue a job that would be identified as explicitly psychology oriented.

In this final chapter, we strive to strengthen the connection between you and your chosen discipline. First, we describe the specifics of the psychological worldview. Beyond demonstrating the characteristics or attributes of psychological thinkers, there are other ways students can keep strong connections to the discipline. We will discuss formal organizations as well as Internet and media resources that can help to keep your psychology interests alive and keep your curiosity about behavior replenished. First, let's examine the distinctive features of the psychological worldview.

WHAT IT MEANS TO BE A PSYCHOLOGICAL THINKER

Specializing in a major also should have a distinctive and profound influence on a student's way of thinking about the world (Association of American Colleges & Universities, 2013). Education in psychology supports a specific set of values that can't help but change how the student sees the world.

We are going to use some of our favorite quotations to try to capture the differences in temperament and perspective that tend to be fostered by an undergraduate major in psychology. Sometimes a psychology program formally commits to developing these characteristics in the official student learning outcomes they incorporate into their courses; however, for the most part, the list refers to *metacognitive* (i.e., thinking about thinking) attributes that collectively set psychology majors apart from others in liberal education that we discussed in Chapter 4.

"You see, but you do not observe."
—*Sherlock Holmes (Sir Arthur Conan Doyle)*

Students regularly experience the necessity of being a careful observer when they are trying to make sense of behavior. They learn that effective observation is derived from careful definitions of behavior that make it easy to measure the behavior. Measurement is an essential feature of psychology that ensures observers are all observing the same thing and can track changes in behavior over time. Observers also learn to distinguish between merely describing behavior and attributing motives to behavior. Nearly all courses emphasize the importance of objective observation in making sense of behavior. **Psychological thinkers are observant.**

"In God we trust. All others bring data."

—W. Edwards Deming

Psychologists advocate making decisions based on empirical evidence. They tend to disavow personal testimony as a flawed source for cause–effect conclusions. When confronted with a claim about behavior, psychology majors learn to ask, "What's the evidence?" If the conclusions don't derive from well-controlled empirical research ("Was there a control group?"), the psychologist is likely to decline to get on board. Psychologists prefer to take the stance of being amiable skeptics; that is, they have a generally questioning attitude toward the conclusions that most other people take for granted. **Psychological thinkers are empirically oriented.**

"Research is formalized curiosity. It is poking and prying with a purpose."

—Zora Neale Huston

Many of our students describe a common phenomenon when they return home from college. At some point during their family reunions, someone is likely to ask, "Why do you have to *analyze* everything?" A good background in psychology provides a great foundation on which curiosity can thrive Psychologists deploy their curiosity in scientific investigation. They poke and pry with an eye toward thoroughly understanding behavior. **Psychological thinkers are curious.**

"Everything should be made as simple as possible, but not simpler."

—Albert Einstein

Before being educated in the ways of psychological thinking, people tend to be satisfied with simplistic explanations. For example, consider why new kindergartner "Kimmie" is so shy. A simplistic approach might suggest her shyness is genetic, that she inherited the condition from her very shy mother. However, a seasoned psychological thinker knows that such a simple answer is not adequate in explaining the complex origins of shyness. Psychological thinkers make the assumption that most behaviors usually have more than one cause ("What is Kimmie's home environment like?" "Do you see her only in situations that bring out her shyness, such as public gatherings?"). They challenge themselves to look for additional factors when others would be satisfied with a simple, shallow answer. **Psychological thinkers expect complexity.**

"Neurosis is the inability to tolerate ambiguity."

—Sigmund Freud

One of the cardinal characteristics of the psychological thinker is the capacity to tolerate ambiguity. No matter how sincere the curiosity, some phenomena will not yield to a satisfying explanation even under the best investigations. Psychologists strive to reduce ambiguity by developing well-controlled research designs but recognize that not all relevant factors may be controllable. Rather than feeling frustrated by absence of answers, psychological thinkers tend to enjoy pondering how much remains unknown and are excited to identify plausible causal factors. **Psychological thinkers tolerate ambiguity.**

"Concision in style, precision in thought, decision in life."

—*Victor Hugo*

The discipline of psychology is at its core a quantitative enterprise. Psychologists believe that a true exploration of behavior requires **precision** in description that lends itself to measurement that, in turn, lends itself to statistical analysis. Psychology majors, especially those who enjoy the research aspects of psychology, learn that there is nothing more thrilling than being able to verify your conclusions with a statistically significant result. Precision also characterizes high-quality psychology writing. **Psychological thinkers strive for precision.**

"The analysis of character is the highest human entertainment."

—*Isaac Bashevis Singer*

As long as there is behavior to observe, a psychological thinker is unlikely to be bored. For example, a grocery line becomes a great laboratory to see principles of reinforcement in action. A sales negotiation demonstrates principles of persuasion. The goods offered in a kitchen store manifest human creativity and problem solving. On the other hand, we think the opportunity for psychological thinkers to entertain themselves by careful observation has been diminished to some degree by the omnipresence of smartphones. Being drawn into the small screen substantially reduces the time that can be spent merely watching, analyzing, and appreciating the human condition. **Psychological thinkers are easily entertained.**

"When people talk, listen completely. Most people never listen."

—*Ernest Hemingway*

Psychological thinkers develop a deep appreciation for the richness of communication. They recognize why undivided attention is so hard for humans to sustain but grasp how empowering it can be. They know that meaning lies not just in what is said but in what goes unspoken. They pay attention to subtleties and nuances of speech and body language. **Psychological thinkers tend to be intentional communicators.**

"Empathy is about finding echoes of another person in yourself."

—*Mohsin Hamid*

Many experiences in the undergraduate psychology major help to develop empathy. Certain aspects of the formal curriculum (e.g., group projects, interviewing exercises) provide opportunities to see conditions from the perspective of another person. Basic counseling techniques (e.g., paraphrasing, questioning) give students the language and strategies with which to be empathic. Increased empathy reduces the human tendency to judge and to dismiss others' points of view. **Psychological thinkers are empathic and nonjudgmental.** For a meaningful example of someone whose writing career reflects the principle of finding commonalities with others, see *A Major Success Story: Transcending Tragedy.*

"It is time for parents to teach young people early on that in diversity there is beauty and there is strength."

—*Maya Angelou*

One way that the discipline of psychology has dramatically changed is in its capacity to acknowledge and encourage the value of diversity. When the discipline began, it was clearly the enterprise of privileged white men. Things slowly started to change, beginning with the ascension of Mary Whiton Calkins, a brilliant female student denied entrance to Harvard in 1890 because of the school's policy of excluding women from enrolling. Although Calkins was not able to be a registered student at Harvard, she was allowed to study there under William James and soon became his favorite student (Furumoto, 1980). Calkins not only survived her Harvard snubbing but went on to be president of both

A **Major** Success Story

Transcending Tragedy

Barbara Delinsky, who holds a BA in psychology, is no stranger to tragedy. At age 8, she lost her mother to breast cancer. She courageously faced her own midlife breast cancer diagnosis, but survived surgery and treatment to write a nonfiction account of her experience. *Uplift: Secrets from the Sisterhood of Breast Cancer Survivors* summarizes practical ideas and stories of resilience from survivors and their support network. All profit from her work goes into a fund to support a research fellowship at Massachusetts General Hospital. In addition to *Uplift*, she has published more than 20 novels under her own name and under various pseudonyms. Her books have appeared on the *New York Times* bestseller list more than a dozen times.

Barbara didn't start out with any inkling that she would be not just a popular but an award-winning writer. In her blog, she recounts the story of being kicked out of Honors English in high school for failing to meet her writing deadlines. She says that she became inspired to write by reading about three famous women writers and simply set her mind to emulating their success. After 3 months of effort, she sold her first book. She established success in the romance genre, then her writing deepened into more complex treatments of marriage, parenthood, and friendship, capturing the emotional crises in our lives. She says, "Readers identify with my characters. They know them. They *are* them. I'm an everyday woman writing about everyday people facing not-so-everyday challenges." She attributes her success to her work ethic, typically putting in an 11-hour workday in the office over her garage.

Along the way, Barbara served as a researcher with the Massachusetts Society for the Prevention of Cruelty to Children and as a photographer and reporter for the *Belmont Herald*. How might her major have helped with her career?

Information from: http://barbaradelinsky.com/biography/biography.

the American Psychological Association (APA) and the American Philosophical Association (APS).

The field has changed with regard to race as well. In *Even the Rat Was White* (2003), a compelling look at the history of the field of psychology, Robert Guthrie identified the struggles that African American psychologists went through in the early years of the discipline. Over time, psychologists recognized the narrowness of their traditions and developed formal mechanisms to broaden and deepen their views, expanding the range of what is studied in the discipline. **Psychological thinkers are enthusiastic about diversity.**

"Service to others is the rent you pay for your room here on earth."
—*Muhammad Ali*

One of the main purposes of psychology has always been to solve problems, whether they be the intense intra- and interpersonal difficulties that are in the realm of clinical psychology or the practical applications that involve research psychology. Researchers address all manner of issues, from combating obesity to increasing awareness about the environment to reducing bullying on the playground. At its core, psychology is a helping profession. **Psychological thinkers are service oriented.**

"Life is a long lesson in humility."
—*James M. Barrie*

When Jane took her introductory psychology course, she experienced a critical moment when the lecturer described defense mechanisms. It was startling to recognize that humans actively distort their thinking to protect themselves. It was even more startling to recognize that she also engaged in such distortions. The idea of defense mechanisms explained a great deal, particularly how two people can be in the same space but not share the same reality. As cognitive research has flourished, we have a better understanding of how human judgment and decision making can produce the wrong conclusions. If we genuinely grasp the variety of ways that humans (including ourselves!) can make missteps, then it follows that we should exercise greater caution when in conflict and resist the impulse to need to be right. This humility should allow psychological thinkers to be open about other possibilities. **Psychological thinkers are tentative in their conclusions.**

The list of attributes we have explored in connection with learning to think like a psychologist is not exhaustive, but includes some of the key differences that tend to set psychological thinkers apart from others. We recognize this discussion presents the psychological thinker as an idealized form. Those trained in a psychological perspective lose their tempers, say things they regret, jump to conclusions, and demonstrate the myriad other human characteristics that complicate matters. But psychological thinkers have less fettered access to the tools that can help them build a peaceful, constructive, and creative life. See *Reality Check: How Am I Doing So Far?* to determine your own progress in developing a psychological worldview.

✔ **Reality Check**

How Am I Doing So Far?

Throughout the text we have identified the ways that people who have been trained to think like psychologists differ from those who have not. Time to take an inventory of those skills to see how far you've come and how far you have to go. See if you can describe a personal example of demonstrating each of the attributes discussed in this chapter.

Attribute	Personal example
Observant	
Empirically oriented	
Curious	
Expecting complexity	
Tolerant of ambiguity	
Precise	
Intentional in communication	
Easily entertained	
Empathic	
Nonjudgmental	
Enthusiastic about diversity	
Service oriented	

KEEPING PSYCHOLOGY ALIVE

Undergraduates who make a successful transition into a psychology graduate program will be immersed in the discipline in ways that they might not have been able to anticipate. In contrast, undergraduates who terminate their education after they receive a bachelor's or associate's degree may find themselves pining for the excitement of studying psychology. In this section, we explore some strategies for staying connected to the psychological community after graduation.

Psi Chi and Psi Beta

As described in Chapter 6, the international honor society **Psi Chi** provides a way to maintain intellectual ties to psychology. Psi Chi's mission is to help keep people engaged in and committed to psychology. By performing well as an undergraduate, you can be nominated by your faculty for induction into Psi Chi. Being part of Psi Chi has some career advantages, as its members are those who have shown great potential within the discipline. All members, whether they go on to graduate school or not, can stay abreast of national trends and interesting ideas through the communications Psi Chi sends out, and many people remain part of Psi Chi for the rest of their lives.

A similar honor society exists for the community college level called **Psi Beta**, which recognizes exemplary academic performance and encourages psychology-related service to the community.

Professional Organizations

You don't have to be a member of psychology's most prominent professional organizations to take advantage of the stimulation they offer. Both the APA and the APS have public portals on their websites where they share important new findings and developments in the professional psychology community.

Part of the APA's website is specifically designed for students (http://www .apa.org/about/students.aspx). The pages feature specific advice on applying to graduate school, on securing funding for research, and on writing and doing research. Student members receive copies of the organization's journal (*American Psychologist*) and magazine (*The Monitor on Psychology*). Undergraduates can join the American Psychology Association of Graduate Students (APAGS) for a nominal fee. Student affiliates also have access to the events the APA holds at its national convention that are specifically tailored to students.

The APS, which tends to focus primarily on the psychological research community, also maintains a division to strengthen students' interest (http://www .psychologicalscience.org/index.php/members/apssc/welcome-to-the-apssc). The APS Student Caucus manages student research competitions; has mentoring programs that match undergraduate students with graduate mentors; encourages leadership development through the campus representative program; and offers opportunities to publish work in the "Student Notebook" column of the *APS Observer* magazine and in the online publication "Undergraduate Update."

Specialized professional psychology groups offer incentives to students to become and stay involved in their organizations. By being welcoming to students, the organizations are able to recruit them to be members and leaders in the future, which helps keep the groups vibrant and full. For example, both Jane and Dana are partial to the organization called the Society for the Teaching of Psychology (STP; see http://teachpsych.org/) because its work has the most direct bearing on the way they both earn a living in psychology. There is a formal subdivision for graduate students but undergraduates can also join to take advantage of the teaching-related resources STP offers. Membership is especially useful for new graduate students who are about to begin to teach.

Cinema

Susan Whitbourne (2012) has argued that the Academy Awards tend to be heavily biased toward subject matter that depicts psychological themes. She says, "Audiences are fascinated by heartless murderers, tragic heroes or heroines wrestling with psychological demons, couples who tear each other apart, and families that make their home life a constant nightmare" and concludes that Hollywood's preoccupation with psychological dynamics keeps the audience "glued to the screen" (p. 1).

To promote the connection between psychology and cinema, we provide a list in **Table 12.1** of our favorite psychology-oriented movies that are guaranteed to spark lively conversation. We offer one caveat: Not all Hollywood movies

---

TABLE 12.1

Recommended Films for Sparking Psychological Conversations

A Beautiful Mind (2001): A flawed but engaging treatment of a troubled mathematician. (135 min.)

A Clockwork Orange (1971): A futuristic tale of aversion therapy. (136 min.)

As Good As It Gets (1997): A film about friendship and compulsive disorder. (139 min.)

Awakenings (1990): Encephalitis sufferers get sudden but temporary relief from a new drug. (121 min.)

Black Swan (2010): A ballet dancer breaks down during her role in *Swan Lake*. (108 min.)

Born on the Fourth of July (1989): Ron Kovic becomes a political activist after being disabled in the Vietnam war. (145 min.)

David and Lisa (1962): Sweet romance between two people with mental impairments. (93 min.)

The Deer Hunter (1978): Vietnam veterans try to adjust to postwar life in a small town in Pennsylvania. (182 min).

Fatal Attraction (1987): A married man's one-night stand comes back to haunt him. (119 min.)

Fearless (1993): Personality change in the aftermath of a major airline crash. (122 min.)

Girl, Interrupted (1999): A young woman spends 18 months in a 1960s mental hospital. (127 min.)

Good Will Hunting (1997): A math genius seeks help from a psychologist. (126 min.)

The King's Speech (2010): Stuttering troubles the ascent of a British monarch to the throne. (118 min.)

Kinky Boots (2005): Drag queens, business practices, and friendship intertwine in this story about British boot manufacturing. (106 min.)

Little Miss Sunshine (2006): A funky family reveals wild dynamics as they help the youngest achieve her dream of competing in a beauty pageant. (101 min.)

The Lost Weekend (1945): A chronic alcoholic engages in a 4-day drinking binge. (101 min.)

The Manhunter (1986): An FBI specialist tracks a serial killer. (119 min.)

Memento (2000): Short-term memory loss troubles a man trying to solve a murder. (113 min.)

My Left Foot (1989): A man with cerebral palsy learns to paint with his left foot. (103 min.)

One Flew Over the Cuckoo's Nest (1975): A con man tries to exploit the mental health system and runs into surprising obstacles, including an oppressive nurse. (133 min.)

Ordinary People (1980): Robert Redford's film about a family's attempt to cope with the death of a teenager in the family. (124 min.)

The Perks of Being a Wallflower (2012): An exploration about the challenge of adolescent self-acceptance. (102 min.)

Continued

Platoon (1986): The Vietnam war produces violence and moral crisis. (120 min.)

Rain Man (1988): Two brothers connect despite autism and narcissism. (145 min.)

Requiem for a Dream (2000): Profiles of four New Yorkers struggling with addiction. (102 min.)

The Sessions (2012): Interactions between a sex therapist and her client, a man in an iron lung. (95 min.)

The Silence of the Lambs (1992): A young FBI cadet collaborates with an incarcerated, manipulative killer to catch another serial killer. (118 min.)

Silver Linings Playbook (2012): Two troubled people connect through dancing. (122 min.)

The Snake Pit (1948): A mid-twentieth-century portrayal of inpatient mental health care. (108 min.)

Taxi Driver (1976): A mentally unstable taxi-driving Vietnam veteran attempts to save a preadolescent prostitute. (113 min.)

The Theory of Everything (2014): The life story of Stephen Hawking, the brilliant physicist who has the neurodegenerative disease ALS. (123 min.)

Three Faces of Eve (1957): An abusive childhood fractures a young woman's personality. (91 min.)

Twelve Angry Men (1957): A definitive look at small-group dynamics in the context of a court case. (96 min.)

Vertigo (1958): A Hitchcock film about obsession and acrophobia. (128 min.)

What About Bob? (1991): A wildly disturbed patient upends his therapist's family dynamics. (99 min.)

A Woman Under the Influence (1974): Cassavetes showcases the story of the impact of schizophrenia on family dynamics. (155 min.)

---

accurately portray what we know from psychological science about human behavior. For example, the compelling film *A Beautiful Mind* misrepresents the mathematician John Nash's schizophrenia; people with schizophrenia tend to have auditory hallucinations rather than the visual hallucinations portrayed in the film. Creative license made for a compelling story, if not an accurate depiction, of the symptoms of schizophrenia. Psychological thinkers simply include the conceptual errors in the psychological content of films to the list of elements they analyze when they watch movies. (For further suggestions of psychology-focused films, see Niemiec & Wedding, 2014; Wedding & Niemiec, 2010.)

Web Crawling

So many treasures exist in cyberspace that it is relatively easy to get lost in the exploration of good psychology resources. You are likely to find an array of interesting choices to explore when you pose any question to a search engine. Some of our favorite recent finds include the following:

■ Why do so few men major in psychology?
http://www.apa.org/gradpsych/2011/01/cover-men.aspx

■ Are there too many psychology majors?
http://www.cogdop.org/page_attachments/0000/0200/FLA_White_Paper_for_cogop_posting.pdf

- What are the highest-paying jobs a person can get with a degree in psychology?
  http://www.businessinsider.com/the-5-highest-paying-jobs-you-can-get-with-a-psychology-degree-2011-9
- What is a psychology degree worth?
  https://www.psychologytoday.com/blog/head-the-class

Several organizations continually update their websites with interesting information. For example, *Psychology Today* includes new writings from a number of experts on its blog (http://www.psychologytoday.com/). The website has topic streams (e.g., obesity, creativity, resilience) that are drawn from its archives and can serve as a stimulus for thinking about potential research topics. (Remember that most professors don't consider references from *Psychology Today* to be good primary sources; however, the readability of the magazine can help unlock creativity about what new directions could emerge from the research it reports on.)

Another helpful site, the Social Psychology Network (http://www.socialpsychology.org/blogs.htm), operated by Scott Plous of Wesleyan University, includes links to more than 150 blogs, podcasts, and RSS feeds that feature some of the most important psychologists conducting research today. The site is organized to highlight resources in general psychology and neuroscience; politics and public policy; judgment and decision making; happiness, fulfillment, and life meaning; interpersonal relationships; and teaching and education, among others.

TED (Technology, Entertainment, and Design) Talks have also done a great job of making psychology more accessible to the public. Included among the psychology superstars of the TED talks (http://www.spring.org.uk/2014/02/superstars-of-psychology-10-best-short-talks.php) are the following:

- Philip Zimbardo: "The Psychology of Evil"
- Barry Schwartz: "The Paradox of Choice"
- Alison Gopnick: "What Do Babies Think?"
- Steven Pinker: "Human Nature and the Blank Slate"
- Mihaly Csikszentmihalyi: "Flow, the Secret to Happiness"
- Elizabeth Loftus: "The Fiction of Memory"

A comprehensive list of psychology TED talks can be found at http://www.ted.com/watch/topics/psychology.

Kindred Spirits

Jane likes to claim that good psychology majors can often finish each other's sentences. So, it is great fun to meet new people who have studied psychology because the shared interest in human behavior accelerates bonding. With a conservative estimate of 1 million students taking psychology courses every year (Munsey, 2008), the potential for finding common ground with new college-educated acquaintances is pretty high.

Although only a few psychologists have reached a level of public recognition that they could be considered famous, many famous people have majored in psychology. See **Table 12.2** for a list of recognizable names of people who share your interest in behavior and either started or completed an undergraduate degree in psychology (Halonen, 2011).

TABLE 12.2

Notable People Who Either Started or Finished a Bachelor's Degree in Psychology

Actors

Katherine Hepburn (*Lion in Winter*, *The Philadelphia Story*)

Natalie Portman (*Black Swan*, *Star Wars*)

Brooke Shields (*Suddenly Susan*, *Pretty Baby*)

Selma Blair (*Hellboy*, *Legally Blond*)

Barbara Bach (*The Spy Who Loved Me*)

Marcia Cross (*Desperate Housewives*)

Harry Hamlin (*L.A. Law*, *Madmen*)

John Ritter (*Three's Company*)

Jonathan Frakes (*Star Trek: The Next Generation*)

Claire Danes (*Stardust*, *Homeland*)

Lisa Kudrow (*Friends*, *Web Therapy*)

Ben Browder (*Farscape*, *Stargate*)

Colin Firth (*The King's Speech*, *Bridget Jones's Diary*)

Entertainers

Ted Allen, playwright and wine specialist (*Queer Eye for the Straight Guy*, *Chopped*)

Dana Bourne, science programmer at WGBH

Jerry Bruckheimer, producer (*Pirates of the Caribbean*)

Wes Craven, writer and director (*Nightmare on Elm Street*)

Gloria Estefan, performer and songwriter

Penney Finkelman Cox, producer (*Snakes on a Plane*, *Terms of Endearment*)

Doug Henning and The Amazing Kreskin, magicians

Al Jarreau, jazz singer

Lil Wayne, hip-hop artist

Phil McGraw, media psychologist

Jon Stewart, producer and late-night satirist

J. Michael Straczynski, producer and creator (*Babylon 5*)

Yanni Chryssomallis, New Age musician

Artists

Annie Truitt, minimalist artist

Elyn Zimmerman, landscape artist and sculptor

Athletes

Herb Brooks, Olympic hockey coach

Gina Carana, mixed martial artist

Natalie Coughlin, Olympic swimmer

Tim Duncan, NBA player

Mia Hamm, soccer star

Wendy Norris, NASCAR pit reporter

Doctor

Benjamin Carson, pediatric neurosurgeon and presidential candidate

Educators

Norman B. Anderson, CEO, American Psychological Association

Sissela Bok, ethicist

Continued

Alan Leshner, CEO, American Association for the Advancement of Science

Judith Rodin, director, Rockefeller Foundation, and former president, University of Pennsylvania

Peter Salovey, president, Yale University

Beverly Daniel Tatum, president, Spelman College

Entrepreneurs

Gary Bridge, senior vice president, CISCO Systems

Peter Butterfield, president and CEO, KIA Motors America

Richard Chaifetz, founder and CEO, Compsych Corp Employee Assistance Programs

Tom Dillon, manager of rail operations, Ringling Bros. and Barnum & Bailey

Jamie Dimon, CEO, JPMorgan Chase

Hugh Hefner, *Playboy* founder and publisher

Mark Zuckerberg, Facebook creator and founder

Guy Kawasaki, Apple promoter

Jim McCann, founder, 1-800-Flowers

Irene Rosenfeld, Kraft Foods executive

Politicians

Ken Blackwell, diplomat

Tipper Gore, Second Lady

Marlene Jenning, Canadian politician

Ted Strickland, former governor of Ohio

Hendrik Frensch Verwoerd, prime minister of South Africa

Vaira Vīķe-Freiberga, president of Latvia

Pilot

Chesley "Sully" Sullenberger

Writers

Barbara Delinksy, mystery writer

Abbie Hoffman, political activist (Steal This Book)

Jonathan Kellerman, mystery writer

Henry K. Lee, novelist (The Missing Wife)

John Most, poet

Carol Tavris, pseudoscience debunker

Robert Anton Wilson, novelist

Although not all of the following people were psychology majors, each carved out a special place in history by winning the Nobel Prize for their work on psychological phenomena.

- Ivan Pavlov (1904): Nobel Prize in Physiology or Medicine for his pioneering work in understanding the physiology of digestion

- Herbert A. Simon (1978): Nobel Prize in Economic Sciences for applying economic principles to the decision processes that affect the dynamics of organizations

- Roger Sperry (1981): Nobel Prize in Physiology or Medicine for his work in establishing the functional specializations of different parts of the brain

- Daniel Kahneman (2002): Nobel Prize in Economic Sciences for carefully differentiating rational and irrational processes that influence decision making

- John O'Keefe, May-Britt Moser, and Edvard I. Moser (2014): Nobel Prize in Physiology or Medicine for discovering cells that provide positioning feedback in the brain

Psychology also has many National Medal of Science Laureates. These include the following psychologists along with the major areas of their contributions:

- Neal Elgar Miller (1964) for learning and motivation
- Harry Harlow (1967) for comparative and experimental psychology
- B. F. Skinner (1968) for broad impact on understanding human behavior
- Herbert Simon (1986) for decision-making and problem-solving
- Anne Anastasi (1987) for individual differences and testing
- George A. Miller (1991) for language and cognition
- Eleanor J. Gibson (1992) for perceptual development in childhood
- Roger N. Shepard (1995) for visual spatial perception
- William K. Estes (1997) for learning and memory
- Duncan Luce (2003) for mathematical behavioral models
- Gordon H. Bower (2005) for cognitive psychology
- Michael I. Posner (2008) for neuroscience and brain function
- Mortimer Mishkin (2009) for memory and perceptual processes
- Anne Treisman (2011) for perception and attention
- Albert Bandura (2015) for social cognitive theory

The Alumni Opportunity

Just because you graduate, it doesn't mean that your connection to your undergraduate major is over. Most psychology departments welcome attention from their graduates, and faculty particularly like to know what directions their students' lives have taken. Many departments sponsor an active psychology alumni network. These organizations serve multiple functions because alumni can:

- be outstanding mentors to undergraduate students. Some departments recognize that external mentors can provide additional support for students who are trying to find their way.
- make great "career night" speakers. When students don't have much notion about what the future holds, it helps to hear someone talk about finding a meaningful psychology-related focus.
- provide introductions to other professionals working in areas that undergraduates think might be their calling.
- designate the psychology department to be the beneficiary of their donations. Most universities allow donors to stipulate how their contributions can be used. Creating an endowment for the best student poster or contributing to student travel funds are great ways to pay back on the investment the department made in you.
- galvanize activity across classes for special events, such as celebrating the retirement of a particularly beloved faculty member.

STAYING A FAN OF PSYCHOLOGY

Falling in love with psychology was one of the most satisfying experiences of our lives. We were lucky that the course of our lives facilitated this choice. If we had to do it over, we'd do it again with big smiles. We envy those who are just starting out on the adventure and hope that the *Companion* has provided some insight and guidance that will allow you to fall and stay in love with psychology, too.

THOUGHT QUESTIONS

1. What kinds of attributes tend to characterize the psychological thinker?
2. How can professional organizations support a life-long interest in psychology?
3. What are your favorite movies with psychological themes?
4. How can you use the Internet to stay current with trends in psychology?
5. Who are some famous psychology majors?
6. In what ways can you continue to support your undergraduate program after you graduate?

Appendix A

This appendix contains a sample APA-style student paper. We have included it to illustrate the general characteristics of a solid experimental first effort by a student.

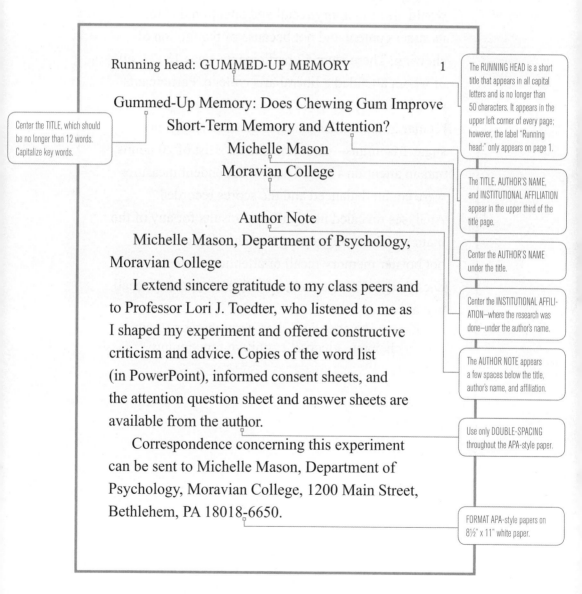

Running head: GUMMED-UP MEMORY   1

Gummed-Up Memory: Does Chewing Gum Improve
Short-Term Memory and Attention?

Michelle Mason

Moravian College

Author Note

Michelle Mason, Department of Psychology, Moravian College

I extend sincere gratitude to my class peers and to Professor Lori J. Toedter, who listened to me as I shaped my experiment and offered constructive criticism and advice. Copies of the word list (in PowerPoint), informed consent sheets, and the attention question sheet and answer sheets are available from the author.

Correspondence concerning this experiment can be sent to Michelle Mason, Department of Psychology, Moravian College, 1200 Main Street, Bethlehem, PA 18018-6650.

The RUNNING HEAD is a short title that appears in all capital letters and is no longer than 50 characters. It appears in the upper left corner of every page; however, the label "Running head:" only appears on page 1.

The TITLE, AUTHOR'S NAME, and INSTITUTIONAL AFFILIATION appear in the upper third of the title page.

Center the AUTHOR'S NAME under the title.

Center the INSTITUTIONAL AFFILIATION—where the research was done—under the author's name.

The AUTHOR NOTE appears a few spaces below the title, author's name, and affiliation.

Use only DOUBLE-SPACING throughout the APA-style paper.

FORMAT APA-style papers on 8½" x 11" white paper.

Center the TITLE, which should be no longer than 12 words. Capitalize key words.

Abstract

Experiments regarding chewing gum's ability to aid or hinder cognitive function have yielded inconsistent results. I hypothesized that flavored chewing gum would assist memory recall and attention due to its sugar content and not because of the motion of chewing. There were 47 participants, ages 18–24, all of whom attended a liberal arts college. Participants were randomly assigned to one of four groups— regular gum, regular mints, sugar-free candy, or sugar-free mints—and were shown a list of 20 nouns and an attention video. The two dependent measures were counterbalanced and the scores recorded. Analyses revealed no significant results for any of the main variables, suggesting that chewing gum does not bolster memory recall or attention scores, nor does the gum's sugar content influence memory recall and attention.

Keywords: attention, short-term memory, gum chewing, glucose, cognitive functioning

The ABSTRACT always appears on page 2. It is labeled with a centered heading.

The ABSTRACT PARAGRAPH is not indented and, for an empirical study, is no more than 120 words in length.

The MARGINS on all sides of all pages are no more than 1 inch wide.

Use LEFT-JUSTIFICATION throughout the paper.

Center KEYWORDS under the Abstract paragraph.

GUMMED-UP MEMORY   3

Gummed-Up Memory: Does Chewing Gum Improve
Short-Term Memory and Attention?

Chewing gum was the first human-made candy—
prehistoric men and women chewed on tree resins and
saps. Every succeeding civilization has shown evidence
of gum chewing. The average American citizen chews
182 pieces of gum per year and the United States
produces 1,000 different varieties of gum (International
Chewing Gum Association, 2005), making gum
production a $3.3 billion industry in America
(Euromonitor International, 2011). Chewing gum's
popularity may be attributed to its increasing association
with benefits such as tooth whitening, breath freshening,
being a source of vitamins, and as a smoking-cessation
or weight-loss aid (International Chewing Gum
Association, 2005). Recent debate focuses on chewing
gum's potential cognitive health benefits.

The topic of chewing gum's effect on cognitive
ability has been highly controversial. Research has
shown inconsistent results; some studies find beneficial
effects while others find adverse effects (Tucha & Koerts,
2012). Studies that found that gum chewing improved
cognitive function also concluded that it impaired
attention (Tucha, Mecklinger, Maeir, Hammerl, &
Lange, 2004). Other studies contest these claims, perhaps
because they use different operational definitions of
attention and diverse scales of measurement, making the
findings extremely difficult to compare.

> The INTRODUCTION appears on page 3.

> Repeat and center the MANUSCRIPT'S TITLE above the opening paragraph of the introduction. Capitalize the title's main or key words. Do not set the title bold.

> PARENTHETICAL CITATIONS use an ampersand (&) instead of "and" but citations appearing outside parentheses use "and" between author names.

Studies that find that chewing gum has a positive effect on cognitive function disagree about whether initial learning affects cognitive functions. Baker, Bezance, Zellaby, and Aggleton (2004) concluded that gum chewing has context-dependent effects on memory. If a person chews gum when initially learning a concept, then they test better if they are also chewing gum when asked to recall information. If they are learning a concept when they are not chewing gum, however, their recall is disrupted by gum chewing. In contrast, Miles and Johnson (2007) concluded that no such context-dependent relationship exists.

Baker et al. (2004) used a sample of 83 undergraduates, ages 18 to 46. Participants were given a written list and 2 minutes to study the list. They were later tested after a 2-minute and a 24-hour delay. Participants either had gum or no gum during both recall and learning, or gum-no gum and no gum-gum for learning and recall. The authors of the study concluded that chewing gum had a context-dependent component, due to differing recall scores, and improved cognitive function.

Subsequently, Miles and Johnson (2007) tried to replicate the experiment. However, they used a smaller sample of only 24 undergraduates, ages 18 to 21. They did not give out the word list but displayed it visually at 5-second intervals. They also ensured that people in the gum-gum conditions

CITE ALL AUTHORS (up to six) the first time their work is used.

After the first citation, CITE THREE OR MORE AUTHORS using "et al."

replaced their gum to ensure that the context of chewing gum (consistency, texture, and flavor) was the same. Their experiment showed that there were no context-dependent effects nor was gum chewing responsible for better cognitive function. The main difference in the studies concerned sample size, and in larger samples, even relatively small differences can be found to reach statistical significance.

A second difference was that Baker et al. presented an actual written list of words, thereby allowing participants to choose which words they wanted to study and recall. Miles and Johnson used an evenly paced, single exposure to each word.

Stephens and Tunney (2004) tested whether glucose availability causes beneficial cognitive effects. However, their procedure had some confounding variables. They used regular drinking water and compared it to glucose-enriched (25 g) water as two independent variables for glucose consumption. From these two variables, they concluded that glucose increased cognitive function, such as memory recall and spatial skills. However, their gum-chewing component was confounded. They used a sugar-free gum and a sugared candy to compare the cognitive effects of chewing gum; this confounds the impact on cognition both of sugar content and of chewing versus a sucking motion. Effectively, they proposed a reasonable theory but failed to properly test it.

GUMMED-UP MEMORY   6

In an attempt to disambiguate chewing gum's effect on memory, I designed a study with an independent variable comprised of four potential mental facilitators: Stride spearmint chewing gum, Stride sugar-free spearmint gum, generic mint Life Savers, and sugar-free mint Life Savers. These conditions account for the effect of sugar content on cognitive functioning as well as the unique properties of chewing gum (i.e., the chewing motion). There were two dependent variables. The first tested memory, defined as the number of words correctly recalled from a 20-item list; and the second tested attention, which was defined as the number of questions correctly answered concerning the content of a YouTube video.

Based upon Stephens and Tunney's theory (2004) that glucose availability causes beneficial cognitive effects, I hypothesized that both the regular Stride chewing gum and the regular mint Life Savers would improve cognitive function due to their sugar content, meaning memory recall and attention improvement are not unique properties of chewing gum and the chewing motion. Participants in the regular mint Life Saver condition may show more improved cognitive function than those in the regular Stride spearmint gum condition due to the elevated sugar content.

APA style supports writing in the first person (ACTIVE VOICE) instead of third person (PASSIVE VOICE). "I designed" is better than "A study was designed."

Present the HYPOTHESIS clearly prior to the Method section.

Method

FIRST-LEVEL HEADINGS appear in boldface.

Participants

Write the METHOD SECTION in the past tense.

Forty-seven (20 men, 27 women) Moravian College students, aged 18 to 24 ($M = 19.85$), participated and most received extra credit in one of their psychology courses. Recruitment was done through the use of flyers in the psychology building. All participants were volunteers who signed up to participate in the experiment. Informed consent was a prerequisite for participation. Participants were assigned to four different groups: the regular Stride spearmint gum group ($n = 12$), the sugar-free Stride spearmint gum group ($n = 14$), the regular mint Life Savers group ($n = 10$) and the sugar-free mint Life Savers group ($n = 11$). All were treated in accordance with the American Psychological Association's Ethical Principles of Psychologists and Code of Conduct.

SECOND-LEVEL HEADINGS appear at the left margin and in boldface.

Italicize STATISTICAL SYMBOLS.

PARTICIPANT INFORMATION includes number, gender, race, age, selection procedure, and any reason for participation.

Use Arabic numerals to represent NUMBERS OF 10 OR MORE.

Materials

The same word list of 20 nouns was presented via PowerPoint to all experimental groups. Each participant was later given a pen and paper to write down recalled items. Each participant received either regular Stride spearmint gum (2 g sugar), sugar-free Stride spearmint gum (0 g sugar), generic mint Life Saver candy (3 g sugar), or sugar-free mint Life Saver candy (0 g sugar). The Rémi Gaillard football video (2007; 3 min 22 sec in length) can

The MATERIAL SUBSECTION describes the nature and purpose of the materials used in the study.

Abbreviate STANDARD UNITS OF MEASUREMENT.

be found on YouTube at http://www.youtube.com/
watch?v=SFsHPFhtEYQ. The question-and-answer
sheets for the Rémi Gaillard video, which functions as
the measure of attention, were also used.

Procedure

Participants were immediately given informed
consent paperwork and reminded that anyone with
diabetes, extensive dental work (e.g., crowns, braces),
or an allergy to gum or mint could not participate.
Participants were then randomly assigned to one of the
four experimental conditions. All papers and surveys
used during the experiment were placed in the coded
envelope and returned at the end of the experiment.

Participants were instructed to chew their gum
or suck their candy. A list of 20 nouns was presented
via PowerPoint at 5-second intervals. Each noun
appeared on a separate slide. After watching the
complete presentation, participants were instructed to
write down all the words that they could recall within
a 2-minute time frame. Papers of recalled words were
collected for scoring. Each word accurately recalled
scored 1 point. Any forgotten or falsely recollected
word received no score (and no penalty).

After being instructed to use a new candy/
piece of gun, participants then watched the Rémi
Gaillard video, which functioned as the attention
component of the study. Participants were given

12 multiple-choice questions regarding the video they watched and the papers were scored in the same manner as the word recall list. To control for any ordering effects, word-recall testing and attention testing was counterbalanced during different sessions of experimentation. The experiment lasted approximately 30 minutes. Participants were debriefed as soon as the data were collected.

Results

Did the sugar in the gum or candy influence recall and attention scores? A 2 (chewing gum vs. sucking a mint) x 2 (sugar vs. sugar-free candy) analysis of variance (ANOVA) revealed no significant difference between gum chewing and candy sucking (F [1, 46] = .250) and no significant differences were detected between the sugar-free and sugared candy (F [1, 46] = 2.755) conditions for memory recall (see Figure 1) and attention to detail (see Figure 2). No interaction was found between the two variables (F [1, 46] = .173), either. One of the factors, mints versus gum, approached a marginal level of significance (p = .104).

In an exploratory analysis of falsely recalled words, the factor of gum versus candy was significant, with gum groups experiencing more false recall (M = .88) than mint groups (M = .33; see Figure 3). However, post hoc testing yielded an

Sections of the APA-style paper appear with NO PAGE BREAKS in between.

Write the RESULTS section in the past tense.

Define ABBREVIATIONS the first time they appear.

Accompany STATISTICAL RESULTS with a verbal description of the findings.

eta-squared of .119, indicating that only 12% of false recall was accounted for by use of gum versus mint candies. The number of correct words recalled and falsely recalled words was negatively correlated at $-.429$ ($p < .01$), meaning fewer false recalls occurred when more correct recalls were made. Self-reported memory ratings had a .244 correlation, a trend at the .10 level. However, no significant correlations were observed between self-reported memory ratings and false recall. Gender, age, and familiarity with the sport in the video had no significant effect on word recall or attention scores.

Discussion

The results fail to support my hypothesis that consumption of regular chewing gum and regular candy during memory tasks improves memory because of the persistent availability of sugar to the brain, contradicting the findings of Stephens and Tunney (2004). Due to the nonsignificant results on memory recall and attention to detail, it appears that chewing gum neither hinders nor abets memory recall or attention, and any differences in score do not result from chewing versus sucking movements, which had been unaccounted for by Stephens and Tunney.

A possible confound was that five participants forgot to wear glasses, rendering their scores on both dependent measures suspect. Of the five participants,

Write the DISCUSSION section largely in the present tense.

DISCUSSION SECTIONS highlight what the findings do and do not reveal.

Note an EXPERIMENT'S LIMITATIONS in the Discussion.

three were in the experimental regular sugared
gum group. In the case of the gum versus candy
comparison, which was close to marginal significance,
it could be argued that a larger sample size could
have led to significant results. Thus, replication of
this experiment may yield more conclusive results
regarding the main effect. However, gum versus
mint candy influences the amount of false recalls that
occur (with candy groups having fewer false recalls).
This could indicate that the chewing versus sucking
mechanism may negatively impact attention and the
motivation to correctly recall words.

    In order to address the issue of falsely recalled
words in future studies, I would add a confidence
interval to the word recall list. A possible explanation
for falsely recalled words is illustrated by the
negative correlation between word recall and falsely
recalled words. Subjects who recalled more words
were less likely to falsely recall words. Therefore,
it is possible that subjects who could not remember
words were willing to just make up words to write
down. Motivation may be a confounding factor
concerning whether words are remembered correctly
and future studies may need to address the motivation
of the participants to actually perform well on the
experimental tasks.

> Present directions for possible future research in the DISCUSSION.

GUMMED-UP MEMORY   12

References

Baker, J. R., Bezance, J. B., Zellaby, E., & Aggleton, J. P. (2004). Chewing gum can produce context-dependent effects upon memory. *Appetite, 43,* 207–210.

Euromonitor International. (2011). *Gum in the US* [Data file]. Retrieved from http://www.euromonitor.com/gum-in-the-us/report

International Chewing Gum Association. (2005). *Fun facts about gum* [Data file]. Retrieved from http://www.gumassociation.org/default.aspx?Cat=4

Miles, C., & Johnson, A. J. (2007). Chewing gum and context-dependent memory effects: A re-examination. *Appetite, 48,* 154.

Stephens, R., & Tunney, R. (2004). Role of glucose in chewing gum-related facilitation of cognitive function. *Appetite, 43,* 211–213.

Tucha, L., & Koerts, J. (2012). Gum chewing and cognition: An overview. *Neuroscience and Medicine, 3,* 243–250.

Tucha, O., Mecklinger, L., Maeir, K., Hammerl, M., & Lange, K. (2004). Chewing gum differentially affects aspects of attention in healthy subjects. *Appetite, 42,* 327–329

Begin the REFERENCE SECTION on a new page.

Use a hanging indent format and double-space APA-STYLE REFERENCES.

APA-STYLE REFERENCES appear in alphabetical order.

Capitalize only the first word in title and subtitle sections of journal articles and books, as well as any proper nouns.

Italicize journal names, book titles, and volume numbers.

Capitalize each word in JOURNAL TITLES with the exception of articles (e.g., the, and) and prepositions (e.g., of) that are shorter than four letters.

Use an ampersand (&) in lieu of "and" for MULTIPLE-AUTHORS REFERENCES.

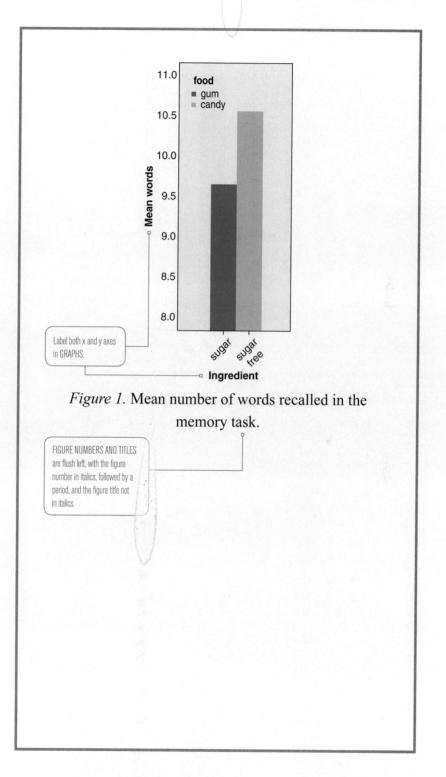

Figure 1. Mean number of words recalled in the memory task.

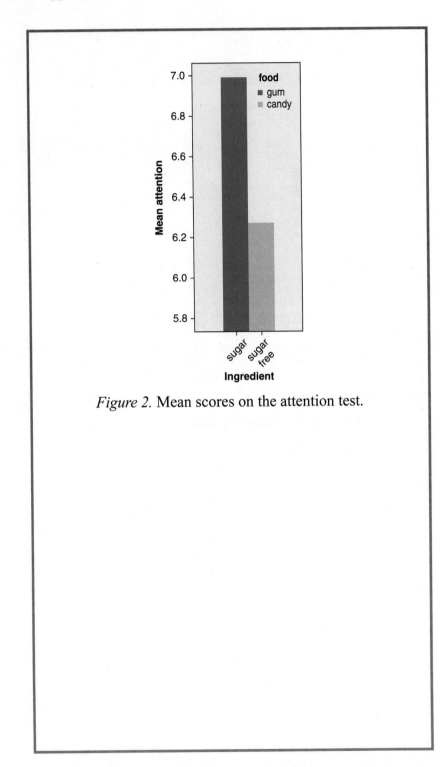

Figure 2. Mean scores on the attention test.

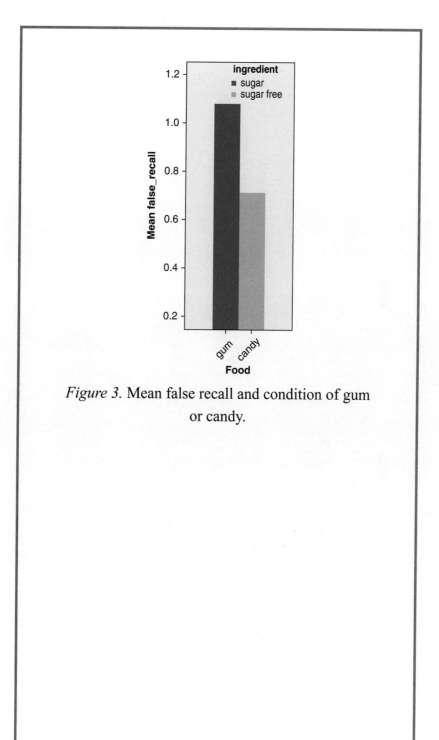

Figure 3. Mean false recall and condition of gum or candy.

Glossary

academic dishonesty Acts that violate authentic performance in academic demands (e.g., cheating, misrepresentation)

ambiguity Conditions of uncertainty

American Psychological Association See *APA*

amiable skepticism An attitude that promotes good-natured challenge of conclusions in the absence of research-based evidence

antiscience major Psychology students who dislike or resist the science elements of the major

APA The American Psychological Association, a national professional psychology organization that addresses practice, policy, research, and educational issues

APA format Writing conventions that psychologists agree to follow to disseminate their work (e.g., active voice, 1-inch margins, section headings)

APA Guidelines for the Undergraduate Psychology Major, Version 2.0 The best practice recommendations sponsored by the American Psychological Association for high-quality undergraduate curricula in psychology

APA style American Psychological Association style, the writing style required for publishing in the majority of research journals in psychology that emphasizes precision, clarity, and an objective (rather than subjective) point of view

APS The Association for Psychological Science, a professional psychology organization that focuses on research and educational concerns

Associate of Arts (AA) degree A type of degree emphasizing liberal arts, conferred at the conclusion of a 2-year program in community college settings and sometimes made available after the completion of the first 2 years of coursework in a bachelor of arts degree

Associate of Science (AS) degree A type of degree emphasizing science and technology, conferred at the conclusion of a 2-year program in community college settings and sometimes made available after the completion of the first 2 years of coursework in a 4-year program

Association for Psychological Science See *APS*

Bachelor of Arts (BA) degree An undergraduate degree conferred upon completion of a 4-year program that emphasizes a background in the liberal arts

Bachelor of Science (BS) degree An undergraduate degree conferred upon completion of a 4-year program that emphasizes a background in science or technology

behaviorism The orientation or school of thought in psychology that emphasizes observable behaviors as the focus of scientific exploration

binge method An ineffective study strategy that concentrates studying intensively in limited sessions rather than spreading study over time

blocked classes A set of classes that a group of students takes together, designed to promote a sense of being in a cohort or learning community

capstone course A course taken near the end of the major that facilitates an integration of learning across courses in the major

career An occupation that tends to provide opportunities for long-term satisfaction and promotion

case notes Written notes documenting interactions with clients that must be written to clinical standards (e.g., objective observations, confidential treatment)

cognitive psychology The branch of psychology that emphasizes both covert (e.g., dreaming and thinking) and overt activity (e.g., observable behavior) as the focus of scientific exploration

coherence All elements working as a whole

committed learner William Perry's term for advanced students who can make decisions and plans despite complex conditions and ambiguity

content-centered approach Teaching strategies that emphasize transmitting the ideas of the discipline typically through lecturing as the primary focus of education

contextual cues Stimulus triggers in the environment that facilitate retrieval of information from memory storage

control or comparison group Participants in an experiment who receive no manipulation or treatment; they provide a controlled comparison with participants who do receive a treatment or manipulation

controlled conditions Research design strategies that ensure participants in all conditions of an experiment are treated equivalently with the exception of the independent variable; this strategy assures being able to judge whether the experimental treatment produces the desired effect

correlational study Research that assesses whether there are positive, negative, or zero associations among variables; correlational studies identify associations among variables, but such associations should not be assumed to be causal-effect connections

cover letter The letter of introduction that accompanies a resume

curriculum vitae (CV) A resume that emphasizes range and quality of performance in academic settings

cyberidentity Personal details available through the Internet

debt load The amount of money owed on the completion of a degree

dependent variable The measurement of participants' responses in an experiment; it is not under the control of the experimenter

Discussion The fourth section of an APA-style report or article that discusses the meaning and implications of a project's results, often identifying questions for further investigation

driftwood major Students who aimlessly float through a major without paying much attention to what will happen in the future

drive-by reading A shallow reading strategy in which the student reads materials too quickly to absorb the most critical information

dualistic learner A concept developed by William Perry to describe a beginning student in the stage of learning in which students tend to see issues in black-and-white terms

EdD An education-focused doctoral degree that prepares clinicians to work in mental health settings, typically with people who are mildly to moderately dysfunctional

Educational Testing Service (ETS) A corporation that creates, administers, and interprets the results of a variety of standardized tests, including the Graduate Record Exam (GRE)

empirical Derived from observation and experience rather than logic and theory

empiricism Developing evidence based on observation and experimentation

exam wrappers Questions aimed at getting students to review their test performance

experiment Research that involves controlled conditions and manipulating variables

experimental group Participants in an experiment who experience a manipulated condition or treatment

fabricating Falsifying or inventing information to appear that research has been done

functionalism The orientation or school of thought in psychology that emphasizes the motives behind and the purposes of behavior

grade point average (GPA) A cumulative, numerical indicator of a student's academic performance that is measured on a scale from 0 to 4.0

Graduate Record Exam (GRE) A high-stakes standardized examination that tests math and verbal skills as well as discipline-specific content; used to make decisions about admission for graduate school

Graduate Study in Psychology (GSIP) An annual publication from the American Psychological Association that lists graduate programs in psychology in the United States and Canada, as well as admission data and related information

grant Funds allocated by an organization to address a specific problem

grant proposal A detailed request for funding to carry out research aimed at addressing a specific problem

guide on the side Teachers who prefer to use a mix of strategies in teaching that emphasize active-learning approaches rather than lectures

header The topmost margin of a research paper; contains the running head on the left and the page number on the right

high-impact practice An activity that facilitates a deeper relationship between the student and his or her chosen discipline, faculty, institution, or community, such as service learning or participating on a professor's research team

hindsight bias Claim that you could have predicted how things would turn out after the outcome became obvious

Holland code A three-letter code that designates which general occupational areas correspond most strongly to an individual's personal preferences

honors program A selective program for students with strong academic potential that offers greater intellectual challenge, increased access to high-impact activities, and enhanced social opportunity when compared to a standard curriculum

humility An intellectual characteristic that acknowledges how little we may truly know; it tends to moderate our sense of self-importance

hypothesis An empirically testable question

independent study A formal opportunity a student arranges to complete work in an area of personal interest

independent variable The variable, controlled by the experimenter, that has at least two levels, one representing the treatment of interest and the other the control group

instructional scaffolding A design feature of an academic curriculum that intentionally sequences experiences (e.g., requiring courses in a specific order) to support learning as cognitive challenges become more difficult

integrity The characteristic that comprises taking personal responsibility and making sound ethical judgments

intentionality Purposefulness in actions

interlibrary loan The process by which people can acquire from other libraries books and journals that aren't available in their home school

internship A volunteer placement in a work setting allowing a student to learn about a particular career and try out professional life in a specific work setting

Introduction The first section of an APA-style report or article that provides an overview and literature review of a research topic

job An activity that produces a source of income

job shadowing Following a professional during his or her typical workday to learn about a particular career

journal entries Personal written reflections that tend to focus on the emotional impact of learning experiences, readings, and class discussions

learning-centered approach Teaching strategies that focus on helping students successfully learn course content through active learning experiences in contrast to lecture

learning community A group of students who gather out of a shared interest (e.g., international students, athletes, psychology majors) and who have access to special high-impact learning designed to address those interests

liberal arts Areas in higher education that provide students with general knowledge rather than specific technical knowledge

Library of Congress Subject Headings (LCSH) A six-volume alphabetized guide of subject headings (search terms), often found in a library's reference department that assists in conducting searches

literature review Research that summarizes what is known about a particular topic

Materials Subsection of Method section of an APA-style report or article that describes any equipment, surveys, questionnaires, and the like that were used

meaning A sense of direction in life

memorandum A business memo than can be either a stand-alone document or the body of an email message

mentor An experienced person who provides guidance for those who are new to a profession or activity

Method The second section of an APA-style report or article; provides a detailed, step-by-step explanation about what was done during the course of an experiment or other research investigation

misrepresentation An ethical violation in which a person is dishonest about some aspect of his or her work to gain personal advantage

multiple retrieval cues Enhancing Memory cues that enhance the capacity for recall of ideas

nota bene Latin for *note well*; an alert to the reader to pay special attention to the point being made

novice A beginner

objectivity Maintenance of an unbiased perspective in interpreting behavior

Occupational Information Network (O*NET) An online center dedicated to providing information about a wide variety of occupations

operational definitions Descriptions of behaviors in terms of the procedures required to produce the behavior

oral presentation A research talk that can be given in an informal venue (the classroom) or a formal one (at a conference or as part of a dissertation defense)

participants Subsection of Method section of research or lab report that describes the people who took part in the research

peer review The formal process of evaluating the ideas and argument in a manuscript or other work by other professionals working in the same field

personal statement A written description of an applicant's interest in and plans for attending graduate school; this statement is a standard part of a graduate school application

PhD A doctor of philosophy degree. This degree is scholarly or research focused. Having a PhD indicates that a person knows how to understand and conduct original research within a given discipline.

placebo A substance that presumably has no direct therapeutic effect on behavior that is used in an experiment's control groups

plagiarism The act of taking the ideas of others and presenting them as one's own

portfolio A collection of evidence of your achievements and skills

positive psychology The branch of psychology that focuses on the science of human virtue and happiness

poster A brief, graphic summary of a research project that follows the main sections of APA-style papers (i.e., Introduction, Method, Results, Discussion), highlighting main findings using tables and figures; the researcher stands with his or her poster and explains the nature of the work to interested conference participants

postmortem test review Reviewing and evaluating successes and errors on tests, quizzes, and papers to improve performance in the future

precision Use of the fewest words possible to express an idea accurately and effectively

premature-foreclosure major A student who declares and commits to a major before he or she has developed a reasonable understanding of what the major entails

prerequisite In college, a course that must be completed prior to another course

principal investigator (PI) The lead author on a grant proposal

Procedure Subsection of Method section of an APA-style report or article that provides a chronology of what took place, who said and did what, and when they did so during the course of a study

pseudoscience Explanations that seem scientific but have no scientific evidence to support them

pseudoscientific explanations Explanatory frameworks that purport to describe cause–effect relationships regarding behavior but that lack scientific support for the claims made. Examples include astrology and phrenology.

Psi Beta The honor society for students who study psychology at 2-year or community colleges

PsycARTICLES A database that provides users access to the complete text of electronic articles that were originally published in APA journals

Psi Chi The international honor society for undergraduate psychology majors who maintain high grades (top 35% overall and a minimum 3.0 in the major)

psychological literacy Knowing the content and demonstrating the skills that characterize the thinking of people trained in psychology; the adaptive and intentional application of psychology to meet personal, professional, and societal needs

psychologist A person with an academic background in the scientific study of human behavior; or the designation for clinicians with a doctoral degree

psychology The scientific study of mind and behavior in human and nonhuman animals

psychological advantage The beneficial effects that completing a psychology major has on effective performance in the workplace (e.g., demonstrating appropriate skepticism in the absence of evidence regarding claims about behavior)

psychophysics The branch of psychology that deals with sensation and perception

PsycINFO A reference database maintained and continuously updated by the APA

PsyD A doctor of psychology degree, oriented more toward clinical practice (in contrast to the PhD, who is trained to work in research and academic settings)

Publication Manual of the American Psychological Association The guide to writing and publishing using APA style

random assignment The process that ensures that all volunteers in an experiment have an equal opportunity to serve in either the control or treatment condition

References The section of an APA-style report or article that contains detailed citations for all the research sources used therein

refuge major A student who declares a particular major, usually one that is perceived as easier, after being unsuccessful in another major

relativistic learner According to William Perry, a person who recognizes and accepts that there are few hard and fast truths

replication The process of repeating an experiment to confirm the original results

research assistant (RA) Someone, often a student, who volunteers to help a faculty member conduct his or her research; some RAs receive course credit while others are paid or simply help out in the lab or other setting for the educational experience

Results The third section of an APA-style report or article; describes the specific findings observed following an experiment or other research investigation

resume A brief summary that outlines a job applicant's personal, educational, and professional qualifications

retrieval The process by which we access information in memory

running head An abbreviated title of the paper that appears in the upper left corner of every page of an APA-style research paper

sage on the stage Teachers who prefer lecture over other teaching methods

scientific method An approach characterized by hypothesis testing, careful observation and experimentation, manipulation and measurement of variables, rigorous analysis, and replication

search terms Key words that are used to find relevant literature in a search

self-assessment The process by which we estimate the quality of our own performance

self-regulation The capacity to manage personal and professional demands

sleep deficit Getting an insufficient amount of sleep, which interferes with the recovery and replenishing of the brain and body

spaced learning Learning distributed over time rather than in one major study or cram session

SPSS® A powerful statistical program designed to identify relationships among sets of variables

SQ3R method A traditional study strategy that entails five steps: survey, question, read, recite, and review

structuralism The orientation in psychology dedicated to mapping the capacity of the senses

structured interview questions A company's standard set of questions that all prospective employees are asked during an interview

technical report A report that outlines the process, progress, or results of a technical or scientific research problem

terminal degree The level of education typically recognized as the highest degree available (doctoral or master's degrees) in an academic or professional track; for some professions, obtaining the terminal degree may be required to enter the field

theoretical orientation In psychology, a specific approach to understanding, diagnosing, and treating disorders

thesis A written summary of research conducted by an undergraduate (a senior thesis), or an investigation done as part of earning a master's degree

time diary A record of how a person allocates time to activities during the day

trait model An explanatory framework used to explain enduring personality characteristics

unstructured interview questions Informal questions asked by untrained interviewers during an employment interview

variable An element or feature in a research design that can be changed

verbatim When the content of a communication (e.g., lecture, message) is duplicated word for word

vocation A professional calling

wishful thinking Hoping for the best and sometimes not actively working to achieve that outcome

work–life balance The degree of harmony or strain that exists between occupational and personal elements in a worker's life

References

American Psychological Association. (2010). *Publication manual of the American Psychological Association* (6th ed.). Washington, DC: Author.

American Psychological Association. (2013, August). *APA Guidelines for the Undergraduate Psychology Major: Version 2.0*. Washington, DC: Author. Retrieved from http://www.apa.org/ed/precollege/about/psymajor-guidelines.pdf

American Psychological Association. (2014). Careers in psychology. Washington, DC: Author. Retrieved from http://www.apa.org/careers/resources/guides/careers.aspx?item=4

American Psychological Association. (2015). Divisions. Retrieved from http://www.apa.org/about/division/

American Psychological Association. (2016). By the numbers: How do undergraduate psychology majors fare? *Monitor on Psychology, 47(2)*, 11.

American Psychological Association. (2016). *Graduate study in psychology 2016*. Washington, DC: Author.

APA Center for Workforce Studies. (2015). How many psychology bachelor's-degree holders work in STEM occupations? *Monitor on Psychology, 46(5)*, 17.

Appleby, D. (2000). Job skills valued by employers who interview psychology majors. *Eye on Psi Chi, 4(3)*, 17.

Appleby, D. C. (2011, August). Academic integrity and the student-athlete. Lecture presented during IUPUI Student-Athlete Orientation Program. Indianapolis, IN.

Arkowitz, H., & Lilienfeld, S. O. (2009, January 27). Lunacy and the full moon: Does a full moon really trigger strange behavior? *Scientific American*. Retrieved from http://www.scientificamerican.com/article/lunacy-and-the-full-moon/?page=2

Arum, R., & Roksa, J. (2011). *Academically adrift: Limited learning on college campuses*. Chicago, IL: University of Chicago Press.

Association of American Colleges & Universities. (2013). What is a 21st century liberal education? Retrieved from http://www.aacu.org/leap/What_is_liberal_education.cfm

Astin, A. (1999, September/October). Student involvement: A developmental theory for higher education. *Journal of College Student Development, 40*, 518–529.

Barr, R. B., & Tagg, J. (1995, November/December). From teaching to learning: A new paradigm for undergraduate education. *Change*, 13–25.

Benjamin, L. T., Jr., Cavell, T. A., & Shallenberger, W. R., III. (1984). Staying with initial answers on objective tests: Is it a myth? *Teaching of Psychology, 11*, 133–141.

Boneau, C. A. (1990). Psychological literacy: A first approximation. *American Psychologist, 45*, 891–900.

Bringle, R., & Hatcher, J. (1995). A service-learning curriculum for faculty. *Michigan Journal of Community Service Learning, 2*, 112–122.

Buehler, R., Griffin, D., & Ross, M. (1994). Exploring the "planning fallacy": Why people underestimate their task completion times. *Journal of Personality and Social Psychology, 67*(3), 366–381.

Bureau of Labor Statistics. (2013). Occupational employment statistics. Washington, DC: U.S. Department of Labor. Retrieved from http://www.bls.gov/oes/2013/may/oes_nat.htm#19-0000

Bureau of Labor Statistics. (2014). Occupational outlook handbook: Psychology. Retrieved from http://www.bls.gov/ooh/life-physical-and-social-science/psychologists.htm

Celeb Net Wealth. (2016). Dr. Phil McGraw net worth and annual salary. Retrieved from http://celebnetwealth.com/dr-phil-mcgraw-net-worth-and-annual-salary

Cherry, K. (2014). 10 ways psychology can improve your life: Practical ways to apply psychology in everyday life. About.com. Retrieved from http://psychology.about.com/od/psychology101/tp/applying-psychology.htm

Cherry, K. (2014). What is a hindsight bias? Retrieved from http://psychology.about.com/od/hindex/g/hindsight-bias.htm

Clay, R. A. (2012, March). What's behind the internship match crisis? *gradPSYCH Magazine.* Washington, DC: American Psychological Association. Retrieved from http://www.apa.org/gradpsych/2012/03/cover-match-crisis.aspx

Council of Graduate Schools Ph.D. Completion Project. (2008). *Program completion and attrition data.* Retrieved from http://cgsnet.org/phd-completion-project

Cranney, J., & Dunn, D. S. (Eds.). (2011a). *The psychologically literate citizen: Foundations and global perspectives.* New York, NY: Oxford University Press.

Cranney, J., & Dunn, D. S. (2011b). Psychological literacy and the psychologically literate citizen: New frontiers for a global discipline. In J. Cranney & D. S. Dunn (Eds.), *The psychologically literate citizen: Foundations and global perspectives* (pp. 3–12). New York, NY: Oxford University Press.

Cranney, J., Morris, S., & Botwood, L. (2014). *Psychological literacy in undergraduate psychology education.* New York, NY: Oxford University Press.

Curry, M. (2008, August 25). The war on college cafeteria trays. *Time.* Retrieved from http://content.time.com/time/nation/article/0,8599,1834403,00.html

Darley, J. M. & Latané, B. (1964). Bystander intervention in emergencies: Diffusion of responsibility. *Journal of Personality and Social Psychology, 8,* 377–383.

Dement, W. E., & Vaughn, C. (2000). *The promise of sleep.* New York, NY: Dell.

Diener, E., & Biswas-Diener, R. (2008). *Happiness: Unlocking the mysteries of psychological wealth.* Malden, MA: Blackwell.

Dunlosky, J., Rawson, K. A., Marsh, E. J., Nathan, M. J., & Willingham, D. T. (2013). Improving students' learning with effective learning techniques: Promising directions from cognitive and educational psychology. *Psychological Science in the Public Interest, 14,* 4–58.

Dunn, D. S. (2011). *A short guide to writing about psychology* (3rd ed.). New York, NY: Pearson-Longman.

Dunn, D. S. (2013a). *The practical researcher: A student guide to conducting psychological research* (3rd ed.). Hoboken, NJ: Wiley.

Dunn, D. S. (2013b). *Research methods for social psychology* (2nd ed.). Hoboken, NJ: Wiley.

Dunn, D. S., Brewer, C. L., Cautin, R. L., Gurung, R. A., Keith, K. D., McGregor, L. N., ... Voight, M. J. (2010). The undergraduate psychology curriculum: Call for a core. In D. F. Halpern (Ed.), *Undergraduate Education in Psychology: A Blueprint for the Future of the Discipline* (pp. 47–61). Washington, DC: American Psychological Association.

Dunn, D. S., & McCarthy, M. (2010). The capstone course in psychology as liberal education opportunity. In D. S. Dunn, B. Beins, M. McCarthy, & G. Hill (Eds.), *Best practices for teaching beginnings and endings in the psychology major: Research, cases, and recommendations* (pp. 155–170). New York, NY: Oxford University Press.

Dunn, D. S., Saville, B. K., Baker, S. C., & Marek, P. (2013). Evidence-based teaching: Tools and techniques that promote learning in the psychology classroom. *Australian Journal of Psychology, 65,* 5–13.

Eagan, K., Stolzenberg, E. B., Ramirez, J. J., Aragon, M. C., Suchard, M. R., & Hurtado, S. (2014). *The American freshman: National norms fall 2014.* Los Angeles, CA: Higher Education Research Institute, UCLA.

Fischer, P., Krueger, J. I., Greitemeyer, T., Vogrincic, C., Kastenmüller, A., Frey, D., & ... Kainbacher, M. (2011). The bystander-effect: A meta-analytic review on bystander intervention in dangerous and non-dangerous emergencies. *Psychological Bulletin, 137*(4), 517–537. doi:10.1037/a0023304

Furumoto, L. (1980). Mary Whiton Calkins (1863–1930). *Psychology of Women Quarterly, 5,* 55–68.

Gardner, P. (2007). *Moving up or moving out of the company? Factors that influence the promoting or firing of new college hires.* Collegiate Research Brief 1-2007. East Lansing, MI: Michigan State University.

Gurung, R. A. R. (2013). Introduction. In S. Afful, J. J. Good, J. Keeley, S. Leder, & J. J. Stiegler-Balfour (Eds.), *Introductory psychology teaching primer: A guide for new teachers of PSYCH 101* (pp. 3–5). Retrieved from http://teachpsych.org/ebooks/intro2013/index.php

Guthrie, R. V. (2003). *Even the rat was white: A historical view of psychology* (2nd ed.). New York, NY: Allyn & Bacon.

Halonen, J. S. (2002, Winter). Love on the boundary: When the personal and professional collide. St. Petersburg, FL: National Institute for the Teaching of Psychology.

Halonen, J. S. (2011). Are there too many psychology majors? [White paper.] Invitation issued by the Board of Governors of the State University System of Florida. Retrieved from http://www.cogdop.org/page_attachments/0000/0200/FLA_White_Paper_for_cogop_posting.pdf

Halonen, J. S. (2012). Are there too many psychology majors? [White paper.] Invitation issued by the Board of Governors of the State University System of Florida. Retrieved from http://www.cogdop.org/page_attachments/0000/0200/FLA_White_Paper_for_cogop_posting.pdf

Halonen, J. S. (2013). The Worthies vs. the Great Unwashed: Overcoming psychology's tier problem. *Eye on Psi Chi, 17*(2), 10–12.

Halonen, J. S. (2014). A makeover for APA's *Guidelines for Undergraduate Psychology. Psychology Teacher Network.* Washington, DC: American Psychological Association. Retrieved from http://www.apa.org/ed/precollege/ptn/2014/02/undergraduate-guidelines.aspx

Halonen, J. S. (2014, January). Why would you want to major in *that?* Desmystifying your psychology major. *Psychology Student Network, 2*(1). Retrieved from http://www.apa.org/ed/precollege/psn/2014/01/why-major.aspx

Halonen, J. S., Bosack, B., Clay, S., McCarthy, M., Dunn, D. S., Hill, G. W., IV., ... Whitlock, K. (2003). A rubric for learning, teaching, and assessing scientific inquiry in psychology. *Teaching of Psychology, 30,* 197–208.

Halpern, D. (Ed.). (2010). *Undergraduate education in psychology: A blueprint for the future of the discipline.* Washington, DC: American Psychological Association.

Hansen, R. S., & Hansen, K. (2014). What do employers really want? Top skills and values employers seek from job seekers. QuintCareers.com. Retrieved from http://www.quintcareers.com/job_skills_values.html

Hayes, N. (1997, July). The distinctive skills of a psychology graduate. *Monitor on Psychology*, p. 33.

Henriques, G. (2014, January 18). Psychology's fragmentation trap. In Theory of Knowledge [Blog]. *Psychology Today*. Retrieved from http://www.psychologytoday.com/blog/theory-knowledge/201401/psychologys-fragmentation-trap

Herd, C., Waide, M. P., & Cohn, T. (2009, June 7). Walking the tightrope: Setting appropriate boundaries within faculty-student relationships. Paper presented at the National Meeting of the Teaching Professor Conference. Washington, DC.

Hettich, P. (2004, April). *From college to corporate culture: You're a freshman again.* Paper presented at the Annual Meeting of the Midwest Psychological Association, Chicago, IL.

Higher Education Research Institute (HERI). (2013, January). Your First College Year Survey 2012. *HERI Research Brief.* Retrieved from http://www.heri.ucla.edu/briefs/YFCY2012-Brief.pdf

Higher Education Research Institute (HERI). (2015, October). Findings from the 2015 Your First College Year Survey. *HERI Research Brief.* Retrieved from http://www.heri.ucla.edu/briefs/YFCY/YFCY-2015-Brief.pdf

Holland, J. (1996). Exploring careers with a typology: What we have learned and some new directions. *American Psychologist, 51,* 397–406.

Holland, J. (1997). *Making vocational choices* (3rd ed.). Odessa, FL: Psychological Assessment Resources.

Hunt, M. (1961). *The story of psychology.* New York, NY: Random House.

James, W. (1961). *Psychology: Briefer course.* New York, NY: Harper & Row (Original work published 1892).

Kahneman, D. (2011). *Thinking fast and slow.* New York, NY: Farrar, Straus, & Giroux.

Kahneman, D., & Deaton, A. (2010). High income improves evaluations of life but not emotional well-being. *Proceedings of the National Academy of Sciences of the United States of America, 107*(38), 16489–16493. doi:10.1073/pnas.1011492107

Kahneman, D., Krueger, A. B., Schkade, D., Schwarz, N., & Stone, A. A. (2006). Would you be happier if you were richer? A focusing illusion. *Science, 312,* 1908–1910.

Kalwarski, T., Mosher, D., Paskin, J., & Rosato, D. (2014). *Money* magazine's best jobs in America. Retrieved from http://people.uncw.edu/guinnc/MoneyMag.html

Keith-Spiegel, P., & Weiderman, M. W. (2000). *The complete guide to graduate school admissions: Psychology and related fields.* Hillsdale, NJ: Erlbaum.

Kendra, C. (2014, December 14). What can I do with a master's degree in psychology? About.com. Retrieved from http://psychology.about.com/od/psychologycareerfaq/f/masters-in-psychology-jobs.htm

Kimble, G. A. (1984). Psychology's two cultures. *American Psychologist, 39,* 833–839.

King, A. (1993, Winter). From sage on the stage to guide on the side. *College Teaching, 41,* 30–35.

Konnikova, M. (2014, June 2). What's lost as handwriting fades. *New York Times.* Retrieved from http://www.nytimes.com/2014/06/03/science/whats-lost-as-handwriting-fades.html

Korkki, P. (2010, September 11). Job satisfaction vs. a big paycheck. *New York Times,* BU10.

Kuh, G. D., Kinzie, J., Schuh, J., & Whitt, E. J. (2010). *Student success in college: Creating conditions that matter.* San Francisco, CA: Jossey-Bass.

Kuther, T. L. (2014). You missed class: What do you do? About.com. Retrieved from http://gradschool.about.com/od/survivinggraduateschool/a/missedclass.htm

Landrum, R. E. (2001). I'm getting my bachelor's degree in psychology—What can I do with it? *Eye on Psi Chi, 6*(1), 20–22.

Landrum, R. E. (2002, Winter). Maximizing undergraduate opportunities: The value of research and other experiences. *Eye on Psi Chi, 6*(2), 15–18.

Landrum, R. E., Beins, B. C., Bhalla, M., Brakke, K., Briihl, D. S., Curl-Langager, R. M., ... Van Kirk, J. J. (2010). Desired outcomes of an undergraduate education in psychology from departmental, student, and societal perspectives. In D. F. Halpern (Ed.), *Undergraduate education in psychology: A blueprint for the future of the discipline* (pp. 145–160). Washington, DC: American Psychological Association.

Landrum, R. E., & Harrold, R. (2003). What employers want from psychology graduates. *Teaching of Psychology, 30,* 131–133.

Lehman, D. R., & Nisbett, R. E. (1990). A longitudinal study of the effects of undergraduate training on reasoning. *Developmental Psychology, 26,* 952–960.

Leonhardt, D. (2014, May 27). Is college worth it? Clearly, new data say. *New York Times.* Retrieved from http://www.nytimes.com/2014/05/27/upshot/is-college-worth-it-clearly-new-data-say.html?_r=0

Library of Congress. (2012). *Library of Congress subject headings* (34th ed., 6 vols.). Washington, DC: Author.

Light, J. (2010, October 11). Psych majors aren't happy with options. *Wall Street Journal.* Retrieved from http://online.wsj.com/news/articles/SB10001424052748704011904575538561813341020

Lilienfeld, S. O. (2004). Teaching psychology students to distinguish science from pseudoscience: Pitfalls and rewards. Retrieved from http://www.lscp.net/persons/dupoux/teaching/JOURNEE_AUTOMNE_CogMaster_2011-12/docs/Lilienfeld_2004_Teaching_PseudoScience.pdf

Lilienfeld, S. O., Lynn, S. J., Ruscio, J., & Beyerstein, B. L. (2010). *50 great myths of popular psychology: Shattering widespread misconceptions about human behavior.* New York, NY: John Wiley & Sons.

Lopatto, D. (2010, Spring). Undergraduate research as a high-impact student experience. *Peer Review, 27*–30. Washington, DC: American Association of Colleges and Universities.

Love, R. (2007, March/April). Before Jon Stewart. *Columbia Journalism Review.* Retrieved from http://www.cjr.org/feature/before_jon_stewart.php

Lovett, M. B. (2013). Using exam wrappers to promote metacognition. In M. Kaplan, N. Silver, D. LaVaque-Manty, D. Meizlish, & J. Rhem (Eds.), *Using reflection and metacognition to improve student learning: Across the disciplines, across the academy* (pp. 18–52). Sterling, VA: Stylus.

Luo, S., & Klohnen, E. C. (2005). Assortative mating and marital quality in newlyweds: A couple-centered approach. *Journal of Personality and Social Psychology, 88*(2), 304–326. doi:10.1037/0022-3514.88.2.304

Maas, J. B., & Robbins, R. S. (2011). *Sleep for success: Everything you must know about sleep but are too tired to ask.* Bloomington, IN: AuthorHouse.

Martin, D. W. (2007). *Doing psychology experiments.* Belmont, CA: Thompson/Wadsworth.

McCrae, R. R., & Costa, P. T., Jr. (2003). *Personality in adulthood: A five-factor theory perspective.* New York, NY: Guilford.

McGovern, T. V., Corey, L., Cranney, J., Dixon, W. E., Jr., Homes, J. D., Kuebli, J. E., ... Walker, S. J. (2010). Psychologically literate citizens. In D. F. Halpern (Ed.), *Undergraduate education in psychology: A blueprint for the future of the discipline* (pp. 9–27). Washington, DC: American Psychological Association.

Michalski, D., Kohout, J., Wicherski, M., & Hart, B. (2011). *2009 Doctorate Employment Survey.* Washington, DC: American Psychological Association.

Miller, G. A. (1956). The magical number seven, plus or minus two: Some limits on our capacity for processing information. *Psychological Review, 63,* 81–97.

Mueller, P., & Oppenheimer, D. (2014). The pen is mightier than the keyboard: Advantages of longhand over laptop note taking. *Psychological Science, 25,* 1159–1168.

Munsey, C. (2008, September). Charting the future of undergraduate psychology. *Monitor on Psychology, 39*(8), 54.

Murray, B. (2000, January). The degree that almost wasn't: The PsyD comes of age. *Monitor on Psychology, 31*(1), 52. Retrieved from http://www.apa.org/monitor/jan00/ed1.aspx

National Association of Colleges and Employers (NACE). (2014). Class of 2014: Top-paid liberal arts majors. Retrieved from http://www.naceweb.org/s05142014/top-paid-liberal-arts-grad.aspx

National Bureau of Labor Statistics. (2013). May 2013 national occupational and wage estimates United States. Retrieved from http://www.bls.gov/oes/current/oes_nat .htm#19-0000

National Center for Education Statistics. (2015). *2014 digest of education statistics.* Retrieved from http://nces.ed.gov/programs/digest/d14/tables/dt14_325.80.asp

National Sleep Foundation. (2015). Napping. Retrieved from http://sleepfoundation.org/ sleep-topics/napping?page = 0%2C0

Nelson, E., & Fonzi, G. (1995). An effective peer advising program in a large psychology department. *NACADA Journal: The Global Community for Academic Advising, 15*(2), 41–43.

Niemiec, R. M., & Wedding, D. (2014). *Positive psychology at the movies: Using films to build character strength and well-being.* Boston, MA: Hogrefe.

Norcross, J. C. & Castle, P. H. (2002). Appreciating the PsyD: The facts. *Eye on Psi Chi.* Retrieved from https://cms.bsu.edu/-/media/WWW/DepartmentalContent/ Psychology/Docs/PsyD.pdf

Norcross, J. D. (2015, August 7). Undergraduate study in psychology: What APA's national survey tells and warns. American Psychological Association convention, Toronto, Canada.

O'Brien, K. (July 4, 2010). What happened to studying? Boston.com. Retrieved from http://www.boston.com/bostonglobe/ideas/articles/2010/07/04/what_happened_to_ studying/?page = 1

Otto, J., Sandford, D. A., & Ross, D. N. (2008). Does ratemyprofessor.com really rate my professor? *Assessment and Evaluation in Higher Education, 33*(4), 355–368.

Pascarella, E.T., & Terenzini, P.T. (2005). *How college affects students: A third decade of research* (Vol. 2). San Francisco, CA: Jossey-Bass.

Pena, L. W. (2010, August). Understanding the working college student. *Academe.* Washington, DC: American Association of University Professors. Retrieved from http://www.aaup.org/article/understanding-working-college-student#.U7xsFiitbb8

Perry, W. G., Jr. (1970). Forms of intellectual and ethical development in the college years: A scheme. New York, NY: Holt, Rinehart, & Winston.

Plous, S. (1996). Attitudes toward the use of animals in psychological research and education: Results from a national survey of psychologists. *American Psychologist, 51,* 1167–1180.

Plous, S. (1998). *Advice on letters of recommendation.* Retrieved from https://www.socialpsychology.org/rectips.htm

Psychology Career Center. (2014, July 14). Psychologist professor among top jobs in United States. Retrieved from http://www.psychologycareercenter.org/psychology-professor-jobs.html

Psychology Career Center. (2015). Psychologist salary and benefits information. Retrieved from http://www.psychologycareercenter.org/salaries.html

Psychology Graduate School. (n.d.). Debt and income. Retrieved from http://psychologygradschool.weebly.com/debt-and-income.html

Robinson, F. P. (1970). *Effective study* (4th ed.). New York, NY: Harper & Row.

Roese, N. J., & Vohs, K. D. (2012). Hindsight bias. *Perspectives on Psychological Science, 7,* 411–426.

Ronan, G. B. (2005, November 29). College freshmen face major dilemma. Personal finance on NBCNews.com. Retrieved from http://www.nbcnews.com/id/10154383/ns/business-personal_finance/t/college-freshmen-face-major-dilemma/#.U8Ahoiitbb8

Salley, A. K. (2014, June–July). Meet Julian MacQueen of Pensacola. *850 Magazine.* Retrieved from http://www.850businessmagazine.com/June-July-2014/Meet-Julian-MacQueen-of-Pensacola/

Shin, L. (2014, September 30). Is grad school worth it? 7 steps to calculating the ROI. *Forbes.* Retrieved from http://www.forbes.com/sites/laurashin/2014/09/30/is-grad-school-worth-it-7-steps-to-calculating-the-roi/#4edacd2587ae

Smith, S. M., Glenberg, A., & Bjork, R. A. (1978). Environmental context and human memory. *Memory & Cognition, 6,* 342–353.

Sparshott, J. (2015, May 8). Congratulations, class of 2015. You're now the most indebted ever (for now). *Wall Street Journal.* Retrieved from http://blogs.wsj.com/economics/2015/05/08/congratulations-class-of-2015-youre-the-most-indebted-ever-for-now/

Stamm, K., Michalski, D., Cope, C., Fowler, G., Christidis, P., & Lin, L. (2016, February). What are the acceptance rates for graduate psychology programs? *Monitor on Psychology, 47*(2), 16.

Stanny, C. J., & Halonen, J. S. (2011). Accreditation, accountability, and assessment: Faculty development's role in addressing multiple agendas. In L. Stefani (Ed.), *Evaluating the effectiveness of academic development practice: A professional guide.* New York, NY: Routledge.

Stanovich, K. E. (2007). *How to think straight about psychology* (7th ed). Boston, MA: Allyn & Bacon.

Steuer, F. B., & Ham, K. W., II. (2008). Psychology textbooks: Examining their accuracy. *Teaching of Psychology, 35,* 160–168.

Stoloff, M., McCarthy, M., Keller, L., Varfolomeeva, V., Lynch, J., Makara, K., ... Smiley, W. (2010). The undergraduate psychology major: An examination of structure and sequence. *Teaching of Psychology, 37*(1), 4–15. doi:10.1080/00986280903426274

Taylor, S. E., & Brown, J. D. (1994). Positive illusions and well-being revisited: Separating fact from fiction. *Psychological Bulletin, 116*(1), 21–27. doi.org/10.1037/0033-2909.116.1.21

Thaiss, C., & Sanford, J. F. (2000). *Writing for psychology.* Boston, MA: Allyn and Bacon.

Watson, J. B. (1913). Psychology as the behaviorist views it. *Psychological Review, 20,* 158–177.

Weaver, R., & Qi, J. (2005). Classroom organization and participation: College students' perceptions. *Journal of Higher Education, 76*(5), 570–601.

Wedding, D., & Niemiec, R. M. (2010). *Movies and mental illness: Using films to understand psychopathology* (3rd ed.). Boston, MA: Hogrefe.

Weimer, M. (2013, May 8). Helping students understand the benefits of study groups [Blog post]. Retrieved from http://www.facultyfocus.com/articles/teaching-professor-blog/helping-students-understand-the-benefits-of-study-groups/

Whitbourne, S. K. (2012, January 14). Psychology's best movies: And the Oscar goes to...which psychological disorder? *Psychology Today.* Retrieved from http://www.psychologytoday.com/blog/fulfillment-any-age/201201/psychologys-best-movies

Wilson, J. H., & Schwartz, B. M. (2015). *An easy guide to research presentations.* Thousand Oaks, CA: Sage.

Wrzesniewski, A., McCauley, C., Rozin, P., & Schwartz, B. (1997). Jobs, careers, and callings: People's reactions to their work. *Journal of Research in Personality, 31,* 21–33.

Wrzesniewski, A., Rozin, P., & Bennett, G. (2003). Working, playing, and eating: Making the most of most moments. In C. L. M. Keyes & J. Haidt (Eds.), *Flourishing: Positive psychology and the life well-lived* (pp. 185–204). Washington, DC: American Psychological Association.

Zhao, C.-M., & Kuh, G. D. (2004). Adding value: Learning communities and student engagement. *Research in Higher Education, 45*(2), 115–139.

Zimmermann, J., & Neyer, F. J. (2013). Do we become a different person when hitting the road? Personality development of sojourners. *Journal of Personality and Social Psychology, 105*(3), 515–530. Retrieved from http://dx.doi.org/10.1037/a0033019

Name Index

Note: Page numbers followed by n refer to notes; those followed by t refer to tables.

Subject Index

Note: Page numbers followed by f refer to figures; those followed by t refer to tables.